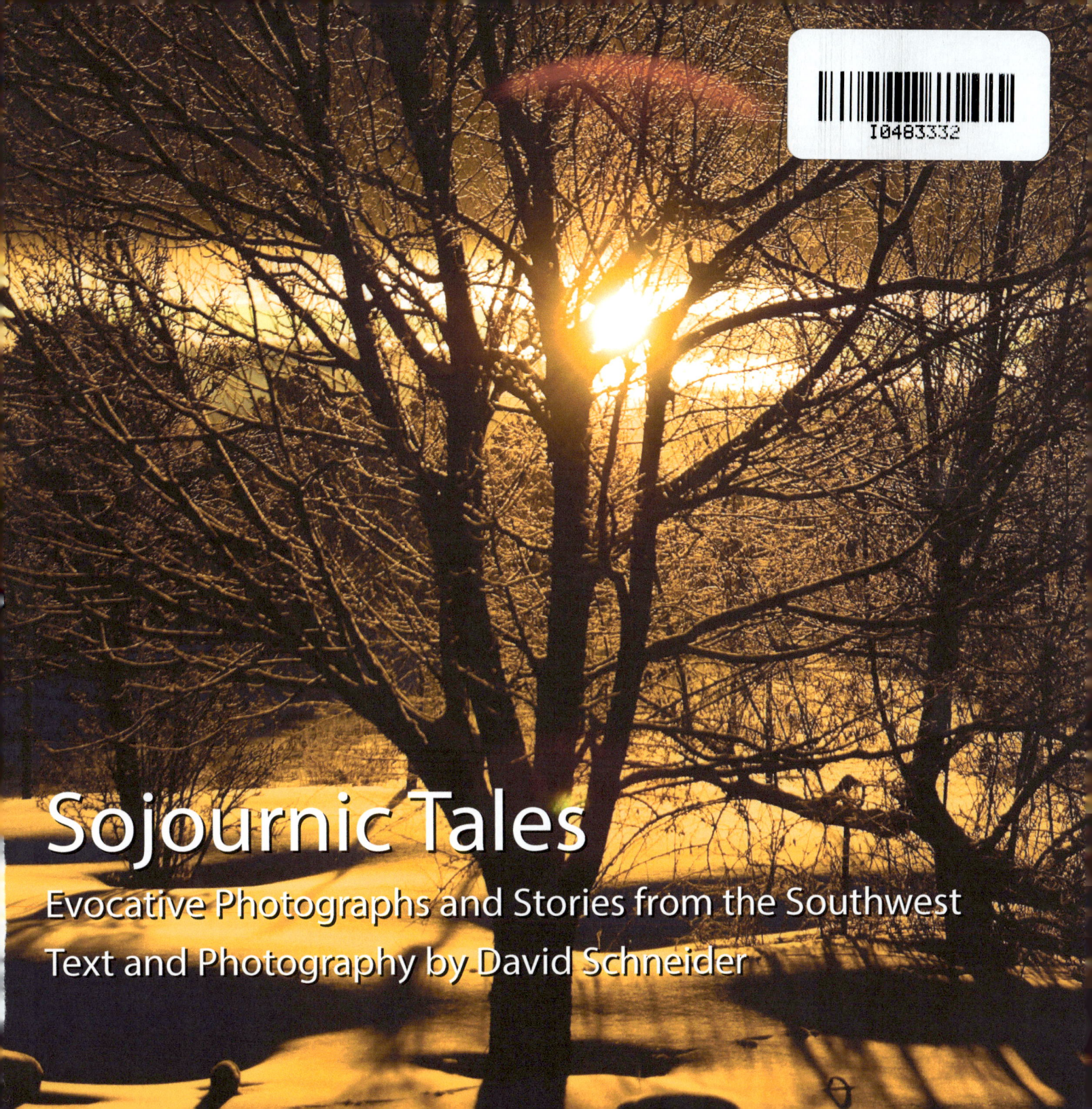

Sojournic Tales

Evocative Photographs and Stories from the Southwest

Text and Photography by David Schneider

Cover: *Infernally Yours*

Title Page: *Dawnting Shadows*

Right: *Ready, Waiting*

Contents Page: *Sand Tracks*

Preface Page: *Bisti Silhouette*

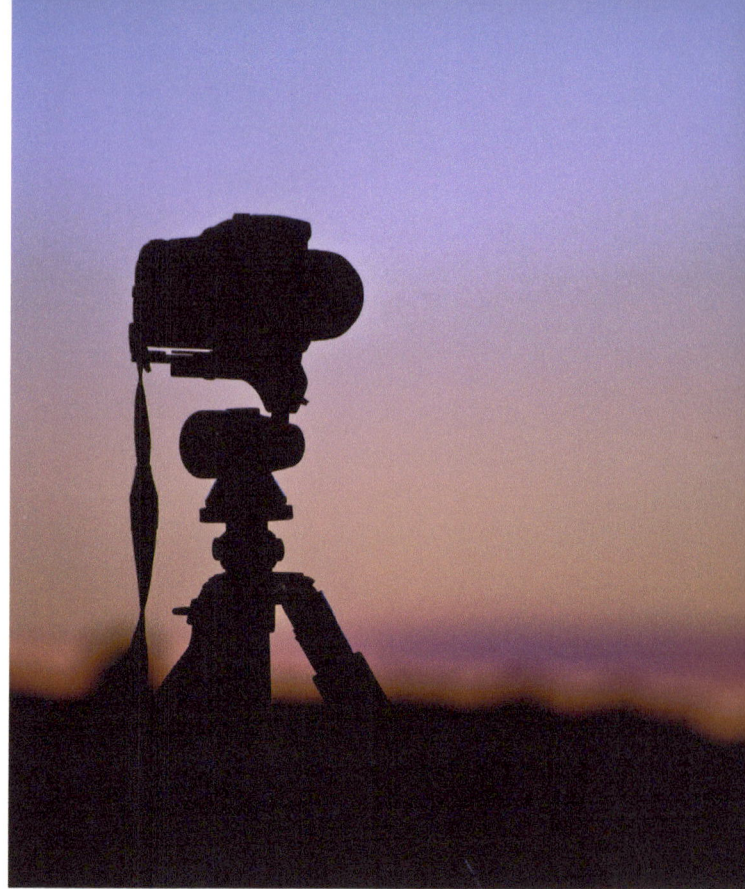

ISBN: 978-0-9838967-1-5

Text and Photography by David Schneider

Edited by Bobbie Christmas

Cover design by Anything Graphic

Created, produced, designed, and printed in the United States

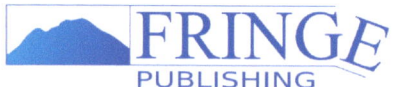

FRINGE PUBLISHING

An imprint of Fringe Innovations

For more information about our books, write Fringe Publishing, PO Box 555, Tijeras, NM 87059, call (505) 750-4PIX, or visit www.fringepublishing.com

Contents

Preface

Photography is a love, a joy, and a driving influence on my life; frankly, so is telling stories, some of which might actually be true. Combining these two delightful activities together into this book has long been a dream of mine, and now it is here in your hands. I am truly humbled and honored that it is.

For me, photography is about the experience at the moment the image was made. What was going on around me? What was I feeling? We won't ponder what was I thinking, because for some reason, I am asked that question quite a lot, usually in an incredulous tone of voice. What was the vignette behind each photo? The accompanying stories strive to explain some of it, briefly, and give some background, or, they might tell a fanciful story that I imagined while I made the image. As for the images themselves, they are neither altered nor overly enhanced. Each image is, by and large, exactly as I experienced it in that fleeting moment of time.

This volume contains some of my favorite images from the Southwest. They represent how I choose to see the world, which is to say a world of beauty and grandeur, a world of eternal mystery and discovery, and mostly, a world of hope.

I hope these images evoke an emotion within you. May they give you peace, hope, a sense of wonder and joy, and a glimpse into the world as I see it, as I envision it might be. May they inspire you with your own vision.

david

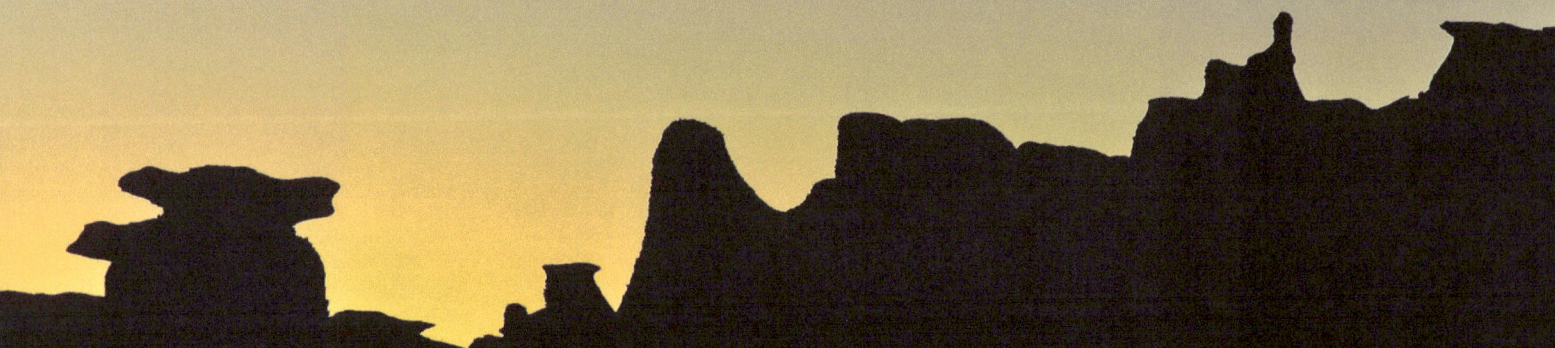

For Mary Beth, my partner, who was by my side for countless thousands of miles as I constantly exclaimed "Oh, look at that!" stopping every moment. Without your steadfast companionship, patience, and love, I could not have accomplished this task.

For Blake and Jessica, my children, who have unconditionally supported me on this journey, may you both always follow your dreams and take your passion with you.

For Mom and Dad, who stuffed me in the back seat of their car when I was a child while they explored America. In so doing you gave me an absolute love for adventure and this world.

For Phil, who shared his wisdom, experience, and advice with me, and most of all, encouragement. I listened, Phil.

Southwest Contrasts

From the tops of tall mountains to the depths of the endless desert; from the sparkling lakes to dramatic sunsets, the Southwest is a land of contrasts. Big versus small, dry versus wet, sand versus snow, the list is long and varied and nearly endless.

Open Road

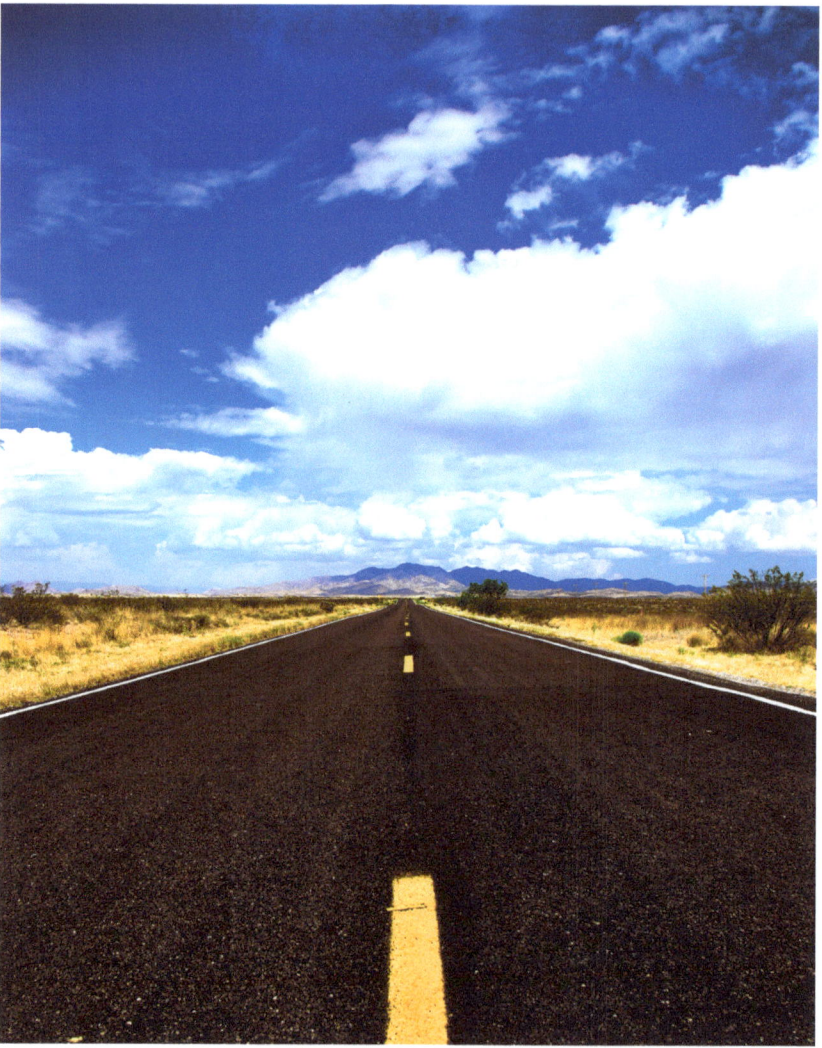

It seems fitting to start our journey with a familiar Southwest shot: a road, any road, every road, that is everywhere and nowhere at the same time. Guiding us on our adventure, it leads us to wonders yet unseen, delivering a bounty of surprises along the way. The road itself is timeless, stretches deep into infinity, and is our guide and companion.

Which road this is exactly, matters not. It is, after all, the open road, and it leads us ever onward.

Telluride Peak

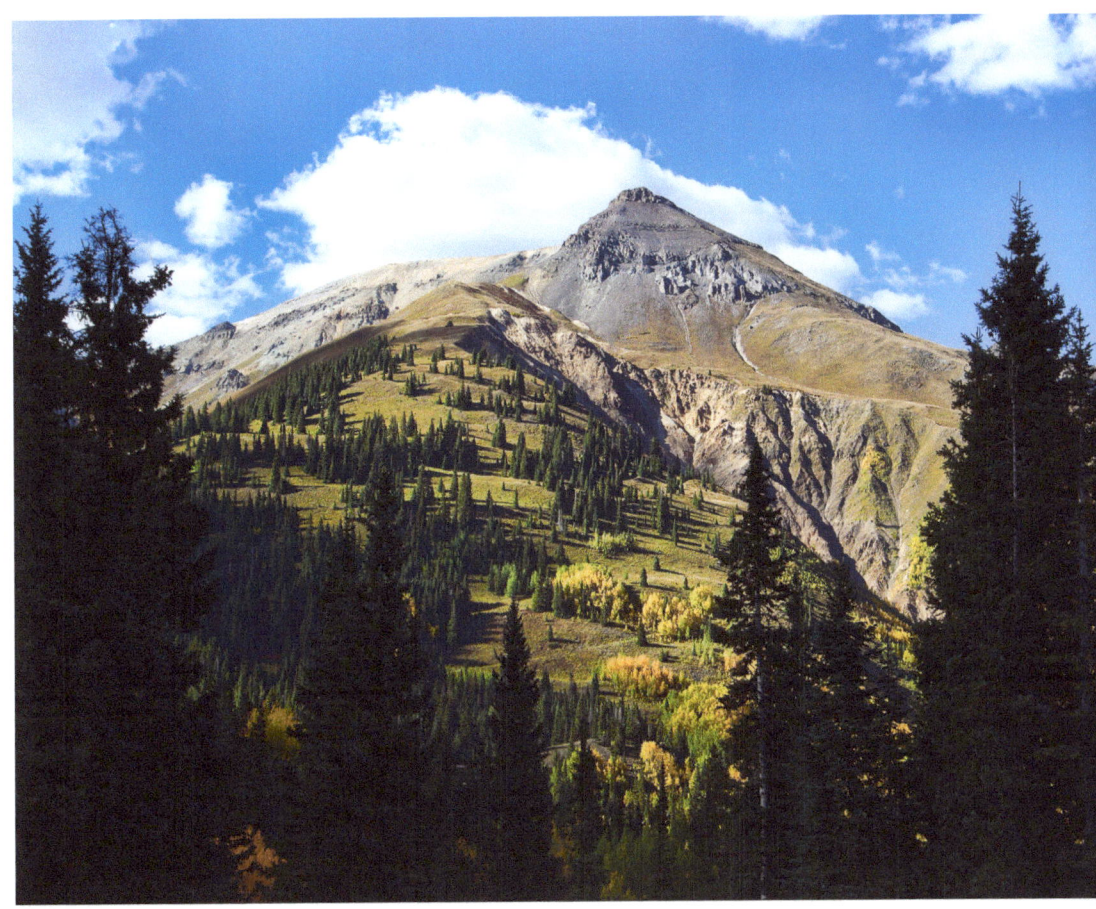

Many places have their location defined by an iconic landmark. Telluride, Colorado, is no exception.

Telluride Peak rises to a lofty 13,478 feet above sea level, making it a very tall mountain indeed, although, to be fair, 227 peaks are higher in the state of Colorado alone. Rising above the town of Telluride, the peak is a symbol of strength and endurance, for one doesn't get to be that tall without a little bit of effort.

Oddly, however, the view of the peak itself from the town of Telluride is blocked by Ajax Peak. Instead, this view is from US 550, just outside of Ouray, peering over the Uncompahgre National Forest. This view is one of my favorites, and it seems like I could just walk right up to the top of the mountain. In actuality, you can, and as walking to the tops of really tall mountains go, this one is not a bad walk at all. Whenever I look at this photo, I feel a deep sense of peace and serenity, yet I also feel the strength of the peak as well.

The early fall setting also lends to the tranquility. Although the evergreens in the foreground will not change to fall colors, their brethren farther up the mountain already have, providing a colorful contrast.

Should you happen to be passing through The Million Dollar Highway (US 550) just south of Ouray, be sure to stop and look for a moment at this million dollar view.

Snowy Vista

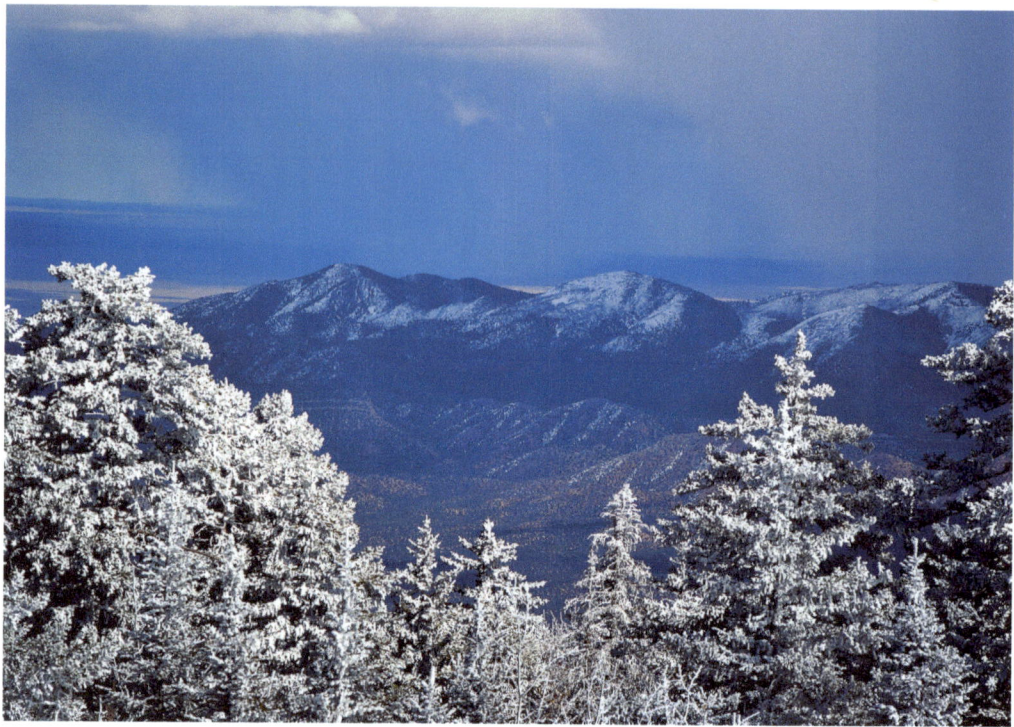

The Sandia Mountains in New Mexico: by some standards a small chain of mountains, but considering that Sandia Peak soars to 10,678 feet, the mountains certainly hold their own.

The weather up on top usually differs dramatically from the lower elevations, as you might expect, although it is often far more different than you might expect, as well. The journey up the mountain is like traveling to an entirely different country, sometimes—it might be spring down below, but up top, it might as well be winter. Oddly enough, that is precisely what happened in this particular photograph.

In late March, it was a beautiful sunny day at the base on the mountain, but by the time I reached the summit, it was far from a spring day. Snow, frost, more snow, and more frost coated the trees, and if you didn't know any better, you would think it was deep winter. A fierce winter storm raged on the next mountain over, and surely we could have been just outside of the Himalayan mountains?

A short time later, the base of the mountain proved us wrong, and spring had indeed sprung.

Snowhere Trail

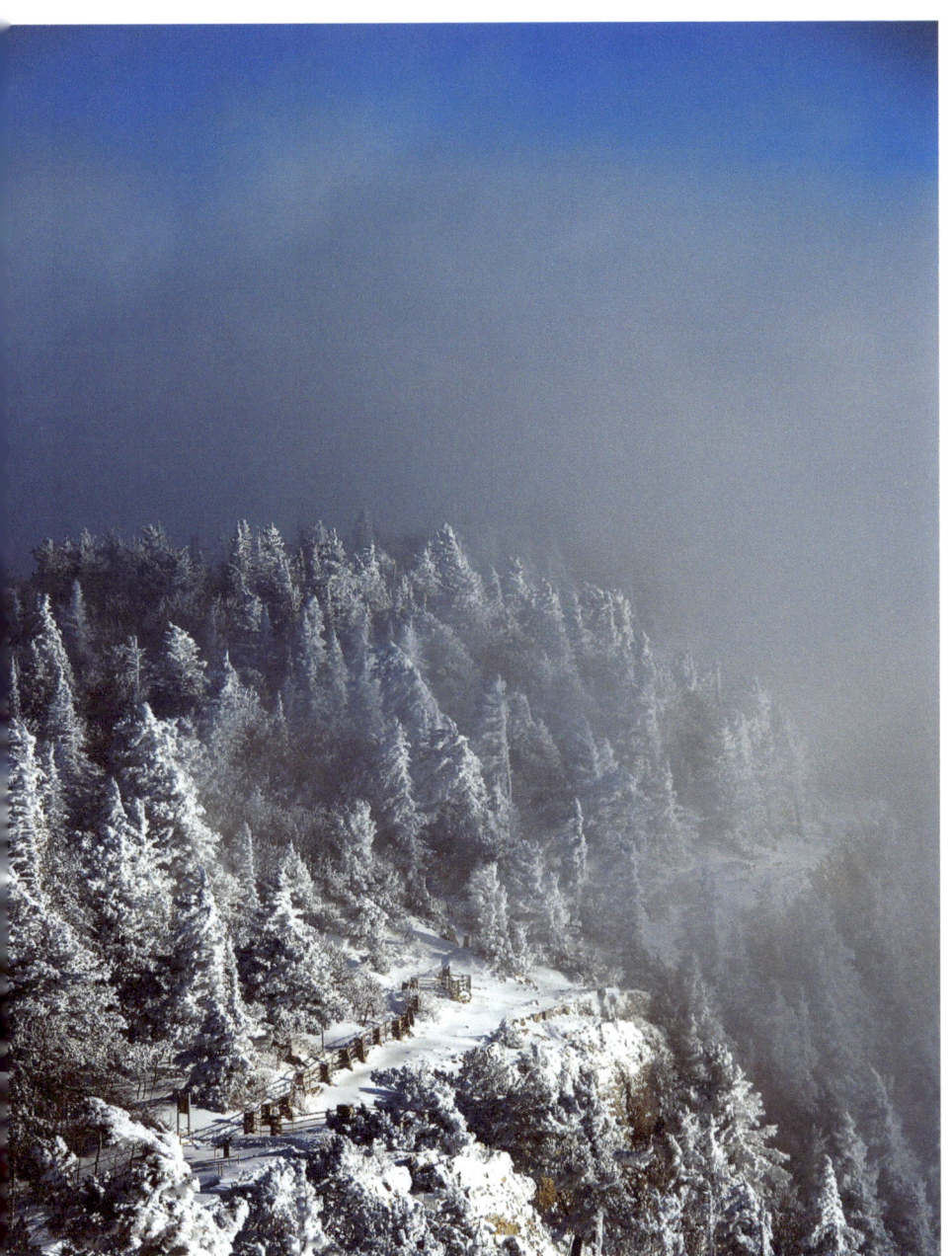

This is one of my most favorite photographs, favorite stories, and favorite titles.

Funny things happen on top of mountains, funny things indeed. The mere mortals who are way down below sometimes can't see what happens, but when you have a bird's eye view, that's a different story.

Despite my love of snow photographs, I rail against the cold, yet for some reason, I keep stepping out in it to create them. Perhaps, I am passive-aggressive toward cold. One winter day I was up on top of Sandia Peak enjoying (if you consider being insanely cold "enjoyment") the day, when, for no good reason, a cloud had the audacity to move over the peak I had happened to be admiring. After asking the cloud politely to move, but it didn't, I realized that an incredible photograph stared me in the face. Naturally, as soon as the cloud saw my camera, it started drifting away, but not before I captured this photograph.

The trail that appears to lead to nowhere intrigued me. Does it continue around the mountain? Does it stop? Does it lead off the edge of the world? No footprints lead down the trail to snowhere.

Foggy Garden

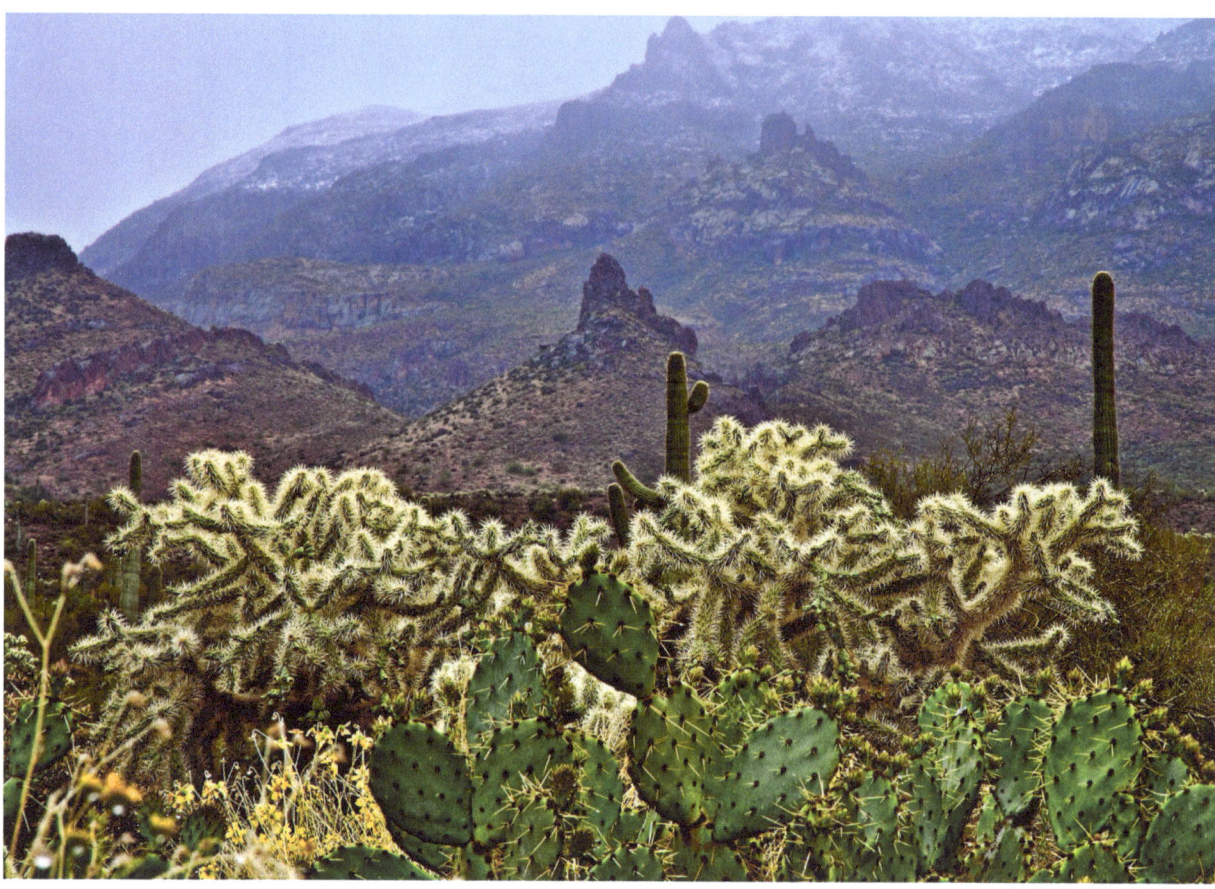

The Superstition Mountains of Arizona have a long and storied history—there's gold in them there hills, you know, or, at least that's what the rumors say. On a misty, foggy day, not that the Superstitions see many of those, the mountains loom foreboding and mysterious, and any gold they might harbor is certainly lost in the fog.

What is not lost in the fog, however, is the blooming cactus of the desert. This clump of cholla and prickly pears, with a couple of saguaros making a cameo appearance, plus a few bright yellow flowers hold forth in their own cheery garden, proving there is treasure in the hills, no doubt.

Desert Snow

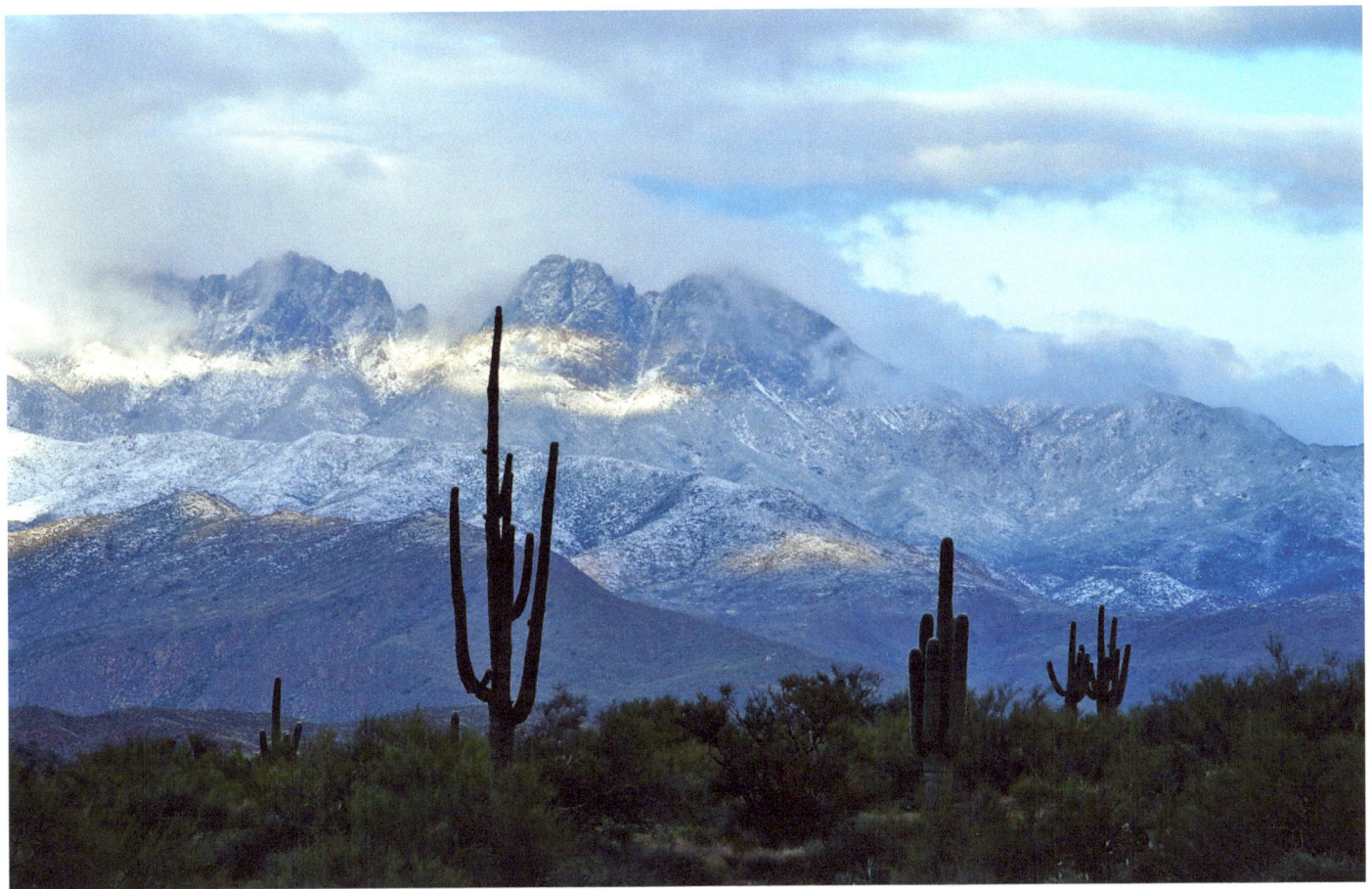

Desert and snow are two things that are not always found together, but in the Superstition Mountains, all sorts of wonders can be found. And often are.

This is the Four Peaks, named for, well, the four peaks. As it turns out, a snowstorm had just rolled through the Superstitions, which is not the most common of events, except when you're me. Snow seems to follow me or find me, no matter how well I try to hide. The storm had completely enveloped the peaks, taking them to itself and hiding them away from the rest of the world. As storms are wont to do, it eventually passed, and as it slowly surrendered its prize, the peaks slowly revealed themselves.

The saguaros stood silent watch to the event and continued their vigil long after the storm had passed.

Snowbound Ranch

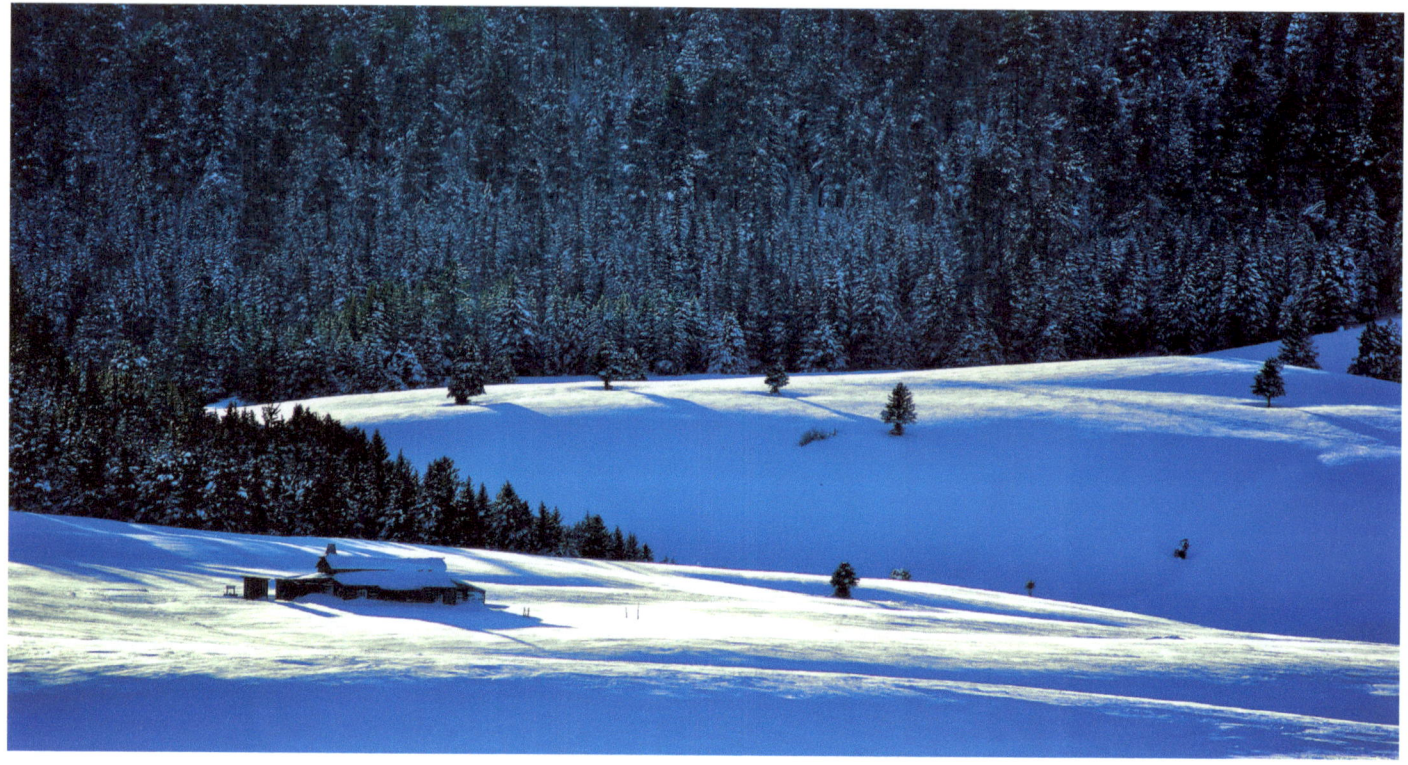

Winter. A time of cold and a time of snow, and in this particular case, a time for a whole lot of that wonderful white powdery stuff.

This ranch is located within the Valles Caldera National Preserve in New Mexico, and from the looks of things, humans don't bother with wintertime occupation. Who can blame them really, for it would probably take somewhere just this side of forever to get through all that snow. And make no doubt about it: this is a lot of snow. Those drifts are significant. What might appear to be a gentle vale is in actuality filled with snow. Appearances can be deceiving.

This photograph was taken late in the afternoon with the dying sun, which provided the long, almost foreboding, shadows. The ranch sits in the lee of a small hill, casting it in shadow. Still, the sun illuminates just the ranch proper, providing a small bit of cheer and warmth to the otherwise cold, cold scene.

The Valles Caldera National Preserve is an interesting place; one, at the moment, full of snow, but snow adds to the charm and serenity that holds it in thrall until the springtime thaw.

Dune's Edge

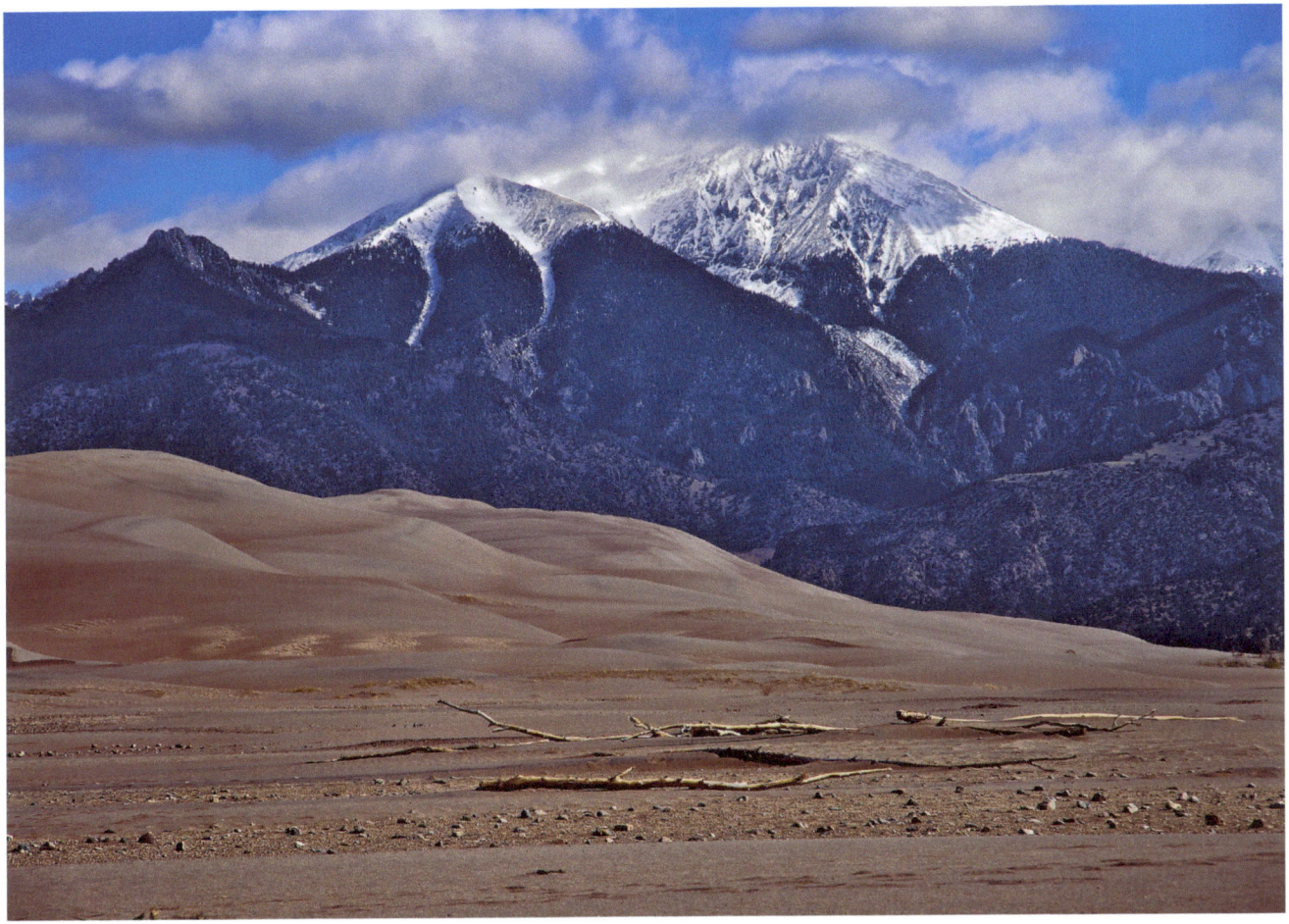

At the edge of the world—the very edge—the boundaries between earth and sky tend to be a little bit murky and ill defined. There, the edges all run together in one big rush, and it is hard to tell where one ends and the other begins. In all likelihood, the edges themselves don't pay quite enough attention, further exasperating the problem. Such a place is found in southern Colorado at the Great Sand Dunes National Park. There the edge of the dune field extends right up to the edge of the Sangre de Cristo Mountains. One moment, there is pure sand as far as the eye can see. The next footstep—the very next one—there is mountain as high as the eye can see. The line is not sharp; it is not distinct; and it is not constant, for it may not even be a line at all.

But really, what else would you expect to see at the edge of the world?

Hanging Lake

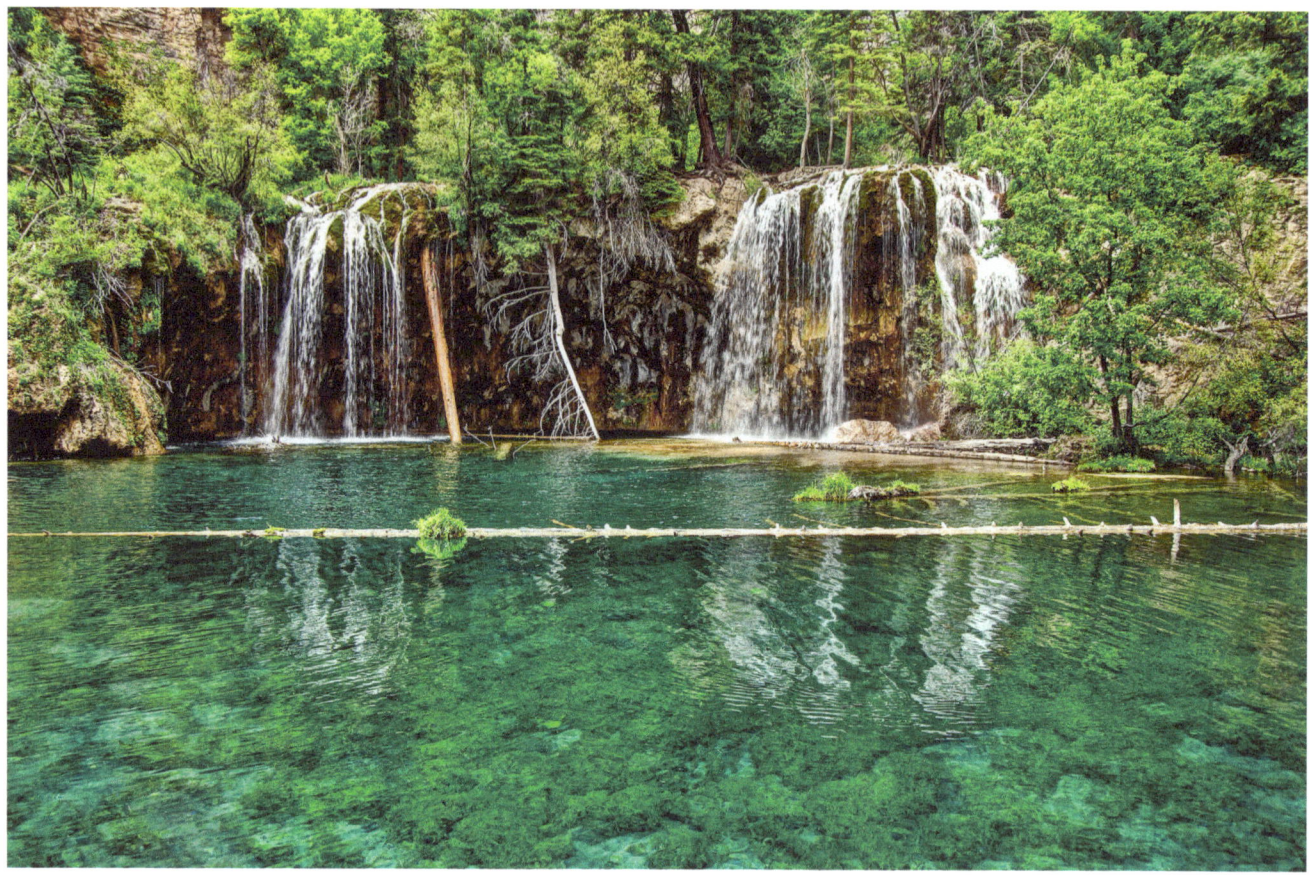

Imagine seeing a small, clear, swift-moving stream before you. Nothing too special there, because our country has countless such places and streams. Even knowing that this particular stream is in northern Colorado doesn't narrow it down too much, since small, swift-moving streams are everywhere there. But if you happen to look up from this stream one thousand feet or so, you would see the miracle that is Hanging Lake.

Hanging Lake is just that, hanging. Nestled in a geological fault one thousand feet above the floor of Glenwood Canyon, it is magical. Fed by twin waterfalls, it boasts a beautiful aquamarine color and a feeling of absolute calm and serenity. By any standard, it is a true marvel. The shoreline is mainly travertine, which gives the water its extraordinary and unusual color. The water is beyond crystal clear, and if weren't for the ripples from the falls, you would never know it was there. The next time you see a small stream at your feet, don't forget to look up. You never know when a lake is there.

Ancient Forest

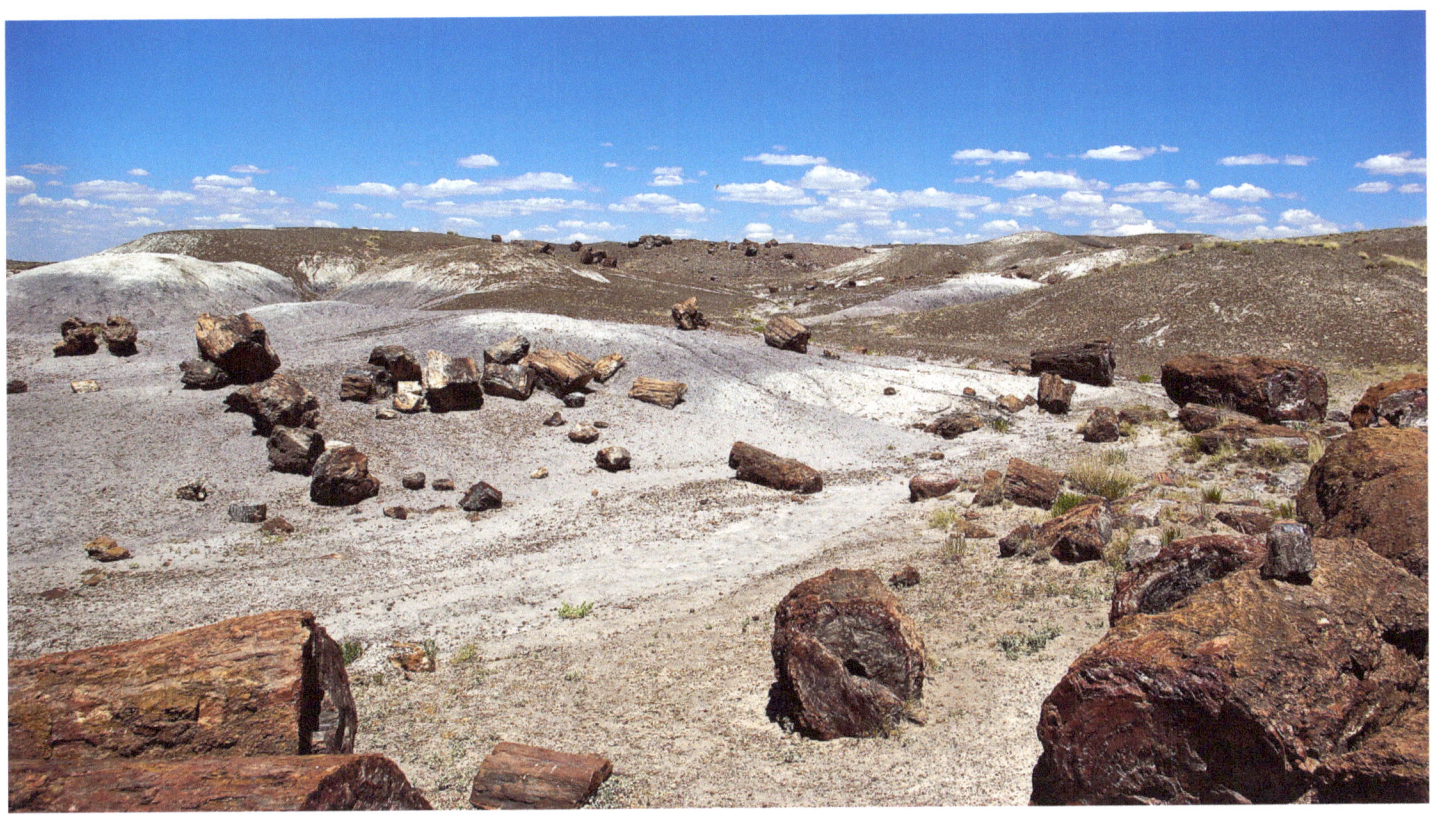

Some extraordinary places on our magnificent planet endure throughout the centuries and even the millennia. These places stand the test of time, remaining as they always are, and as they always will be. Some places, however, are not as lucky, and time takes out its frustration on them. The Petrified National Forest is one of those places.

What was once a lush, rich, and vibrant tropical forest is now arid desert. Tall rainforest trees lie in petrified fragments almost forgotten amid the sand. The winds of the desert and the winds of time now and then again reveal a tree once long lost, but those same fickle winds also hide one that was enjoying the sun. The Petrified National Forest is a treasure, although a desolate and harsh one. It is a stark reminder of a time long past. The vegetation is gone, but the trees remain, and somehow, against the odds, morphed into an extraordinary place that endures forever.

Silverton Afternoon

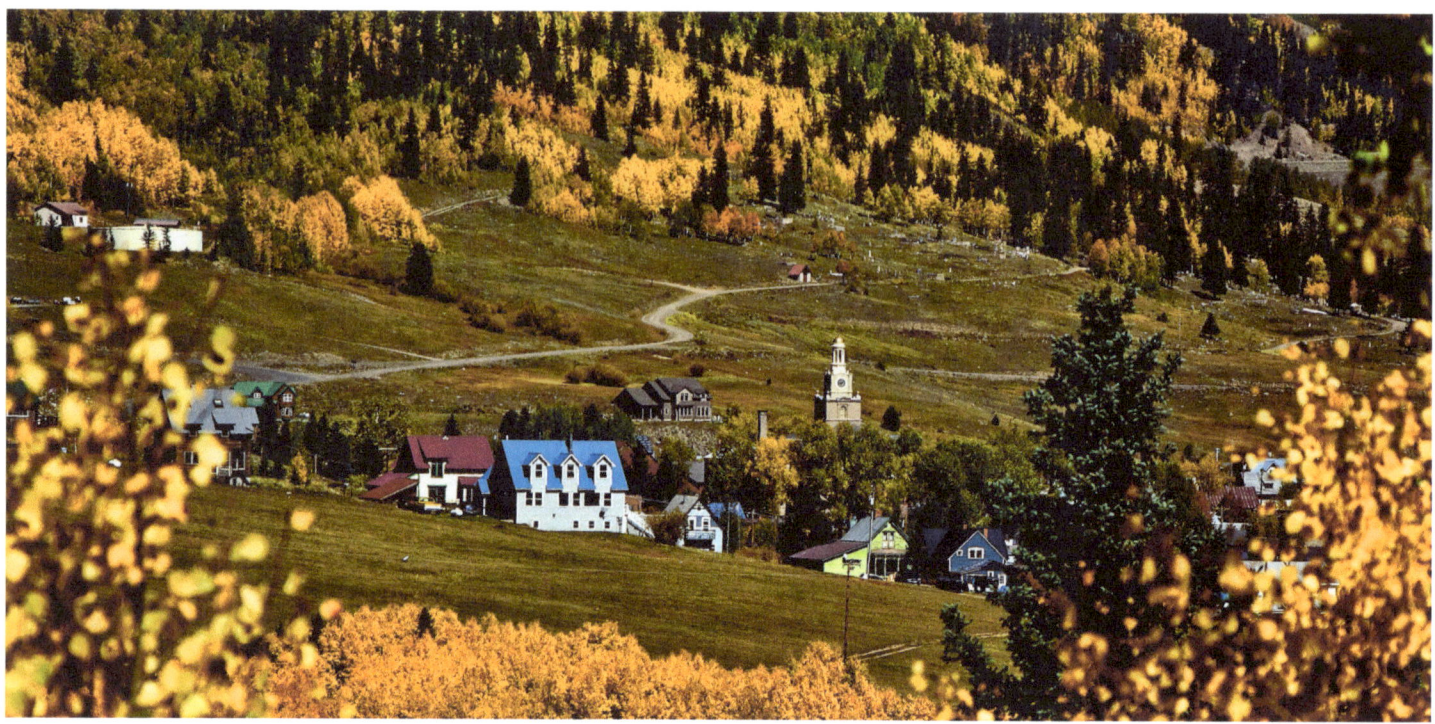

Nestled in a valley along The Million Dollar Highway in Colorado lies Silverton. It isn't the biggest town around, not by a long shot, and on the way in, you can see the entire town and then some, neatly laid out. What it lacks in size, however, it more than makes up for in charm and history.

Silverton is, as one might reasonably expect, a mining town, or at least it was a mining town, before the mines around it played out. Its history is rich and storied, and silver played a significant role in that history. All around the town are the relics of the mining era: mining tools, railroad tracks, equipment, and of course, the mines and mills themselves.

On this autumn day, Silverton was basking in a sunny afternoon. This view is from one of the curves on the approach to town, peering through the aspens in full fall color down into one edge of town. From this vantage, the town is quiet and colorful.

Still, even from this distance and through this time, if you listen closely and carefully, you can hear the sounds of the mines and mills churning out silver for those lucky enough to have found it.

Crystal's Summer

Back in 1892, well before the widespread use of electricity, the need for power tools certainly existed at the Sheep Mountain Mine near Crystal, Colorado. There was silver in that mine, and mining it was backbreaking work. Without a convenient power plant, human ingenuity came to the forefront.

A small, powerful river happened to run nearby: the Crystal River. A power plant was built just above a small fall on the river. A horizontal water wheel ingeniously turned the water motion into compressed air, which was then fed to the mine to power the tools. The mining in the Sheep Mountain Mine became far more efficient. The mine eventually closed in 1917, and the residents of nearby Crystal drifted away. The mine, power plant, and town all faded into the past, as many mining towns eventually do.

Crystal remains a very special place, however, and today, the power plant (now colloquially called Crystal Mill, even though it was never a mill) remain an iconic Colorado location. Although the buildings next to the mill have long since collapsed, Crystal Mill itself remains, standing steadfast against the elements and time. Crystal Mill is also rare in the United States, because few such power plants were ever built in the first place: to have one still standing is a true marvel. Nestled against the river and in between a picturesque stand of aspens, Crystal Mill remains today as a symbol and a sign of Colorado mining at its finest.

Oddly, today the town of Crystal does not have electricity, even though it does have a handful of seasonal residents. In talking to these sons and granddaughters of the original miners, they don't miss it, and life there is idyllic. Time marches on, but not everywhere.

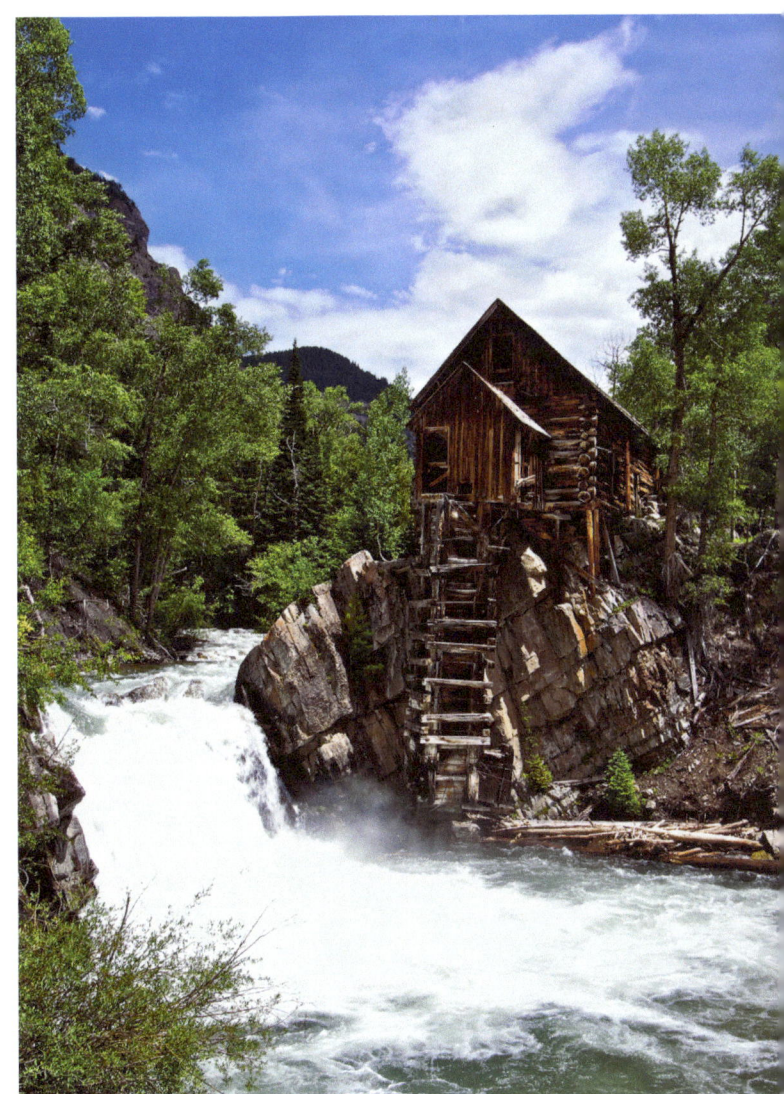

Capilla's Joy

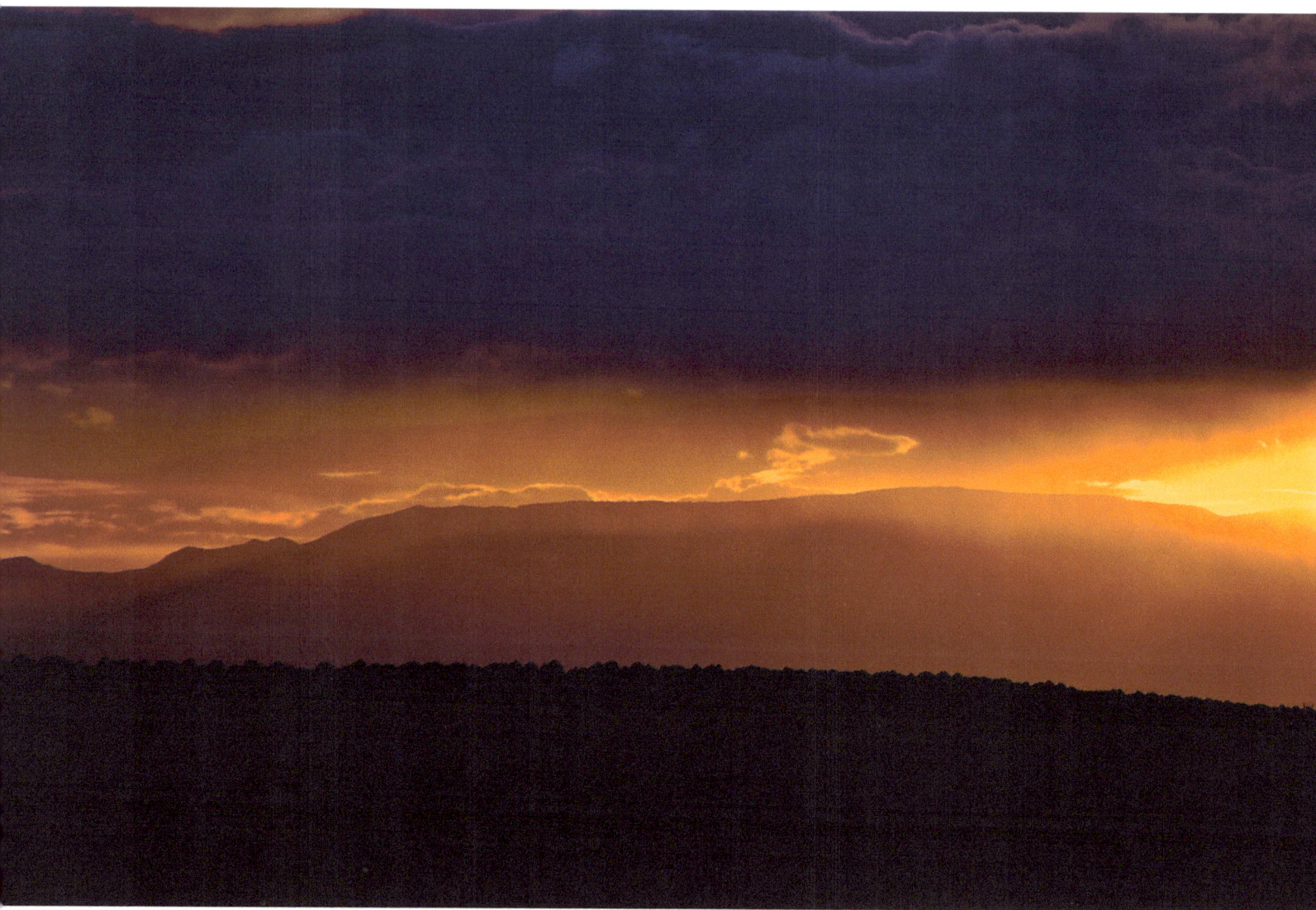

The day was at its end. It had been a long day, and moreover, a drab one. The storm clouds scuttled endlessly through the sky, and the ground below gave up on seeing any bit of the sun. Snow threatened throughout the day, although sometimes nature changed its mind and threatened to rain, instead. In the end, it bothered to do neither. The sun had done its best. Here and there it found a break in the clouds and began to light, and warm, the earth below, but no sooner did it do so

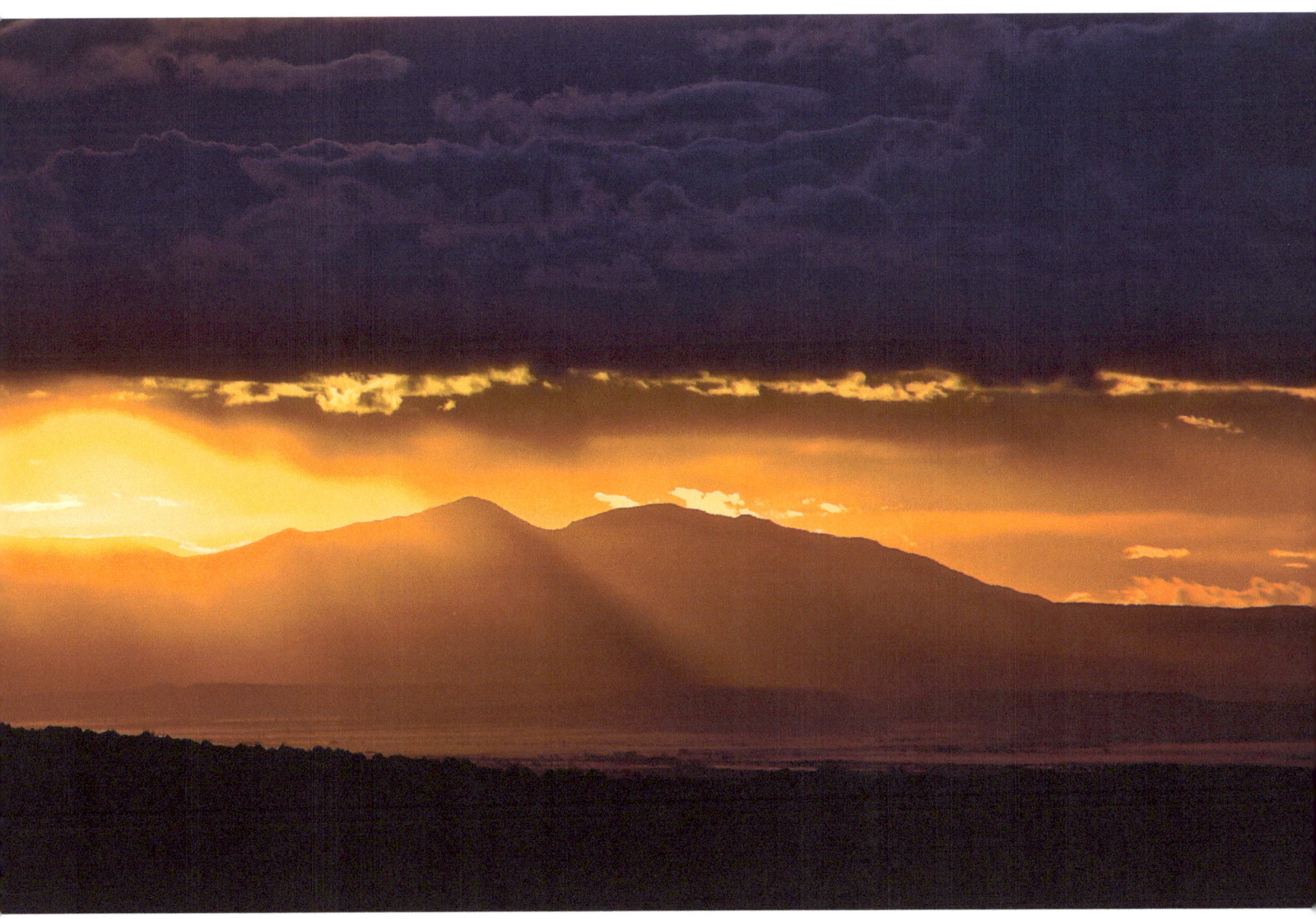

then the clouds found the break and as quickly closed ranks. Waiting until the clouds were preoccupied in the east, the sun slipped westward, as it does every day. At the last moment it found the opening it was looking for, and quickly dropped beneath the unsuspecting clouds. In that instant, the sun's golden rays spread across the land, washing it in the most incredible colors imaginable. Capilla Peak basked in the glory and the joy that was due the day.

Red Rock

The Southwest is often associated with red rocks. Red rocks come in many varieties, from small yet outstanding formations to vast sweeping panoramas.

Classic Wave

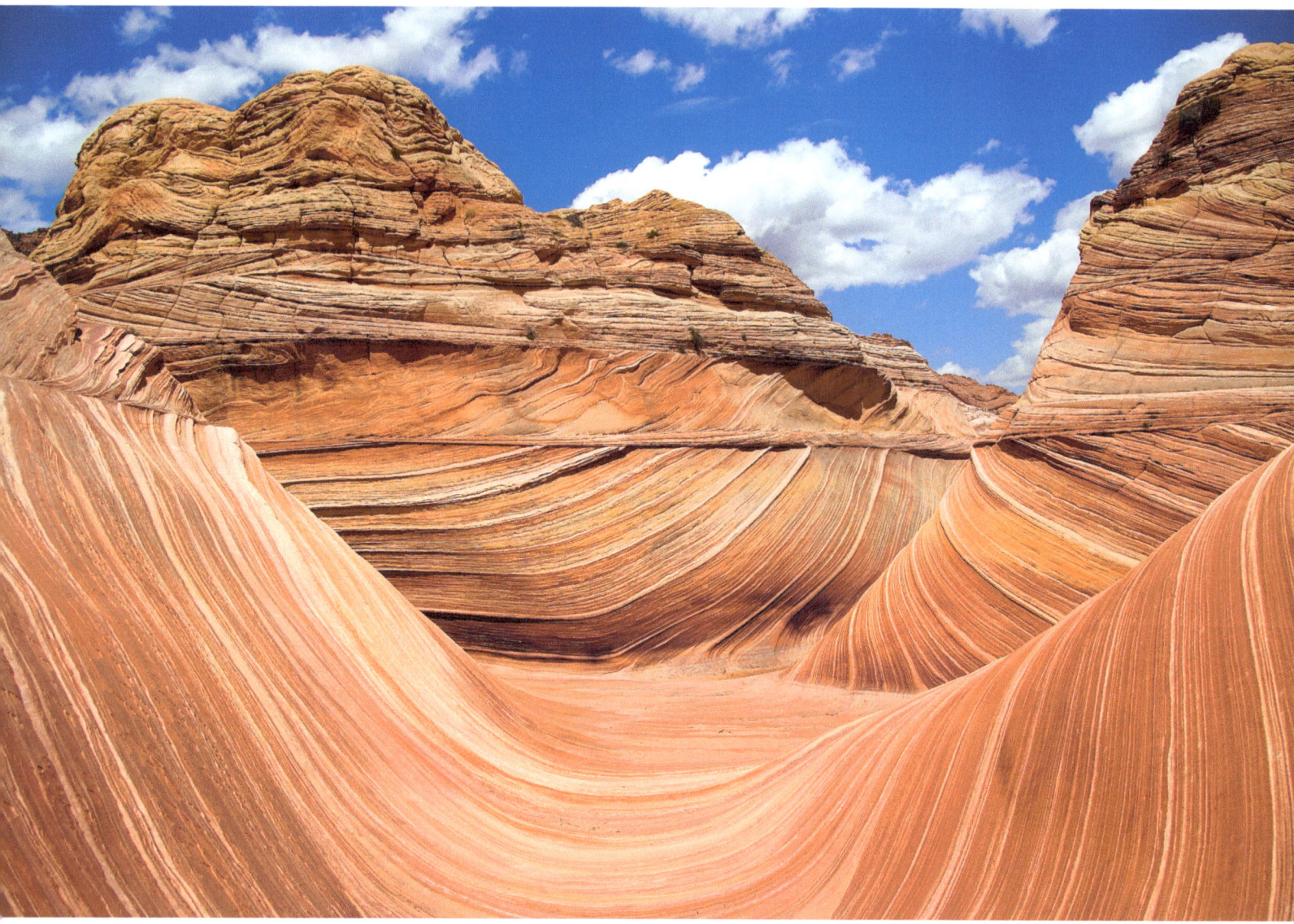

This is the "classic" photograph of Southwest red rocks. Known simply as The Wave, its strong lines, wind-carved through eons of effort, provide a view unlike any other. The sandstone reds and sky blues combine effortlessly to provide a beautiful Southwest palette. Its beauty and magnificence are unmatched anywhere in the world. There is no place quite like The Wave.

Wave Way

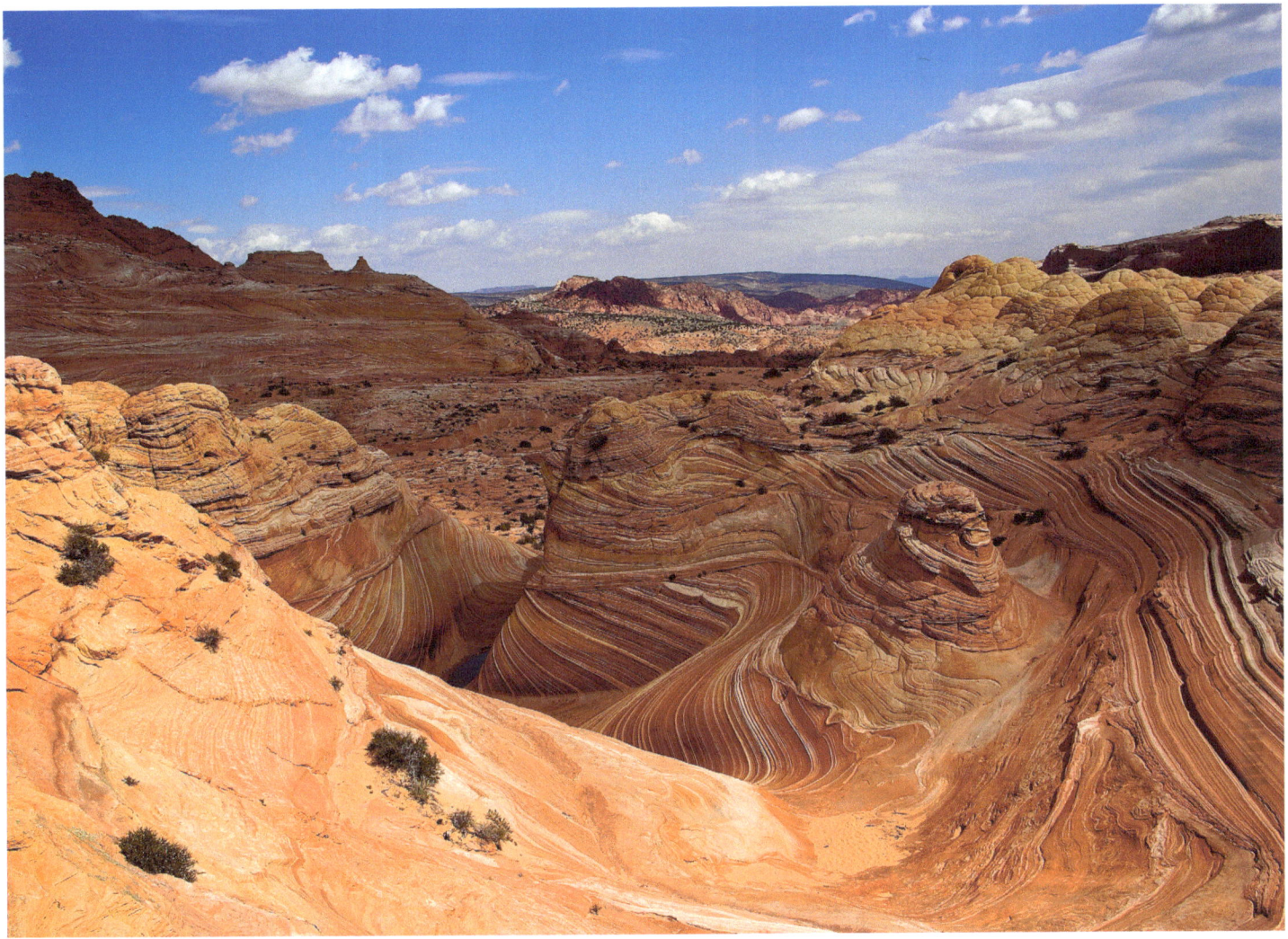

The Wave lies in the heart of in the Paria Wilderness in northern Arizona. No roads or formal trails ease the three-mile trek to it; rather a hiker must follow directions such as "go that way about so far." Still, for those that find it, the beauty of the area is outstanding. The colors and the lines make a tortured and arresting landscape, an almost surreal one that defies the imagination. When you approach The Wave, it doesn't seem like you are coming to anything special, but as you walk out onto the feature, that notion is tossed aside. You can visit The Wave by permit only, and because many folks want to make their own pilgrimage to it, a daily lottery is held to select the lucky few. The Wave is truly a hidden treasure of the desert.

Inspired Valley

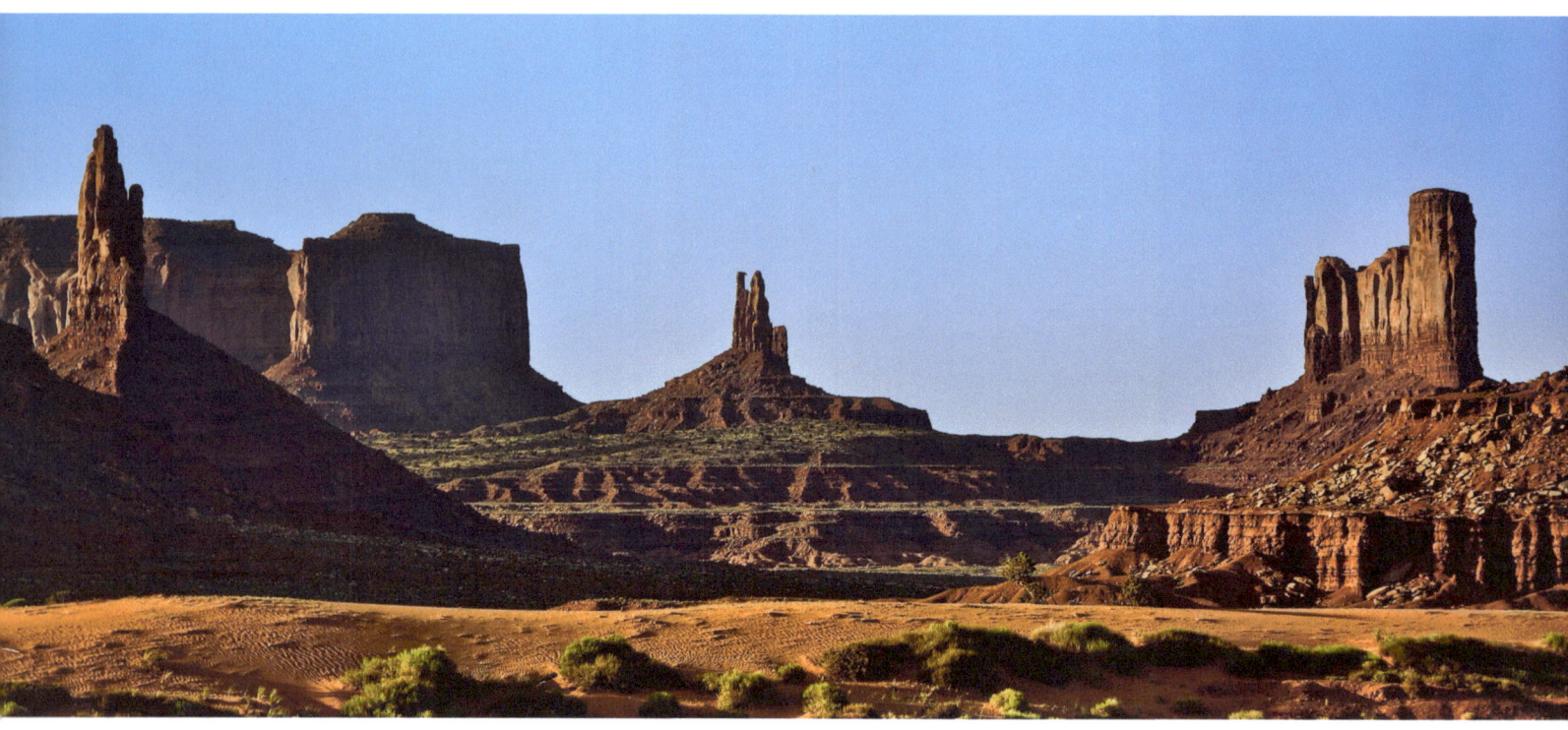

As you look out across the floor of Monument Valley, it is easy to forget exactly where you are. It is hard to remember that you are on Planet Earth or in North America or the state of Arizona or Utah, depending on where you happen to be standing. It is hard to remember that you are not in the time of dinosaurs, too, and it would not be completely unexpected to see one lumber out from in between the rocks over yonder. The landscape is ethereal and distant, in time and space, yet despite that, here it is before you.

The spires that reach up from this section of Monument Valley do so with the hope of touching the sky, not an impossible dream, for their brethren next to them do just that. Make no mistake about it, although these spires look small, they are not. Each is significant in its own right, but when everything around is even bigger, your sense of scale gets a little skewed.

Monument Valley has been the inspiration for much of our Southwest vision, and rightfully so.

Canyonlands Overlook

Canyonlands National Park in Utah has some of the most incredible scenery imaginable. Deep canyons with sheer, steep walls weave through twisted, torn red rock. Rivers run in impossible paths, tearing through the desert. Buttes rise out of nowhere, challenging the sky for supremacy, and all these things are taking place in the first view you see. After that, the views get even more intense.

It is hard to describe, let alone do justice to, this area. It is full of geological surprises wherever you look. It has a few roads, but they are difficult passages and not for the faint of heart.

Still, sometimes if you peer out from an overlook many hundreds of feet above the desert floor, you get a glimpse into and a taste of that world, as in this scene. The Green River, off to the right, wends its way through the area and provides a stark contrast of blues and greens. The early summer day provides warmth to the sky and adds intense reds to the desert, and everything competes for attention.

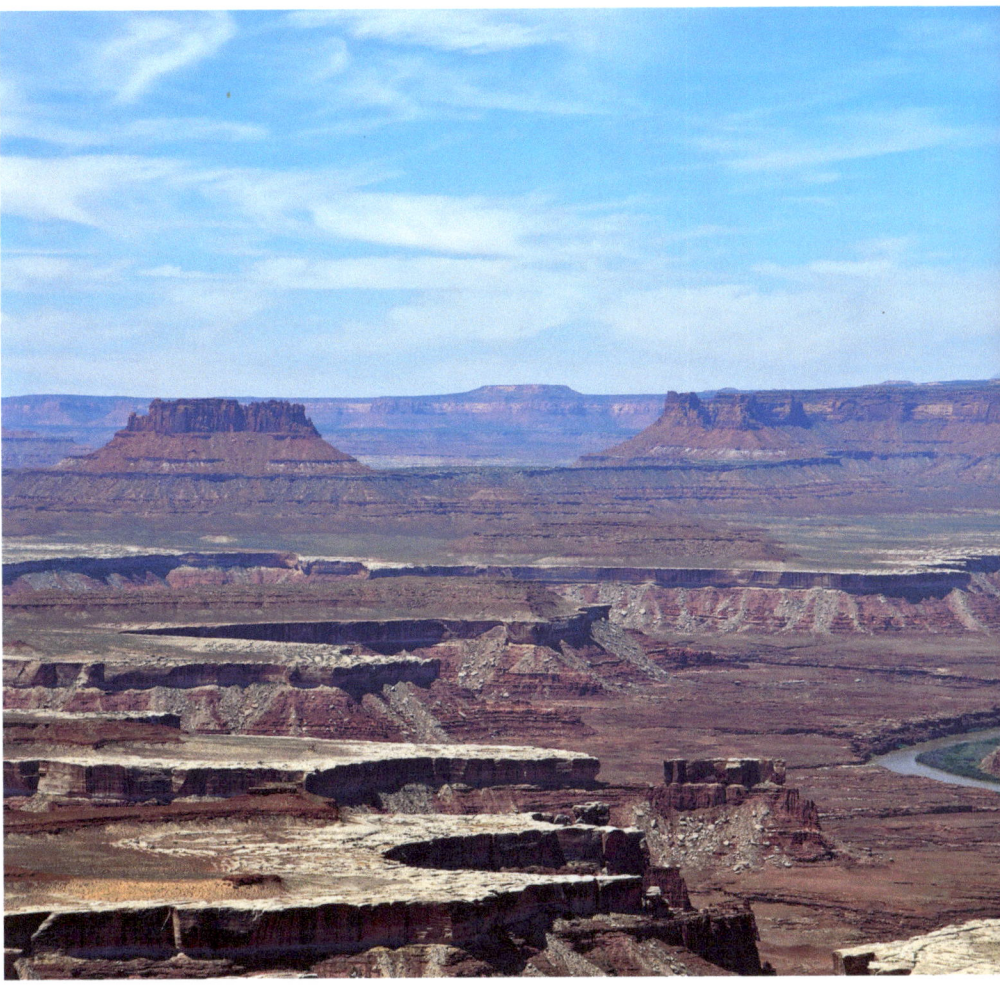

I chose to include this image, harshly lit as it is, to emphasize how unforgiving the desert Southwest is. Despite its overwhelming beauty, it is, at its core, an inhospitable land deeply intolerant of mistakes. Even through the beauty, a sense of hardness pervades the view, and folks must always take heed when traveling in this land.

Canyonlands National Park, and the lesson it teaches, is a sight not soon forgotten.

Delicate Arch

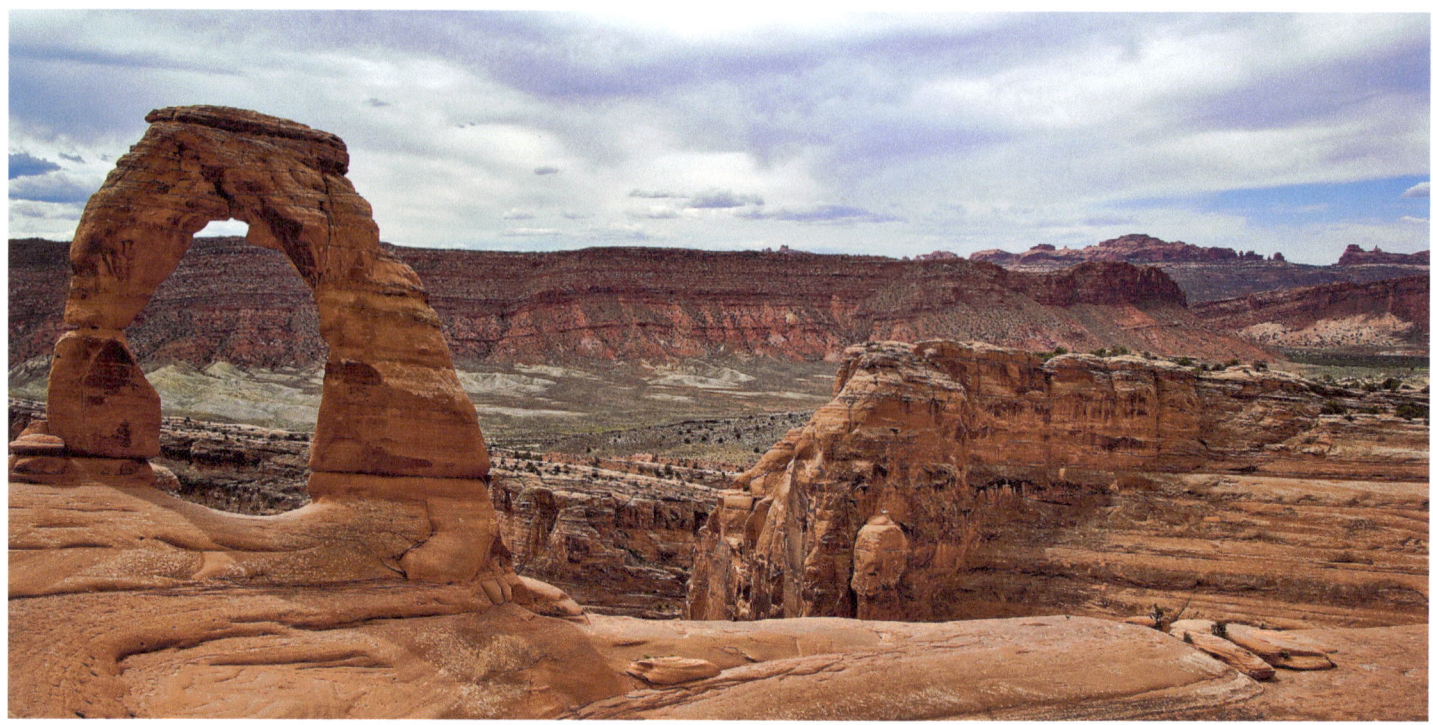

No other arch is as famous or widely known as Delicate Arch in Arches National Park, Utah. Images of it exist everywhere, from books (ahem), to posters, to postage stamps, and even the state of Utah's license plate. Still, that amount of exposure doesn't lessen the sheer beauty of this arch; it enhances it.

Standing fifty two feet tall, the arch is neither small nor particularly delicate. It will, one day, collapse, as all arches do, for time and erosion erases all equally. Until then, however, this arch stands as a monument and symbol of arches everywhere.

Even an overcast day cannot eclipse its grandeur and majesty.

Grosvenor Arch

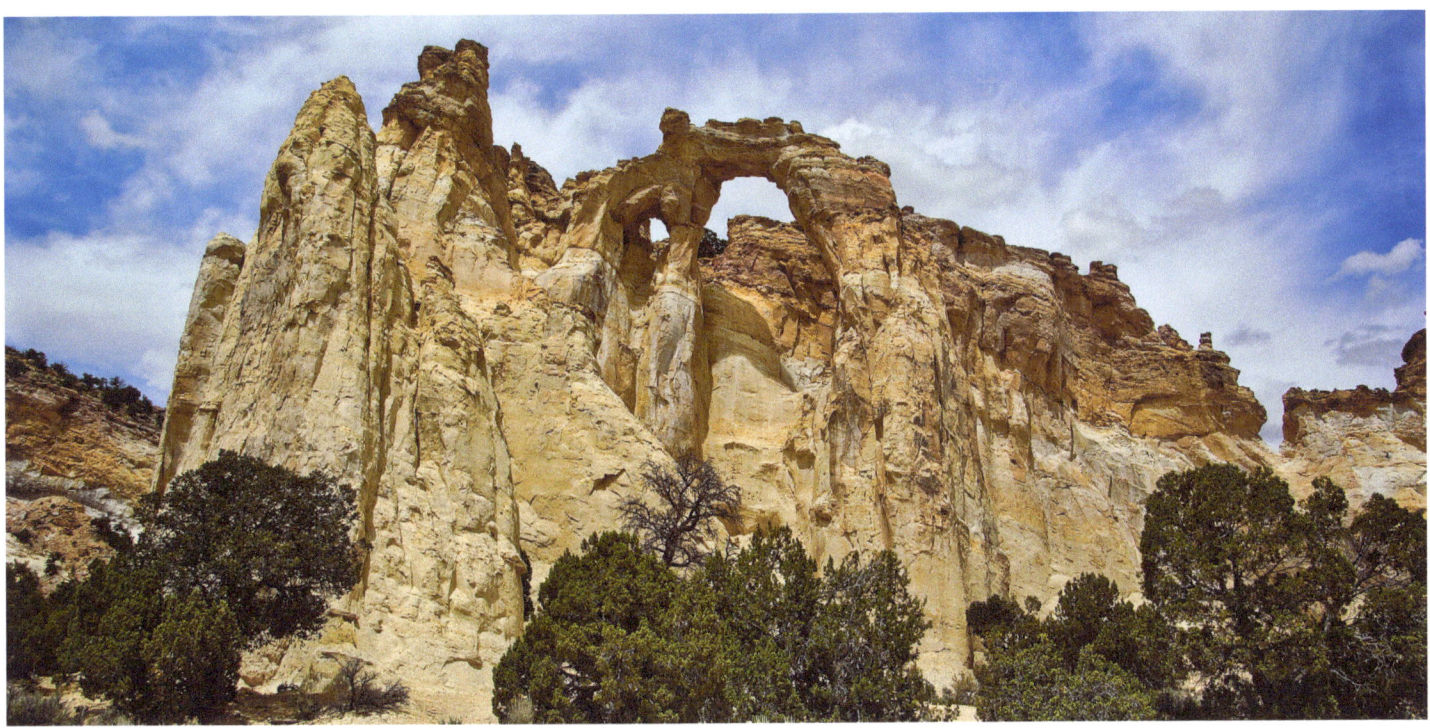

Not every arch is as well known as Delicate Arch, but many are equally spectacular. Take for example, Grosvenor (pronounced as Grove-en-nor) Arch. What makes this arch so interesting and unique is that it is a double arch, plus its main formation stands alone, jutting abruptly out of the surrounding landscape.

Located in the Grand Staircase-Escalante National Monument in Utah, this arch doesn't receive nearly the amount of attention that other arches do. For this reason, it deserved inclusion here, for one of my goals is to celebrate a wide diversity of beauty throughout the Southwest, from the well known to the seldom trod.

When I first encountered this arch, I was speechless. It was an unexpected sight at an unexpected time in an unexpected place, which is probably why it made such a lasting impression on me. It serves me well as a reminder that the raw power of the Southwest is everywhere, and often "just over there."

Bryce Point

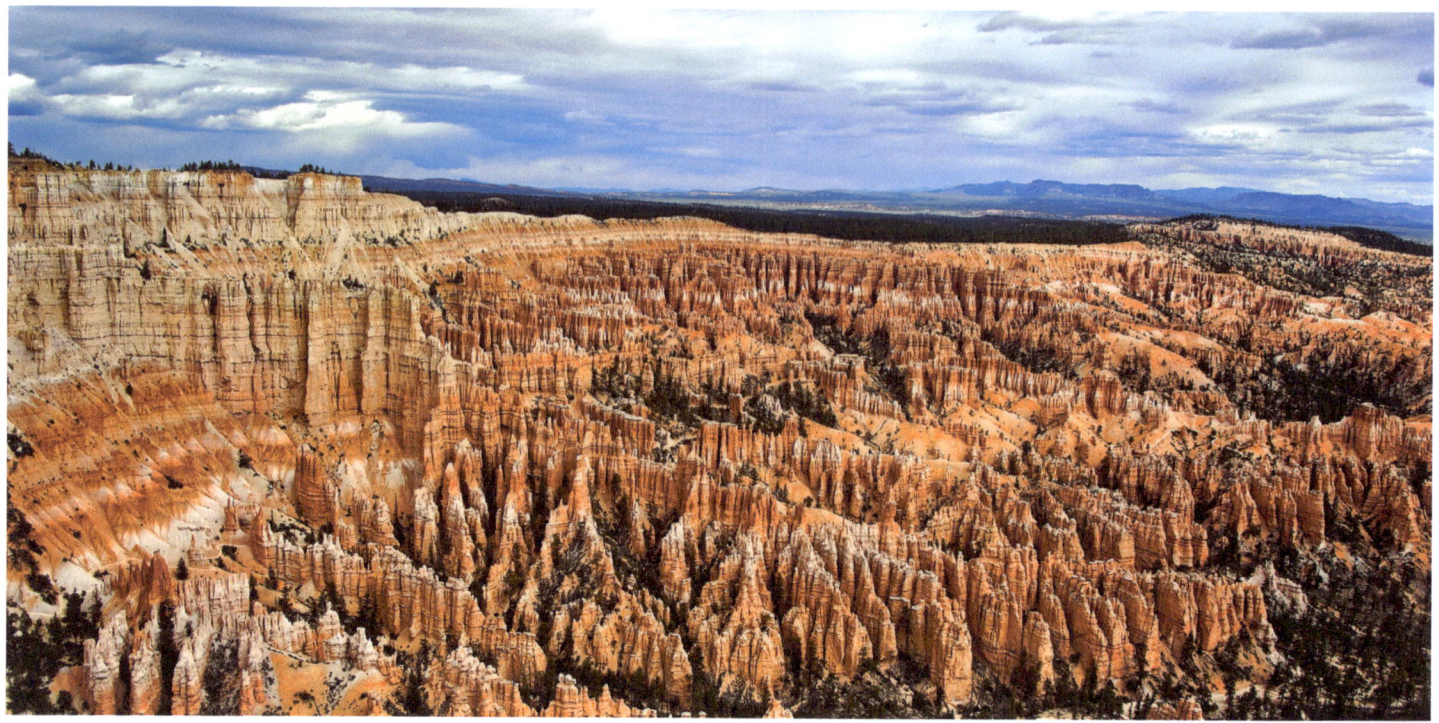

Utah has its share of big, red rocks; that's for sure. It has some amazing soaring rock formations and arches that reach toward the sky. It also has, located in canyons far below the sky, hoodoos.

Hoodoos are fun to spot, often boast multiple bands of color, and typically are conical. When there are a lot of them together, the effect is stunning. Bryce Canyon National Park is the best place to see hoodoos en masse. Here, everywhere one looks, hoodoos abound; countless, innumerable hoodoos from wall to wall of each and every canyon, and those canyons are not small, either. And within the park, Bryce Point is one place where you can readily see the full scope of the hoodoos. From left to right, front to back, as far as the eye can see are hoodoos everywhere, big and small, each with bands of color, and collectively with uniform colors.

It is hard to capture the sheer scale of the hoodoos and how large the area in this photograph encompasses. Ebenezer Bryce said it the very best when he dryly commented that this is a "hell of a place to lose a cow."

Evening Bluffs

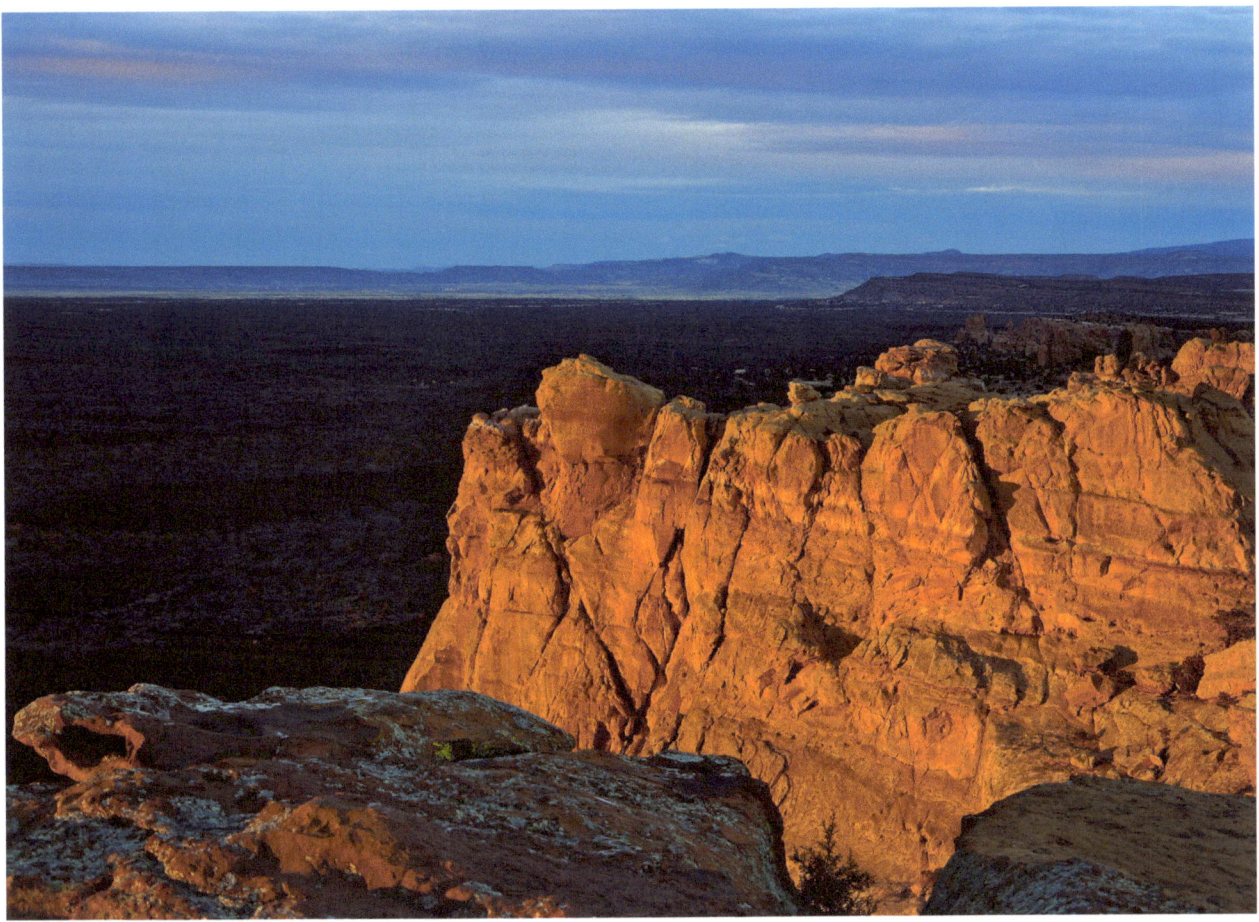

New Mexico can also lay claim to some wonderful red rocks, as exemplified by these sandstone bluffs in El Malpais National Monument. By day, these colorwise unassuming bluffs look out over the vista beyond, and you might pass them with barely a glance at their drab color. Come evening, though, in the rich colors of the waning sun, the bluffs come alive, with reds, oranges, and yellows. As the sun sinks lower, the colors become even more intense, deepening and strengthening. As the sun slips below the horizon, the color drains back out of the bluffs.

Tomorrow, though, the performance takes place again.

Antelope's Light

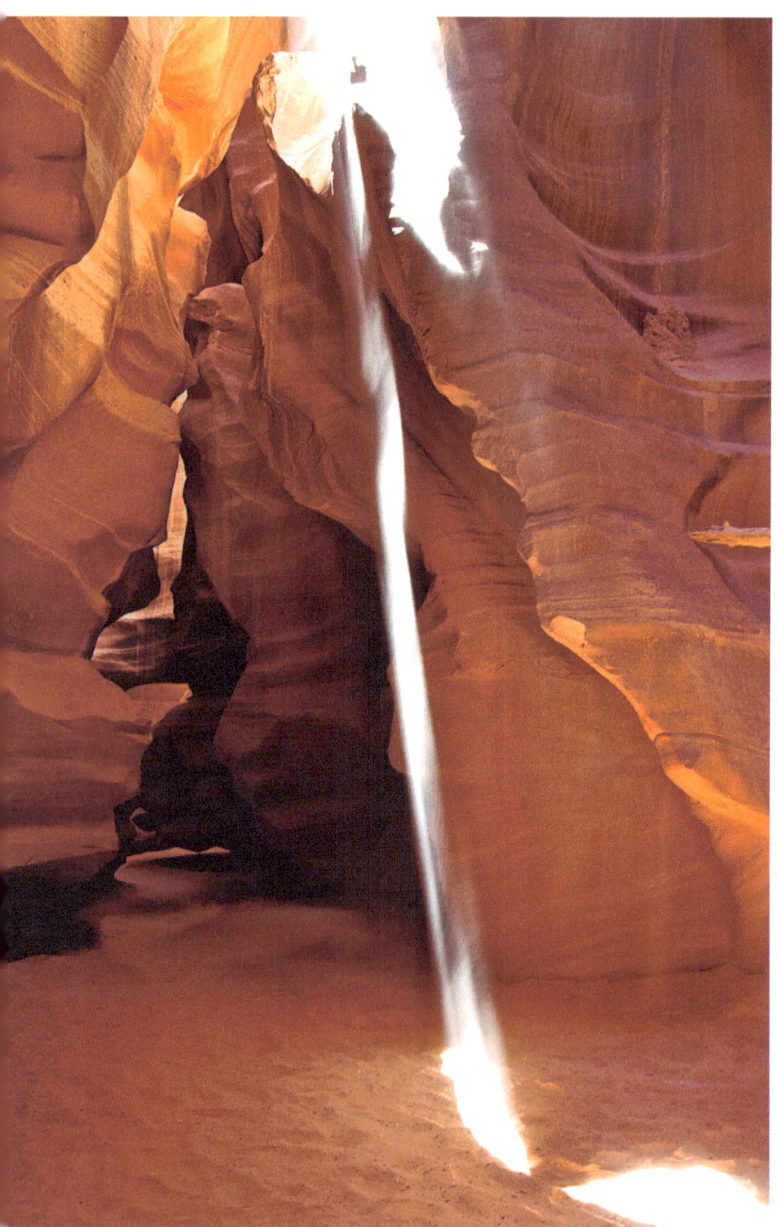

Antelope Canyon is a classic sandstone slot canyon, and along the way happens to be extraordinarily dramatic.

The drama is a result of the confluence of many factors, each incredible in its own right: the combination almost overwhelms the senses. The walls were carved over the centuries and eons by wind and water, and the lines and swirls in them make a remarkable display. Sinewy lines snake through the canyon, drawing the eye along through the twists and turns, back into the deep recesses of a world that surely must lay beyond. Being made of sandstone, the walls hold, yet also reflect the light, causing a wide range of colors, most of them improbable.

From the "normal" color of brown to the highlighted oranges that blend smoothly into yellows, to the oranges that blend smoothly into the reds, the colors vary, wherever you look. As the sun moves overhead, the colors change, providing a constantly shifting scene.

If that phenomenon is not enough, at a certain time of the year, the sun is in the perfect position overhead to shine directly onto the canyon floor. The top, however, is so narrow and the sides so convoluted that the sun rarely reaches all the way to the very bottom. Light beams appear in those few places the sun is able to pierce the gloom, as they strike the floor in a splash of pure, white light. The light beams last mere moments, and they move before your very eyes, so the dance of the light beams is a short one.

Wherever you look, the light of Antelope Canyon is beyond description, ever changing, and impossibly beautiful.

Sand Falls

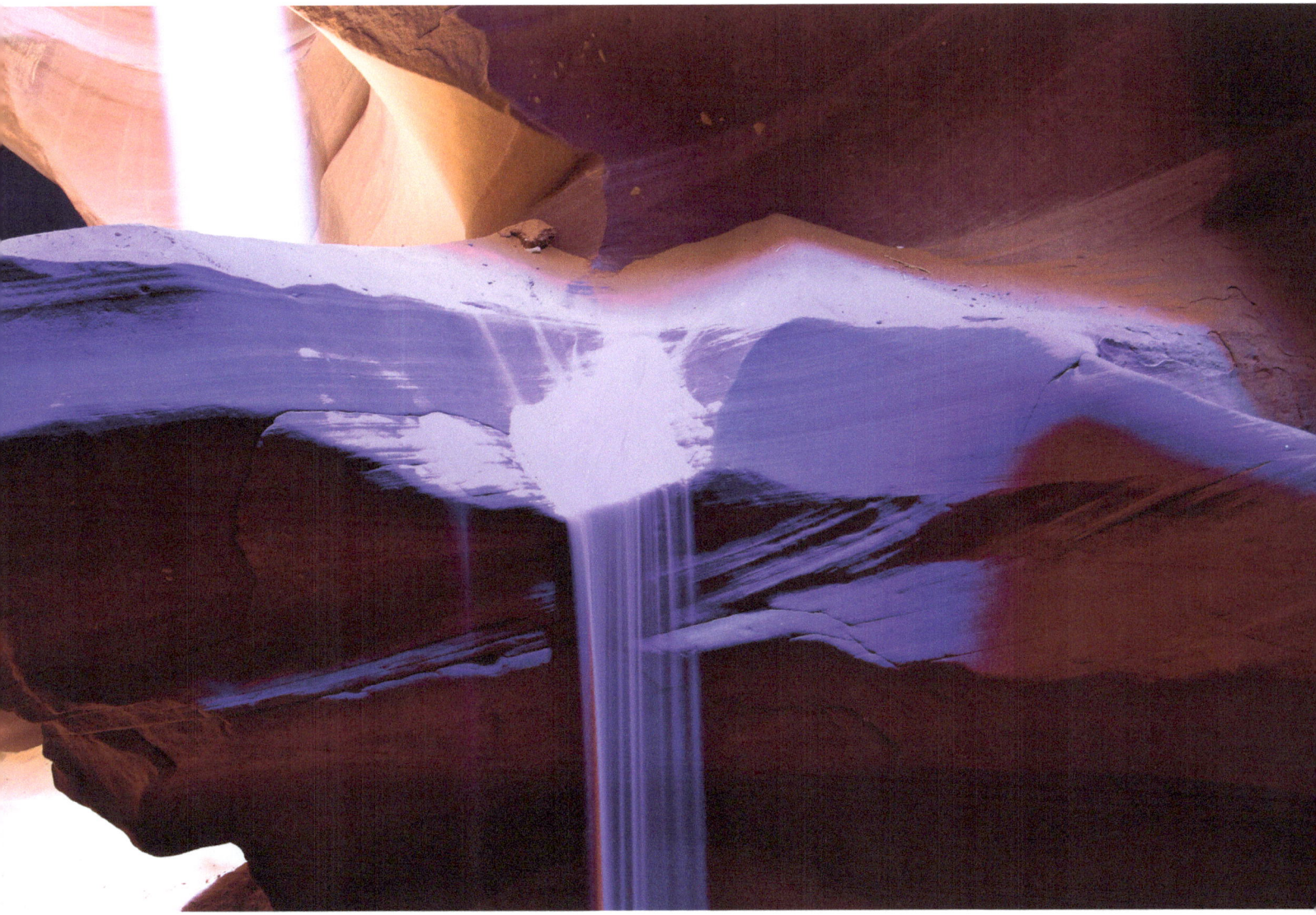

Antelope Canyon is known for its twisty walls and fantastic colors from floor to ceiling. It also has smaller sensations, such as this sand fall. With an intense light beam in the background providing ambient light, the sand fall itself is lit with reflected light only, giving it a violet cast. The sands of time trickle over the edge of the rock, also lit in the reflected violet hues. This is a sight in Antelope Canyon that may be small, but it implies that the sands of time slip away, all the same.

Monte Rojo

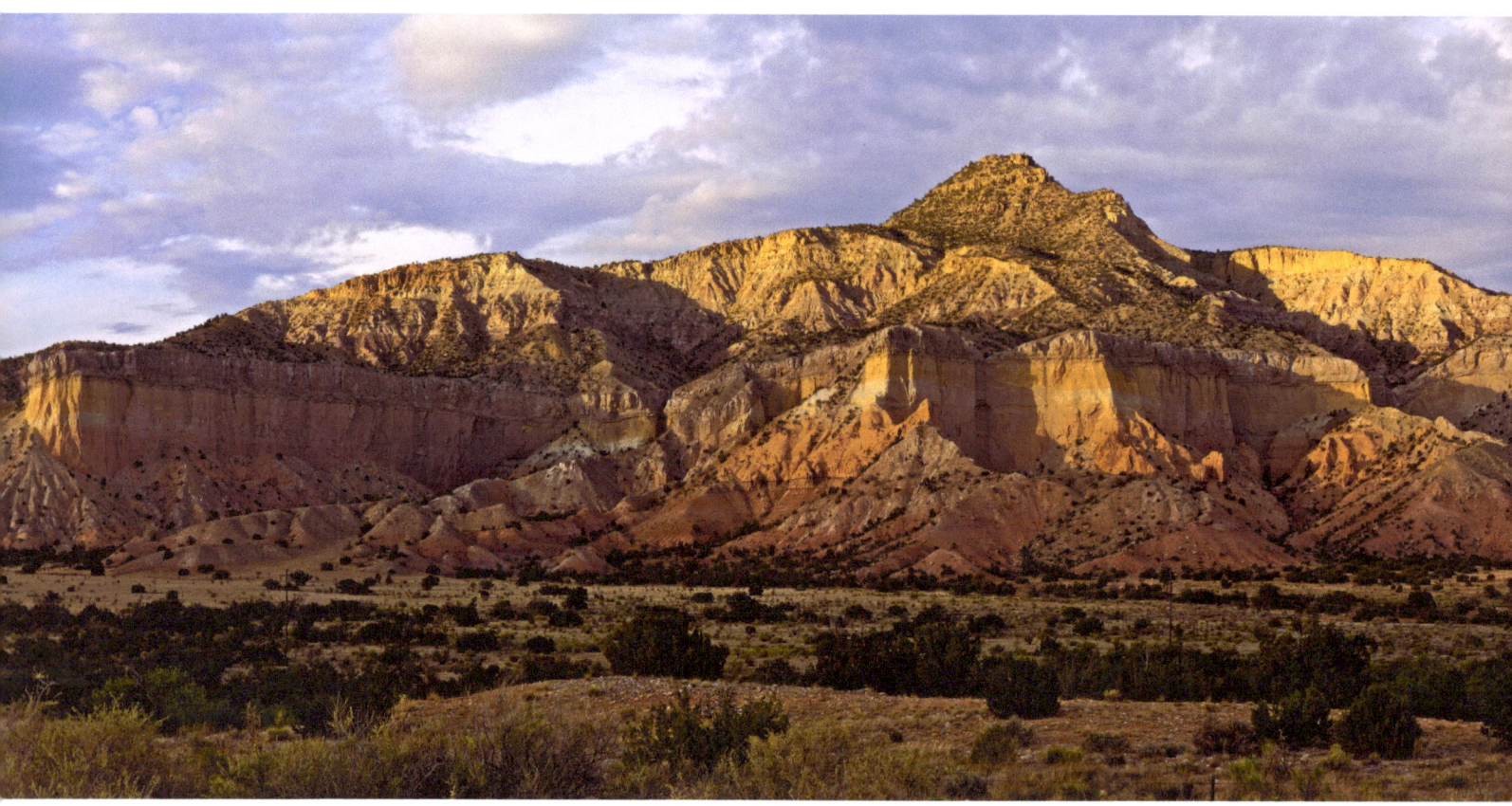

She's still here, painting. If you close your eyes, you can almost see her, hard at work, recording the vast landscape into the canvas before her. Georgia O'Keeffe may have physically left us some time ago, yet her spirit lives on in this area of New Mexico, one of her favorite places, and the subject of so many of her famous landscapes.

Well before her, countless eons ago, this entire area was once a lush, fertile land and home to a great many dinosaurs from the Triassic Period. Several significant finds have been made here, and surely more are waiting just below the red dirt, for those who seek.

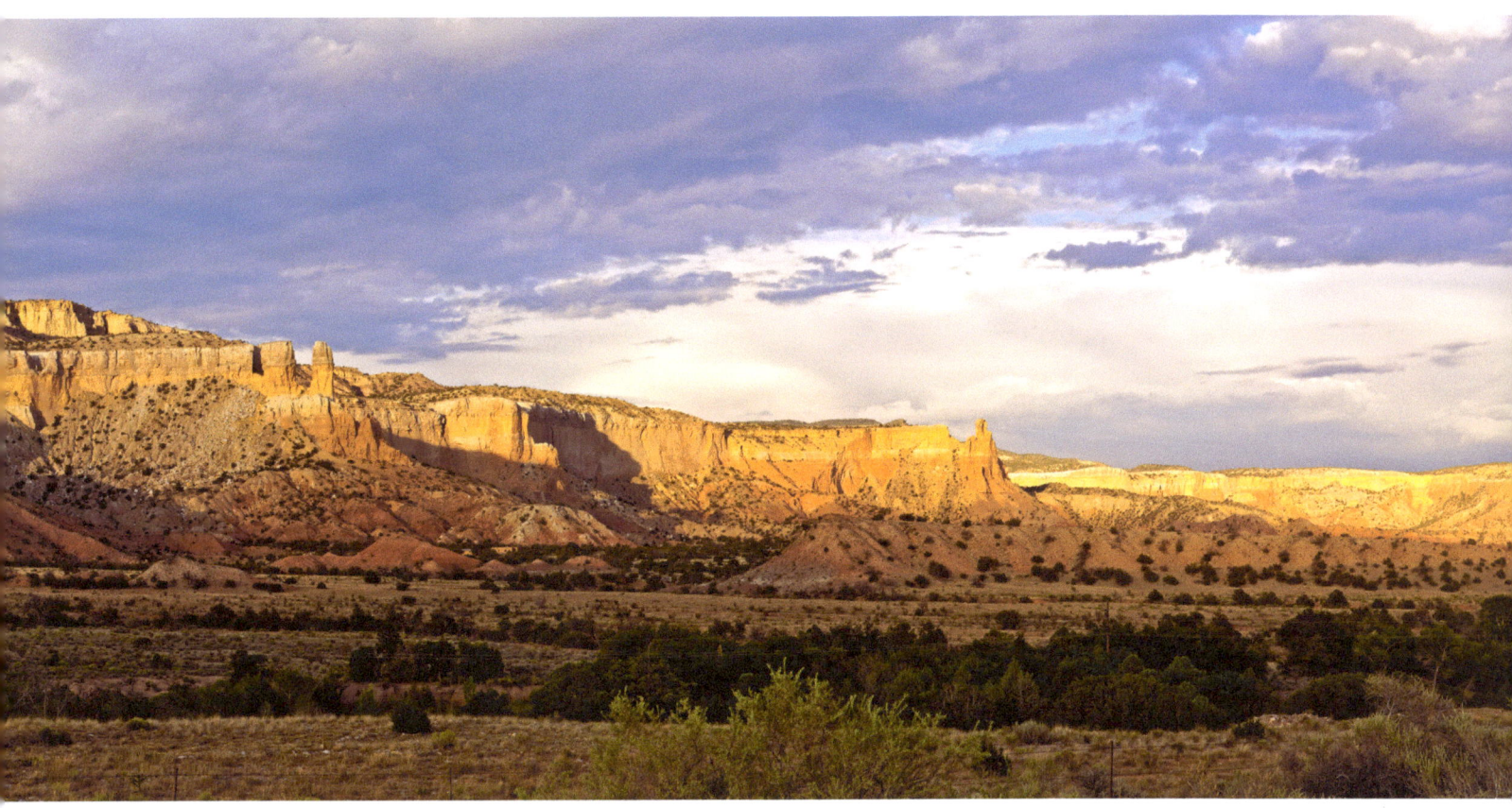

Ghost Ranch has a darker, lesser-known side, as well. It was originally settled back in the 1600s, first by Cristobal Onate, and then more formally by Spanish traders and a military garrison. Staring in the 1800s, however, rustlers used a box canyon there for nefarious activities. Soon enough it became known as Rancho de los Brujos (Ranch of the Witches) and later, simply Ghost Ranch for all those who became a ghost there. Today, however, Ghost Ranch is owned by the Presbyterian Church, and the stories from long ago are just stories.

Or are they?

Visionary Eyes

"The eye is the window to the soul." How many times have we heard that statement? Yet it rings so true. These eyes are exceptional eyes, full of depth and wisdom and perfect windows, each and every one.

Saw-Whet Pose

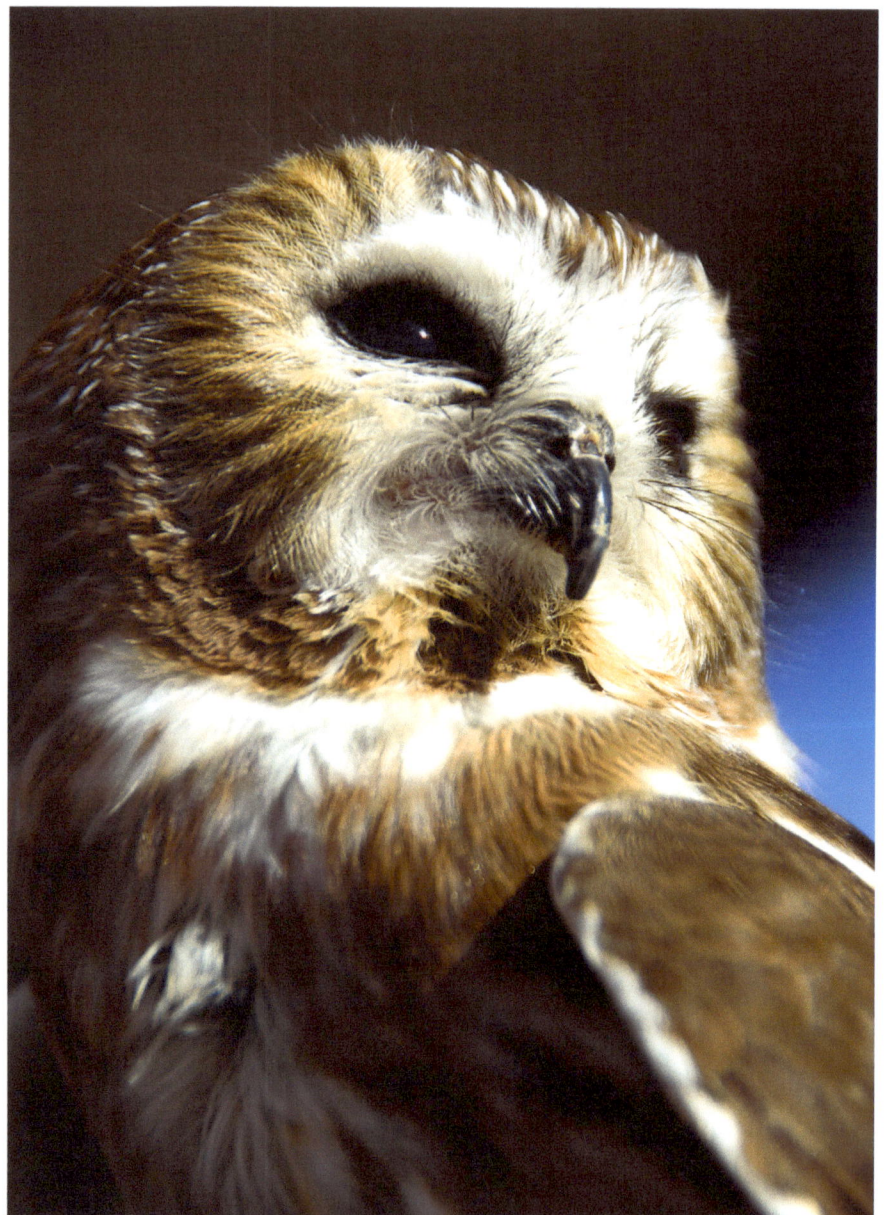

This is a saw-whet owl, captured at the Bosque del Apache National Wildlife Refuge in New Mexico during the Festival of the Cranes. Plenty of dedicated groups are out there taking care of nature when it needs help, and this little guy is a rescue from one such group.

The group is kind enough to let folks meet this little guy, and he was quite a charmer. He seemed to know what a camera was and how to strike a pose. He sat there willingly and happily, I think. Come to think of it, how do I really know the owl was happy? I'm guessing it was. As if just for me, he turned this way and that in the sunlight. He was enjoying the afternoon, and basking in the sunlight. Although it is usually nocturnal, one must make exceptions now and then.

When it comes down to it, is there anything better than spending your afternoon with a posing owl?

Owl Eyes

One of the great things about the Festival of the Cranes is that it is all about the wildlife there, especially birds, and as such, lots of folks come to exhibit and talk about wildlife.

A myriad of birds were there from various wildlife rescue groups, groups that care for those who need help. These people often work diligently to reverse the effects of man on our fragile habitat. These groups desperately need our help so they can save our wildlife. OK, I'll get off my soapbox. Not surprisingly, many of the groups were all about birds, and there in a corner was Wildlife Rescue Inc. of New Mexico, and owls.

Owls are way fun. They are bright, inquisitive, not camera-shy in the least, and they definitely interact with you. They watch you, too, which can be a little unnerving, because of those eyes. The eyes! Here's a hint: don't try to win a staring contest with an owl. You won't. Believe me, this is the voice of experience talking. It's the eyes, you know. That and the fact that they are really sure your name tag says, simply, "Dinner"

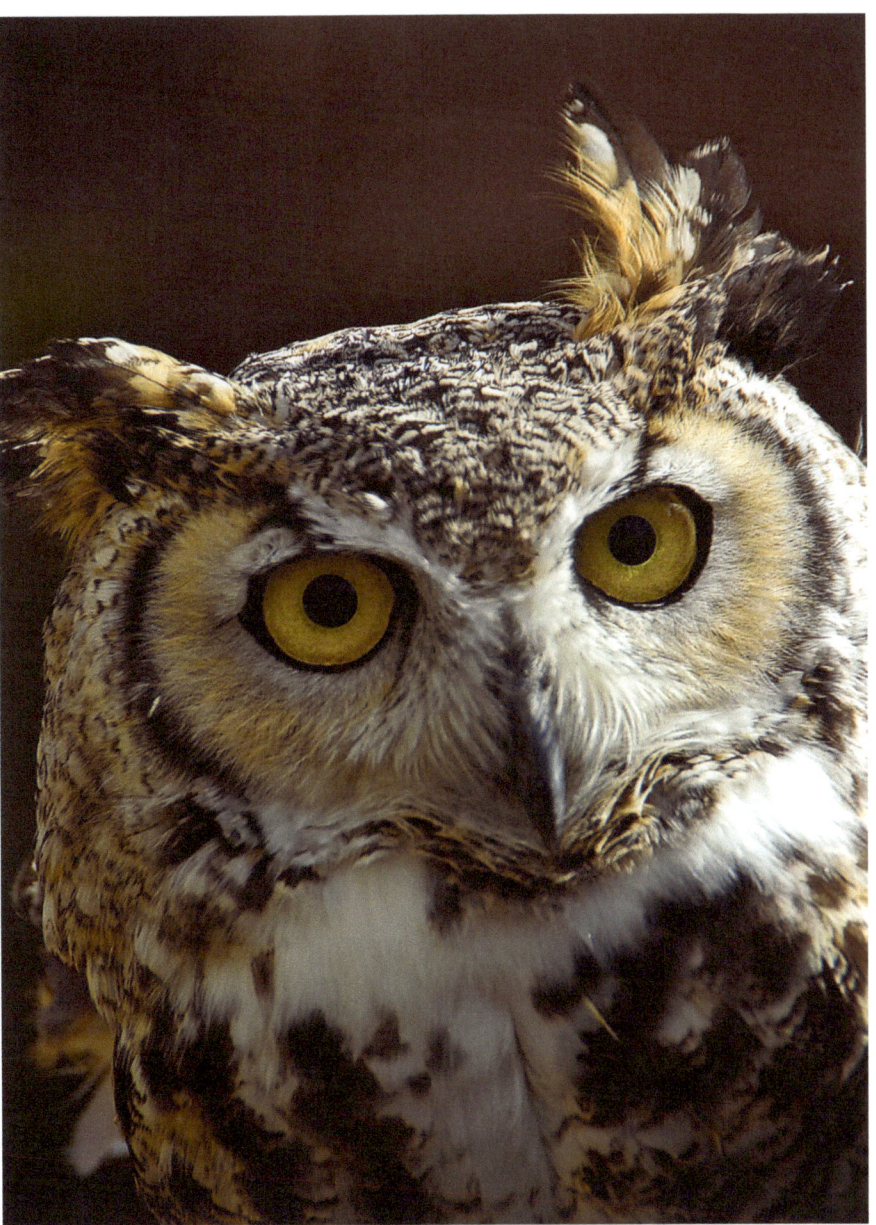

Blue Hoo

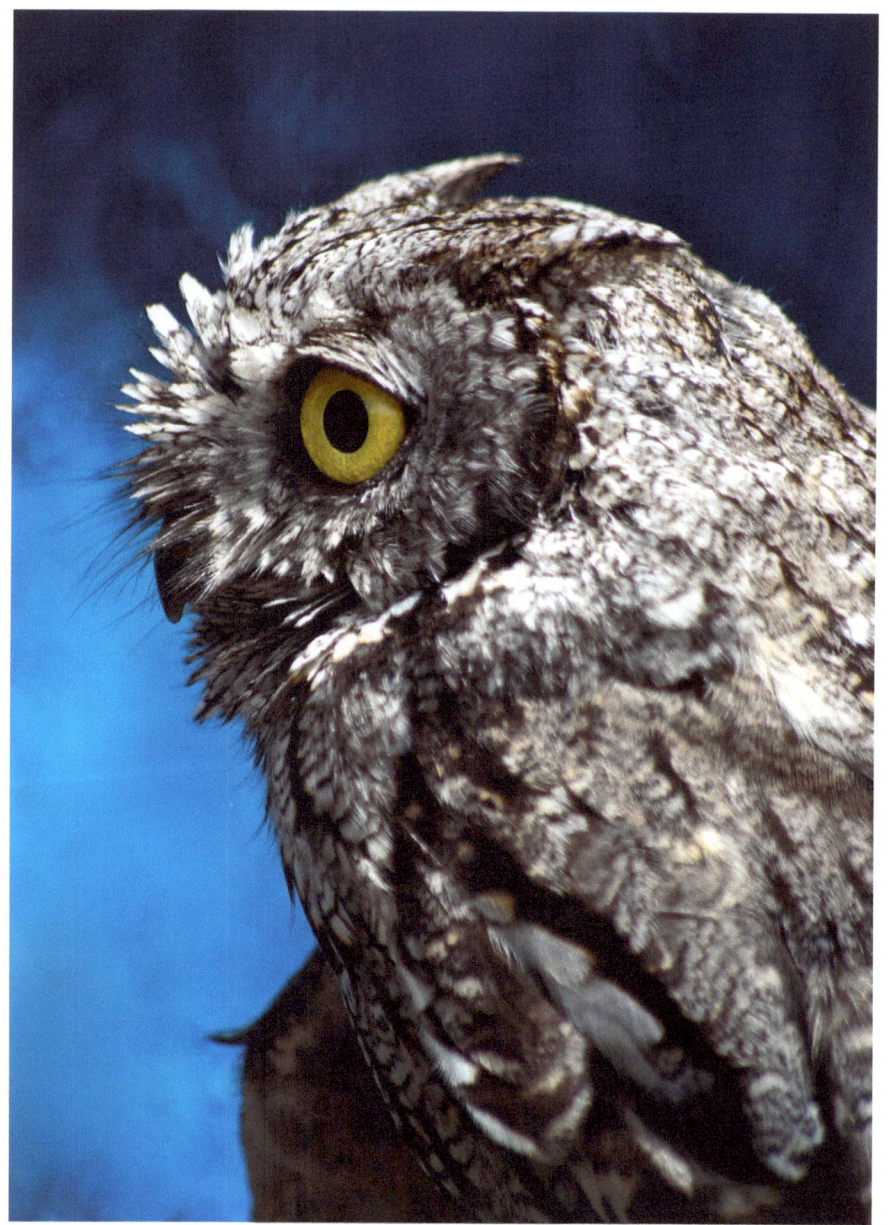

What's in a name, really?

This little fellow, known to us since 1867, has more names than you would imagine; the most common name is the western screech owl, but some of the more fanciful names include dusk owl, ghost owl, mouse owl, cat owl, little cat owl, and, well, let's just say the list is a long one, shall we?

Like all birds of prey, size is no indication of hunting skill, and if you think the list of names for this fellow is long, you should see his dinner menu. If it flies, hops, swims, crawls, slithers, creeps, or even moves, it is fair game. The owl might be only a few inches tall, but he is quite the accomplished hunter.

He's talkative, too. The screech owl doesn't really screech, but does make the all-too-familiar soft and mellow "hoo-hoo-hoo" sound heard throughout western North America.

As you walk through the forest just after sunset and hear that familiar call, you'll know a screech owl is close by. Maybe it is, in owl-speak, swearing up a blue streak. Maybe it is sounding out its territory, or maybe, just maybe, it is saying its name, by whatever name it is called.

Intense Pygmy

Probably close to a million euphemisms compare size to everything else. In all of these, the common theme is that the size of something, often someone, has nothing to do with its attitude or capability or whatever is being compared. Clearly, though, every single one of these platitudes has to draw inspiration from the pygmy owl.

These guys are small, just a few inches high, and they weigh just a few ounces, but they don't know it. Even if you could tell them, they simply would not believe you.

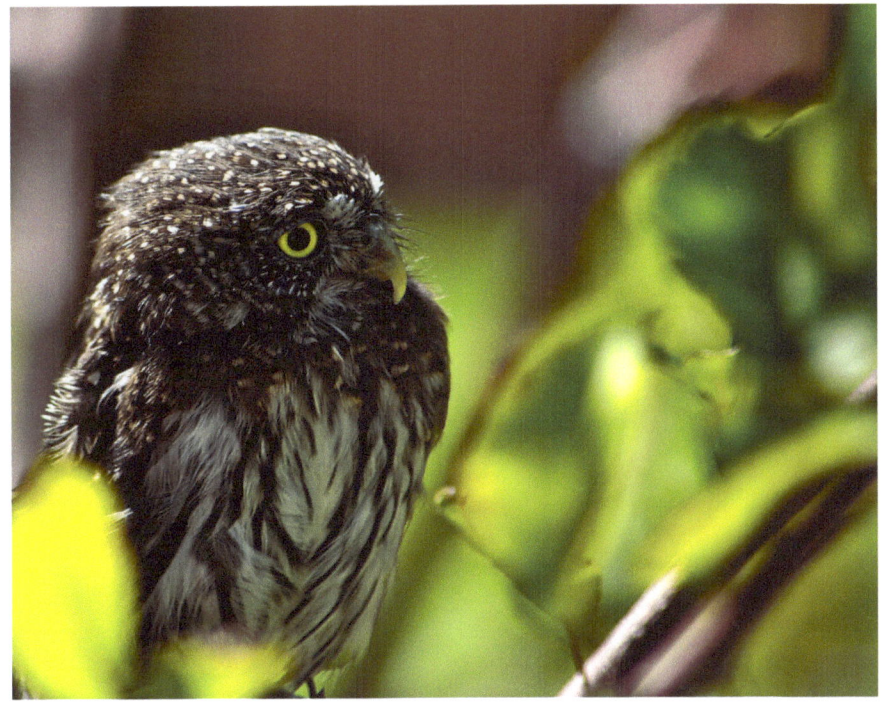

Case in point, this pygmy owl hosted by Wildlife Rescue Inc. of New Mexico. Sure, he's on the small side, but one day workers put him next to a great horned owl—a bird of prey many times larger. Most birds would cower in fear in such an untenable situation. Most birds would do the sensible thing and leave immediately. Most birds would figure, and rightly so, that their number was up, but not this fellow. When he was next to the great horned owl, he sized it up. He measured it. He studied it. And then he decided to have a great horned owl snack. They are afraid of nothing, will take on prey far larger than themselves, and are one of the fiercest predators out there. They have proved the euphemisms on size many times over.

His attitude caused this fellow to be a rescue. In the pose in the upper right he looks perfectly fine; however, should he turn his head so his other eye faces you, you'll understand. He lost his eye picking on another bird, probably another owl, many times his size—and lost the fight.

Today, though, he lives a peaceful, easy life. His days are full of sunshine and safety. But he still dreams of having a great horned owl for lunch.

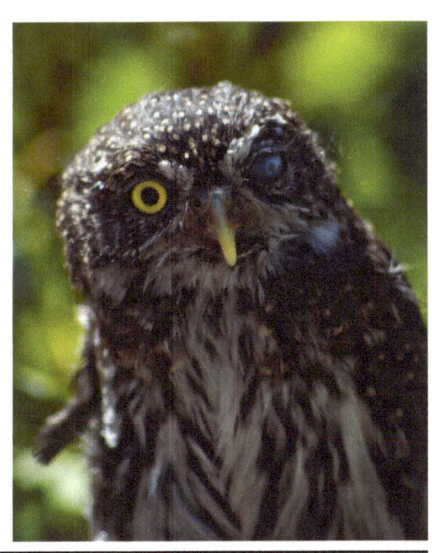

Wolf Prowl

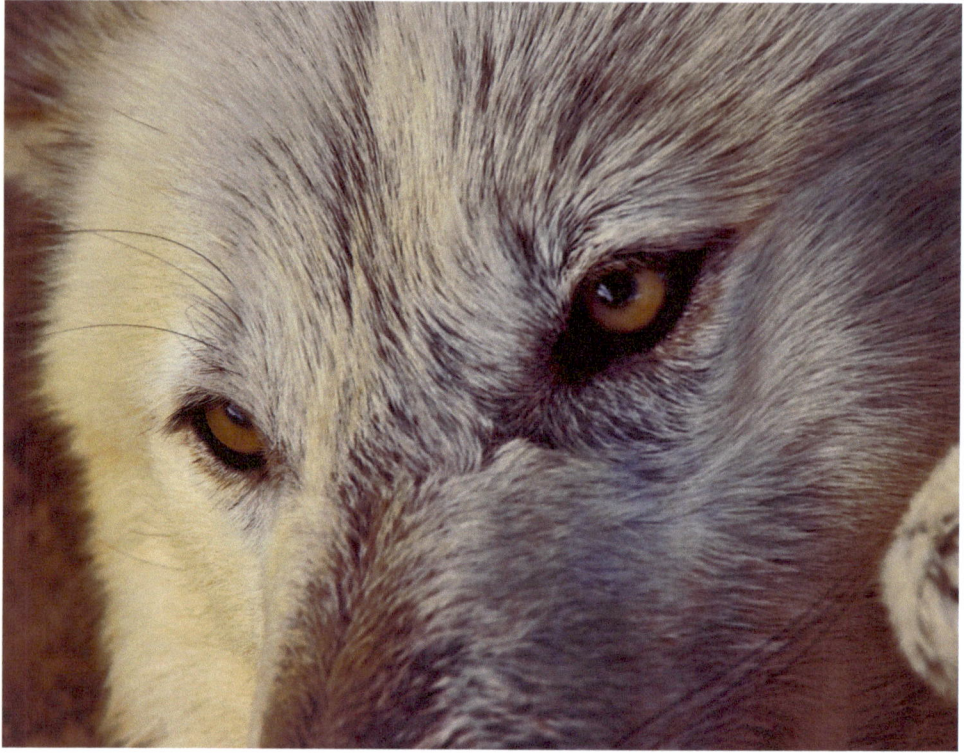

The wolf—a pure white one—was stealthy as only a wolf can be. His eyes had an incredible intensity; golden yellow and bright, seeing the here and now, as well as what lies ahead. Slowly, slowly it crept forward toward its target, drawing ever closer. The afternoon continued, oblivious to what was about to happen. The wolf's attention was focused, though, and the eyes never wavered. Those eyes!

The wolf in question, as it turns out, resides at the Wild Spirit Wolf Sanctuary near Ramah, New Mexico. Dedicated—absolutely, positively, and completely dedicated—to helping wolves who are in need, the good folks here have a passion for them, as you might expect.

Wild Spirit Wolf Sanctuary provides a permanent home for captive-bred wolves and wolf-dogs. It is a non profit organization, and the service it provides is impressive. So is the sanctuary in general, from the well-maintained grounds to the caring staff, including the animals themselves. Without help and guidance, the fate of these wolves would be a far worse one.

The wolf, however, paid no attention to anything except its prowl. That is as it should be.

Wolf Eyes

The eyes have it. Oh, yes, they have it. Fathomless. Intense. Staring right at you and through you at the same time. Yellow in exactly the shade of yellow that eyes should not be. Seeing you, all of you, sizing you up, measuring you, and taking complete stock of you. Non-blinking and non-wavering, the eyes have it.

And they have you.

This pair of eyes belongs to a wolf at the Wild Spirit Wolf Sanctuary. Since Wild Spirit is all about the care and rehabilitation of wolves, you might expect the place to have more than a few wolves in varying stages of wildness, and it does. Some are a little more gentle around humans than others; in fact, some are almost puppy-like in their desire for affection and attention. Some, though, like this guy, let's just say that the question is not entirely answered.

Oh, and that spot of blood? Hard to see, I know, because the eyes hold you, but it certainly leaves room for doubt, doesn't it?

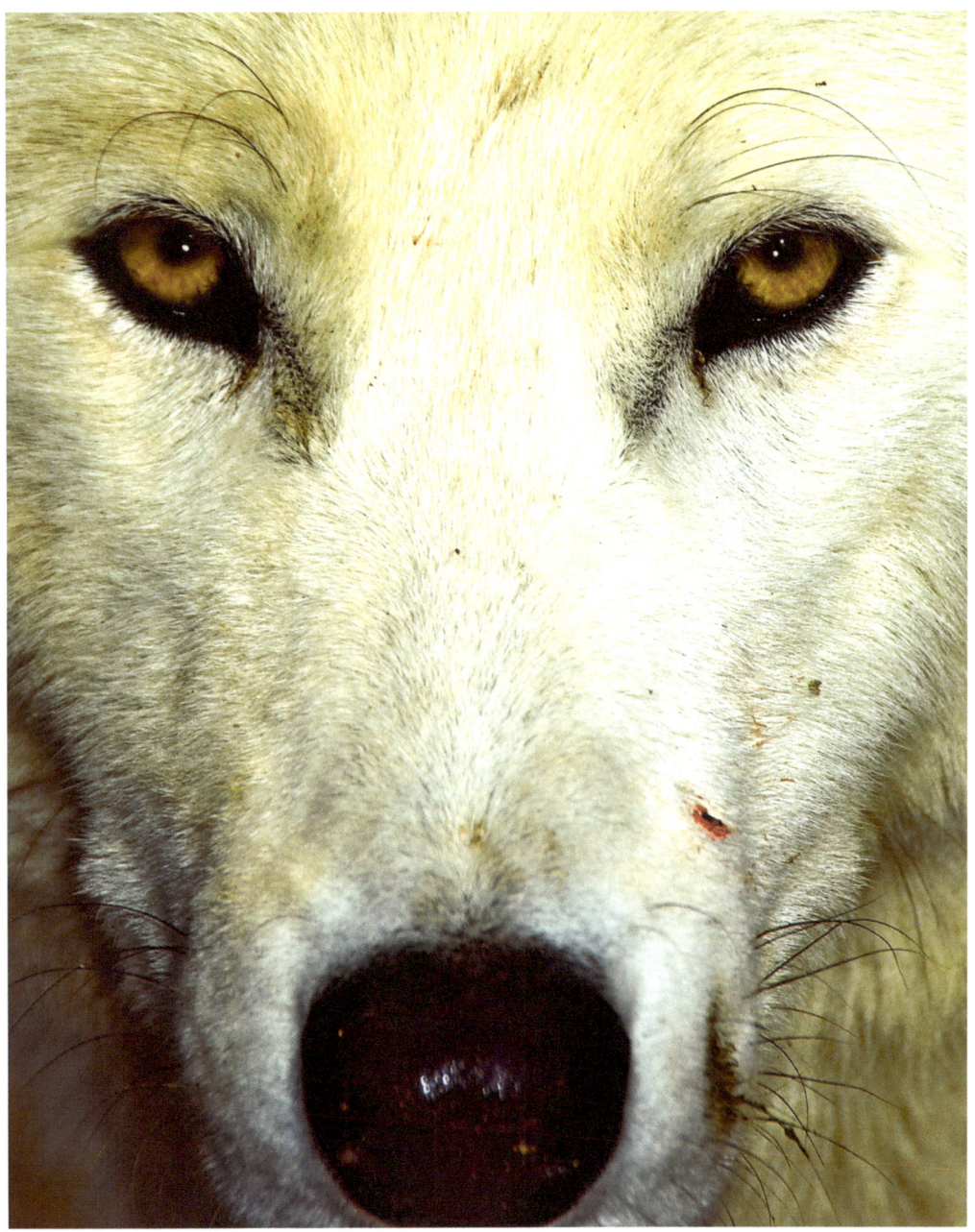

Sunny Fox

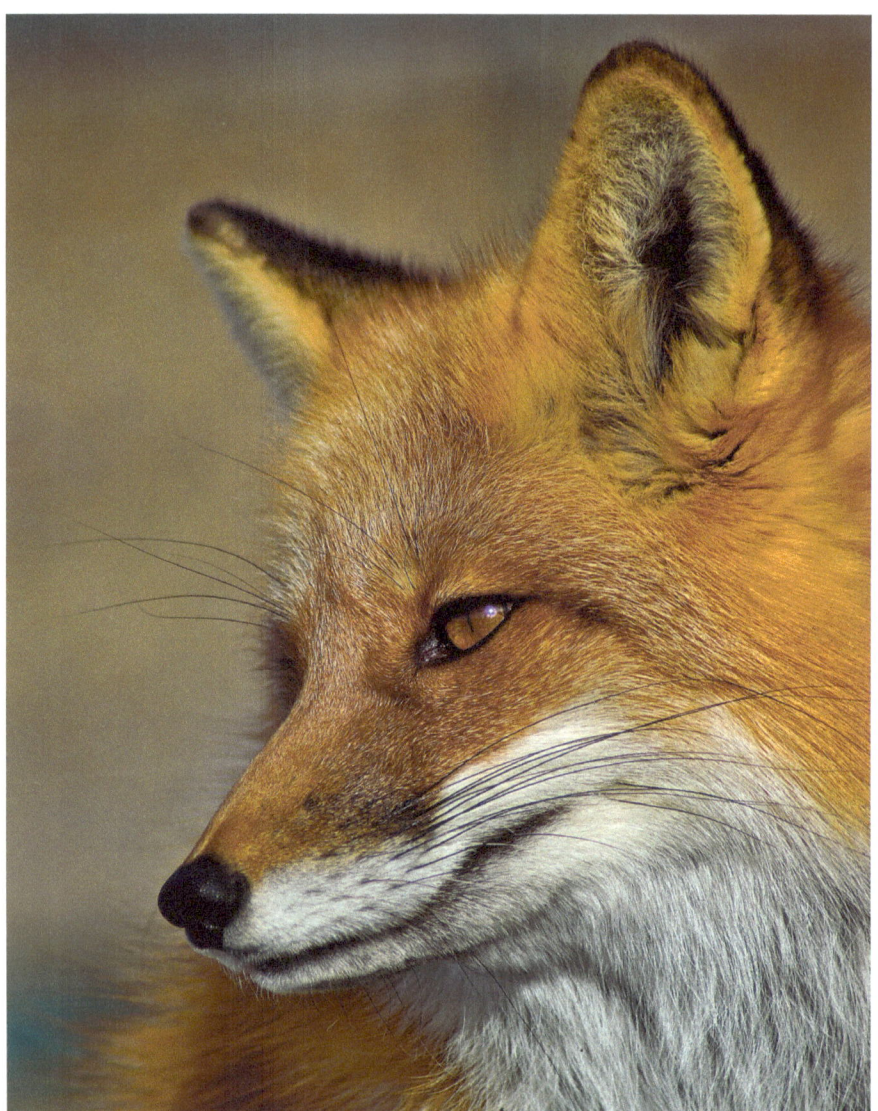

Wild Spirit Wolf Sanctuary is a heartwarming place to visit. The people who work there are dedicated, and I mean devoted, to helping wolves. They care for them, house them, feed them, and do phenomenal work for and with the wolves. More than a few wolves live in the sanctuary, and it is hard to know where to start. Naturally, I started with the one denizen who is not a wolf: the red fox.

This fox hails from the Midwest and was in desperate need of a new home. Being a fox made it harder to place him. Despite the ultimate coolness of being a fox, it also ruled out the obvious choices for a new home, because all the potential places already had a red fox. His situation was not looking good.

Luckily, the folks here took over the fox's care, and he is living out his days in foxy luxury. He's super friendly, very playful, not shy in the least, and best of all, for me, loves to mug it up for the camera.

Meet Romeo. He's foxy, and he's a great guy.

Mischievous Fox

Who knows what mischief lurks behind these deceptively serene eyes? We are, after all, looking into the eyes of Romeo.

Living at Wild Spirit Wolf Sanctuary is living in style for him. Although Wild Spirit is all about wolves, the staff has a soft spot for Romeo, and it shows. He has his own private enclosure, built especially for the mischievous fox. He has all the attention and all the privacy he could want, and his days are good ones.

I was honored that he took some time out of his day to chat with me and get to know me. He is curious, yet cautious. In the end, however, his curiosity won out, and we had an absolutely great visit. We talked about all sorts of foxy things, although he was disappointed when I did not know where he could find the nearest henhouse.

He always had a more-than-mischievous look about him. I asked him what he was about to do, and he avoided the question. I suppose I was better off not knowing. Sly like a fox indeed!

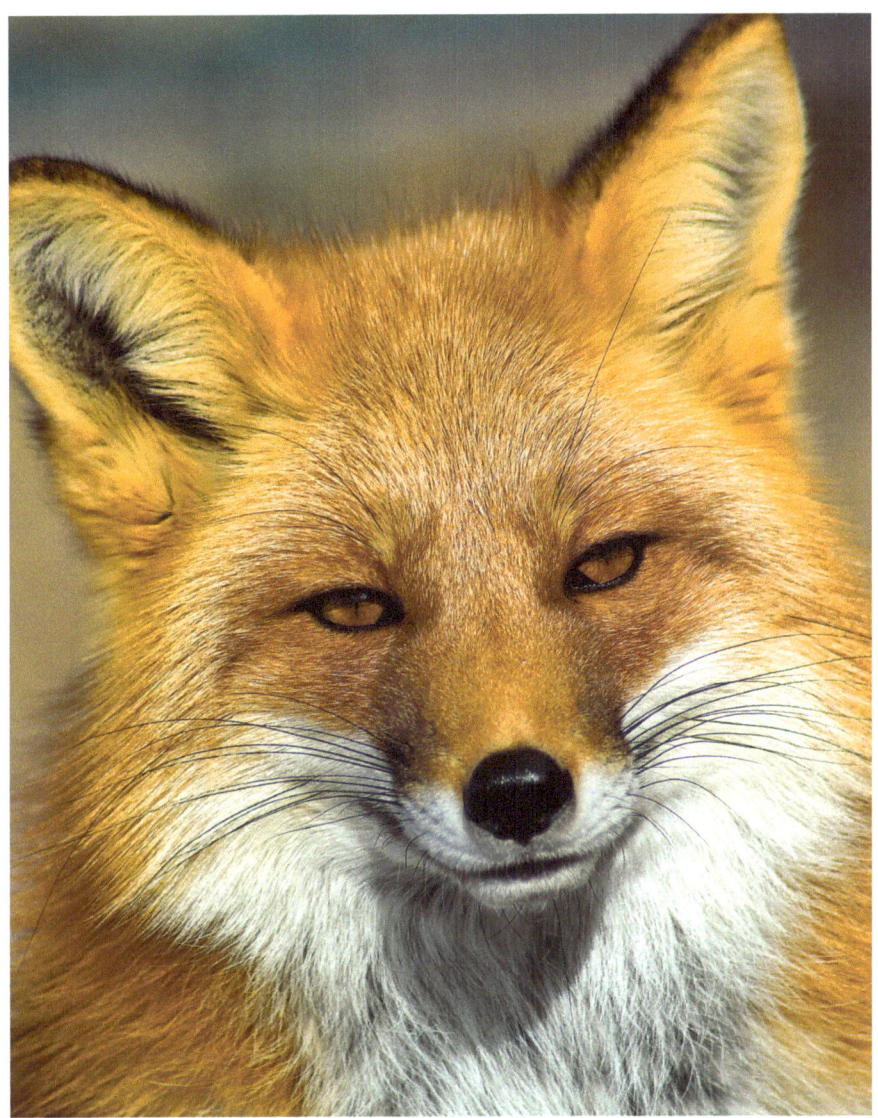

Hawk Eye

The red-tailed hawk, long held sacred and long sought after for falconry, remains a formidable hunter. If you are in North America and look to the skies, chances are you might see one of these powerful birds of prey soaring above.

These are large birds. Very large, actually, and their wingspan can easily be more than four feet. They live a pretty long time, as well, up to twenty years in the wild. No wonder this magnificent bird holds such a revered place among us.

This particular bird was caught as it was looking away from me, but just for a moment. As it turned its head, its eye caught the surrounding trees, and quick as a wink, the photograph was made. Good thing, too, for the instant I made the photograph, it whirled its head back around to look at me long and hard. Those eyes, when they are looking straight at you, hold your attention and make you glad you are big enough not to be considered for lunch.

The fact that it is a rescue hosted by Wildlife Rescue Inc. of New Mexico doesn't mean it doesn't dream big.

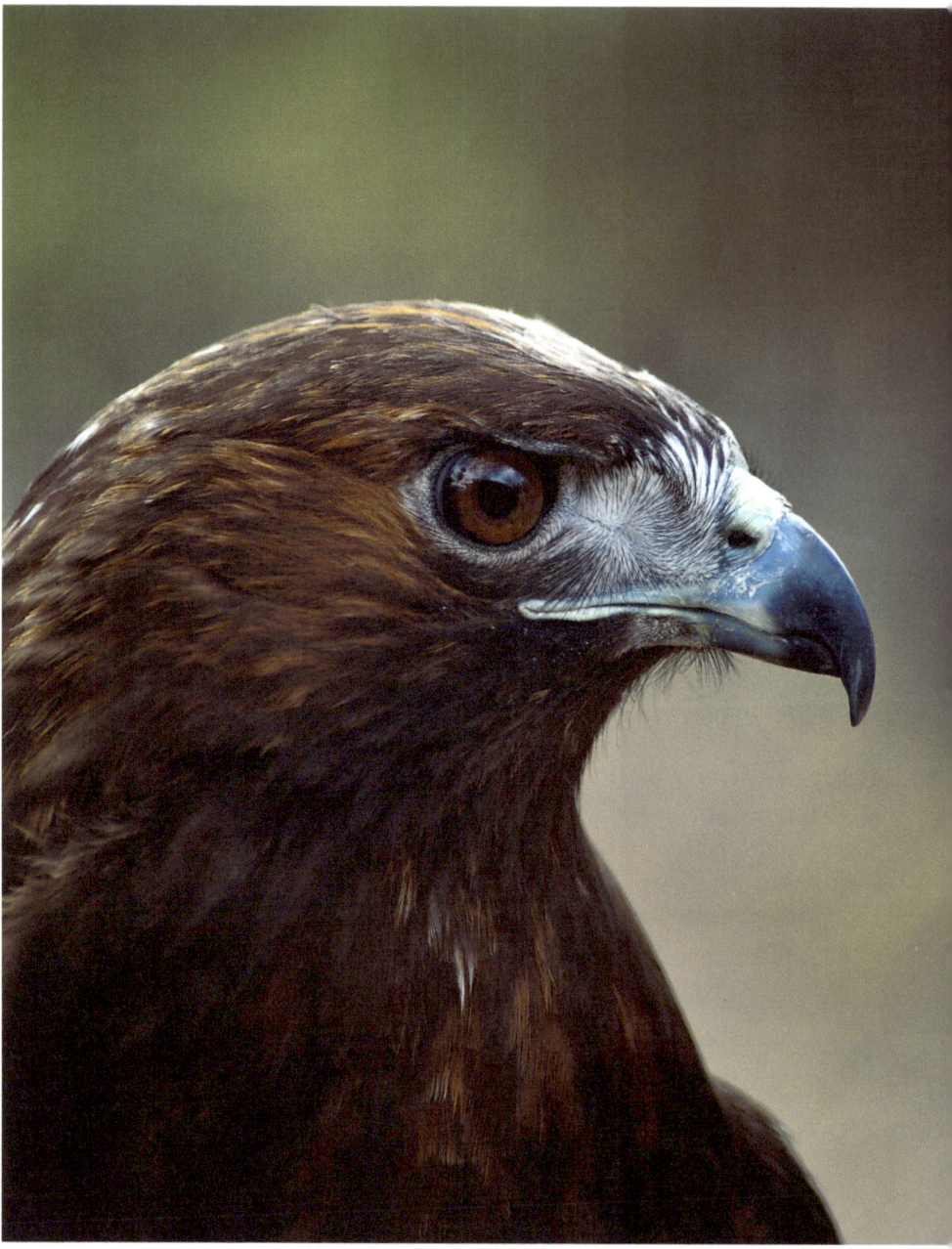

Hawk Standoff

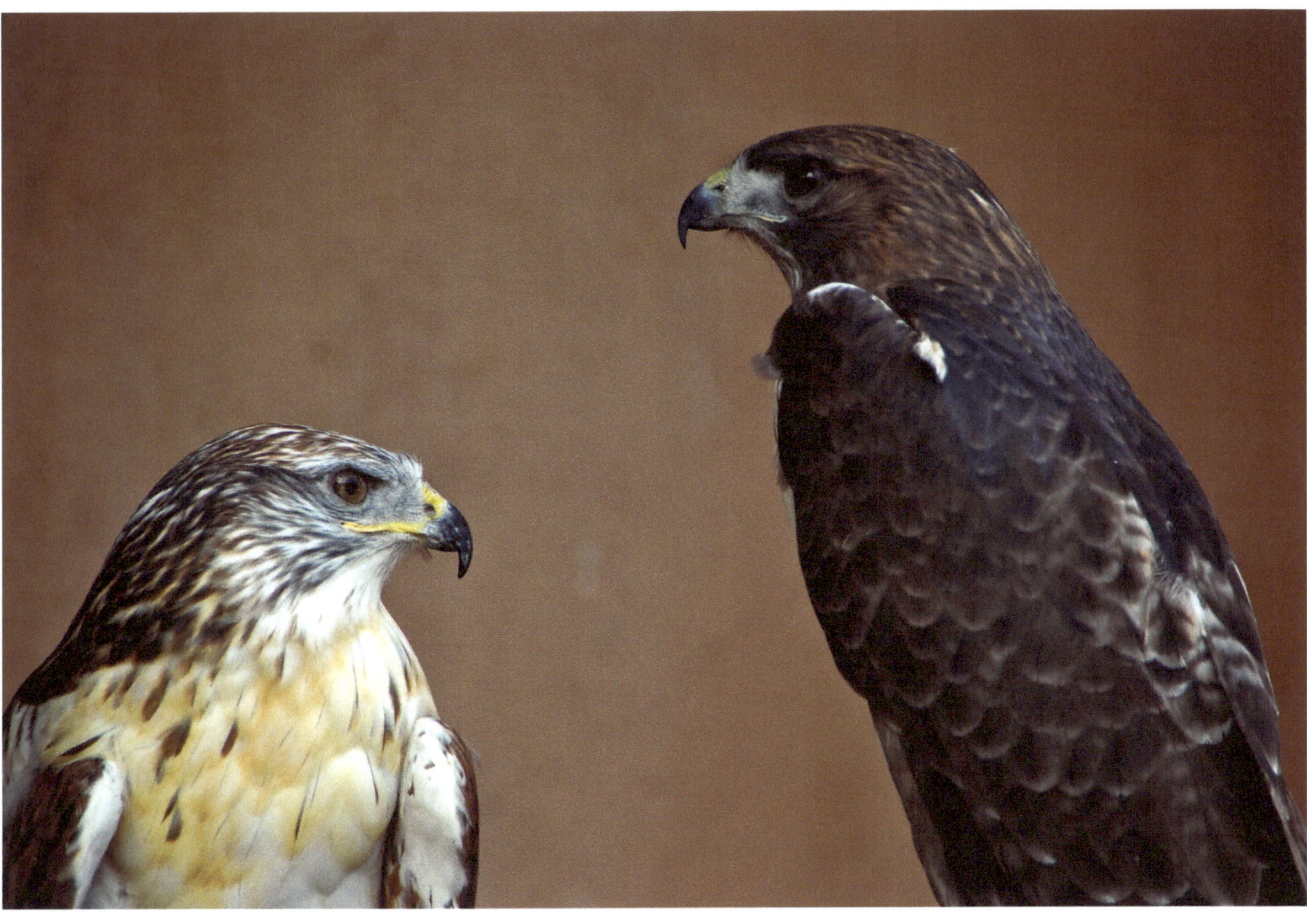

It's reminiscent of the Old West: two weathered gunslingers with a score to settle square off on the dusty dirt street. With malice in their eyes, they size each other up, each planning his draw, each already mentally taking aim. The street falls silent, although plenty of spectators watch, and even the normally blustery winds stop for a moment. Everyone waits to see whose shot is the truest.

In this case, there are a couple of differences from the Old West, though. First off, the "gunslingers" are actually a cooper's hawk, on the left, and a red-tailed hawk, on the right. Although they appear to be squared off, they are actually very familiar with each other, since they are both hosted by Wildlife Rescue Inc. of New Mexico. They don't really have a duel in mind, but rather are just keeping a watchful eye out over a peaceful day. The crowds? Oh, they are there, too, except everyone is admiring these handsome and magnificent creatures, even the wind.

Kestrel Takeoff

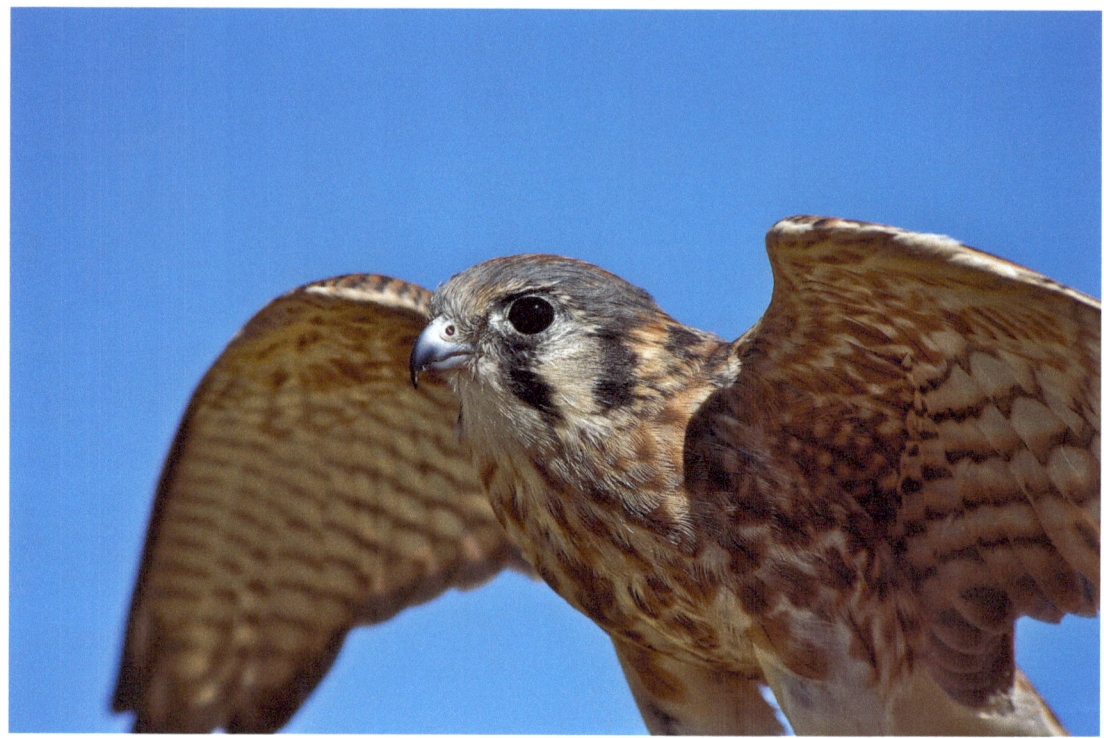

She took one last glance, slowly readied her wings, and then, in a burst that the eye could not follow, she was gone. The female kestrel spotted her prey, adjusted her timing and took off on the hunt. Dinner would be hers soon.

The kestrel is not the largest bird around—in fact, it is small and very common. Still, the bird's size utterly belies its skill, for it is an accomplished hunter. Kestrels are falcons, through and through, which makes them a raptor, as well. Spread through North America, they have little preference as to where they live. City or farmland, either way, they are comfortable.

Furthermore, they play an important role. Their primary diet consists of insects in the summer, switching to small mammals in the winter months. They keep the insect population under control, providing the ever-essential check and balance. Hunting from a perch, they look much like songbirds—they are not.

She rose high into the air, then plunged like a brown streak, her hunt successful.

Kestrel Landing

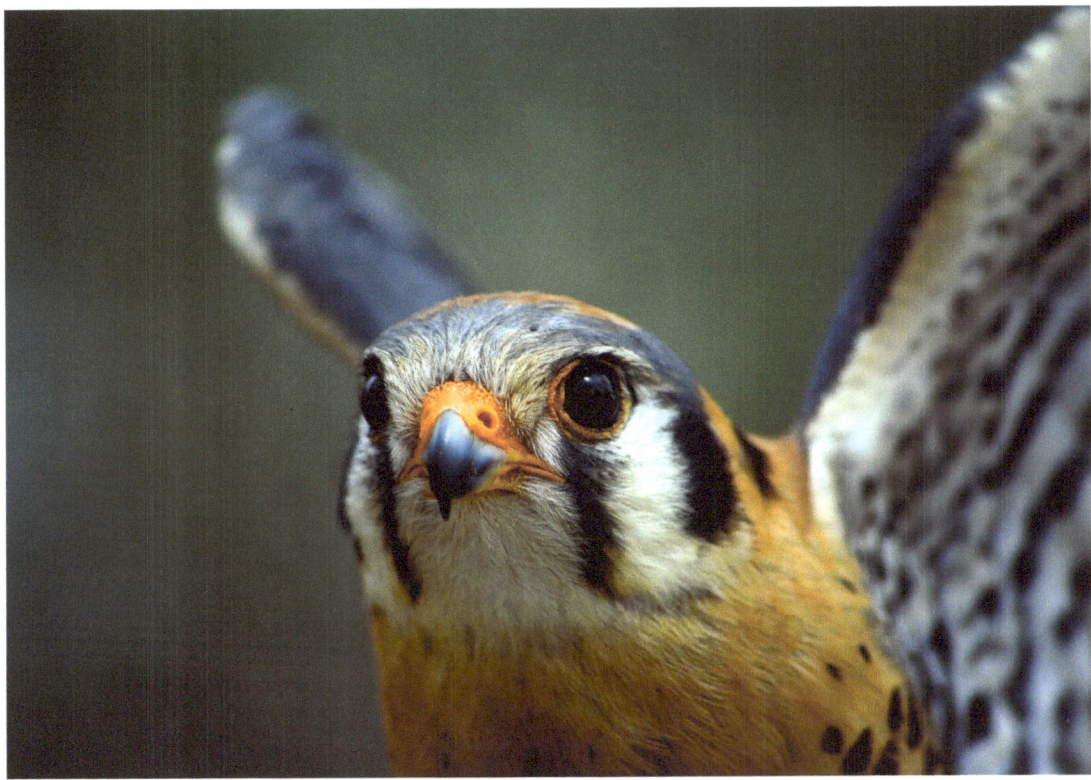

The American Kestrel, small, fast, fierce and deadly; its hunting skills are considerable. It has the distinction of being the most colorful raptor and the most common falcon in North America, ranging throughout almost all of the North American continent. This raptor gets around, and it stays around.

This male happens to be in full breeding color. Note the intense orange around its beak. If you happened to be a female kestrel like the one on the previous page, you would find him quite handsome. He is just landing in this photograph, perhaps to rest, after looking for lunch. Note that this magnificent fellow is being cared for by Wildlife Rescue, Inc of New Mexico.

Being on the wrong end of the American Kestrel, small though it may be, is not something I would care to be. Oh, no, not at all. Come to think of it, I'm not sure that the glint is his eye is all that good news for me.

Reverent Visions

Religion is deeply woven into the fabric of the Southwest, yet time forgets and time remembers without regard to man's desires. Sometimes the grandest of all monuments slips into the dim past, and sometimes the smallest of shrines slips through the centuries. It is not man's place to determine how each meets its fate. Celebrate, then, what we can, and remember well the rest.

Iglesia Solitaria

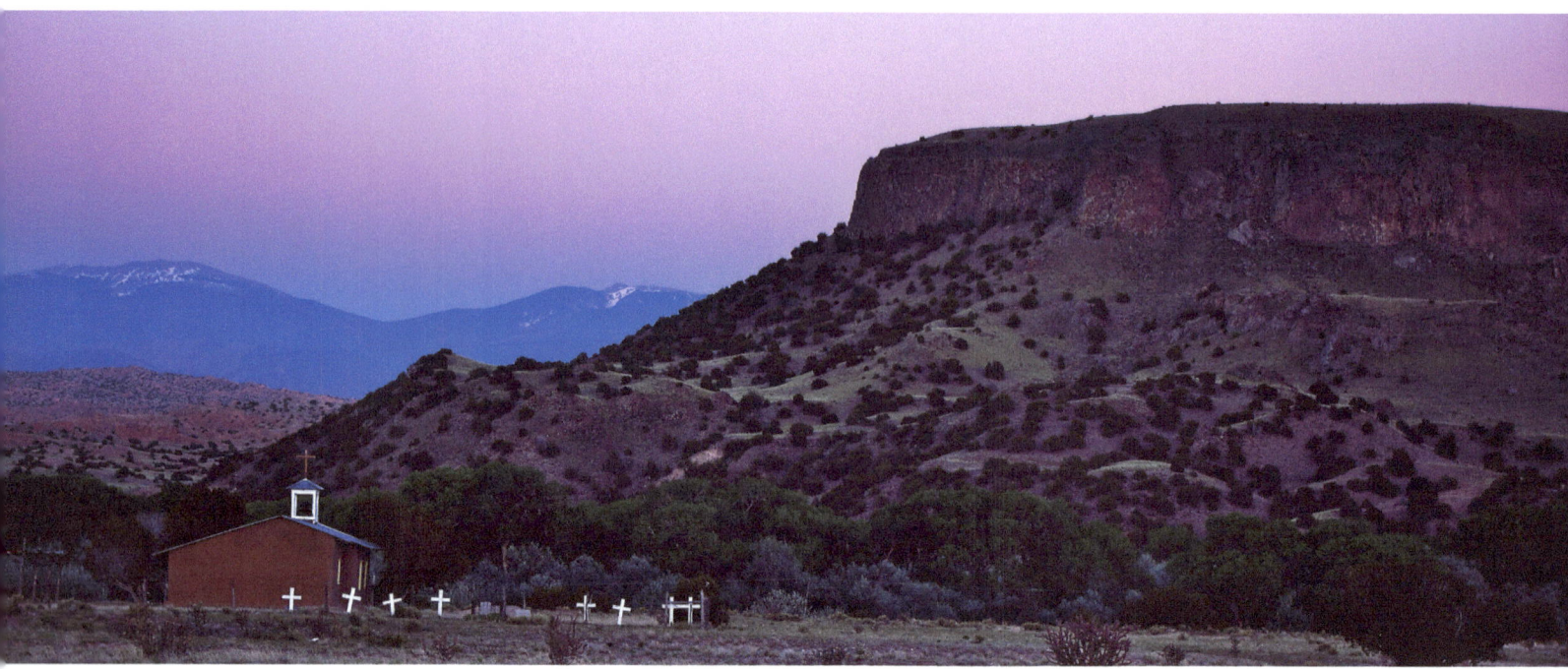

The sun continued the daily journey from east to west and began slipping below the distant mountains. As old Sol dipped below the horizon, the sky transformed from a beautiful blue to a sky extraordinaire, full of pinks and purples of every hue imaginable. The landscape was awash in color, and the serenity of the night began to take hold.

The small church at the foot of Black Mesa, however, had no one to share the evening ritual with. Its doors remained locked, and no one was about. The church was alone. The crosses in front of it lit up with the most ethereal white light; almost glowing from within, they stood out against the falling night, a stark contrast. Small, seemingly forgotten, the church began to fade into the night as the sky lost its color. Just before the night stole the last of the day, a dove rose from the church and into the sky.

The church, as it turns out, wasn't as solitary as it first appeared. Instead, it was a sanctuary, a safe harbor, and a place to rest. As the dove faded into the distance, the church stood fast against the night and the crosses glowed even brighter. Lonely and solitary the building was, once again, but for only a short while. For only a short while.

Stormy Mission

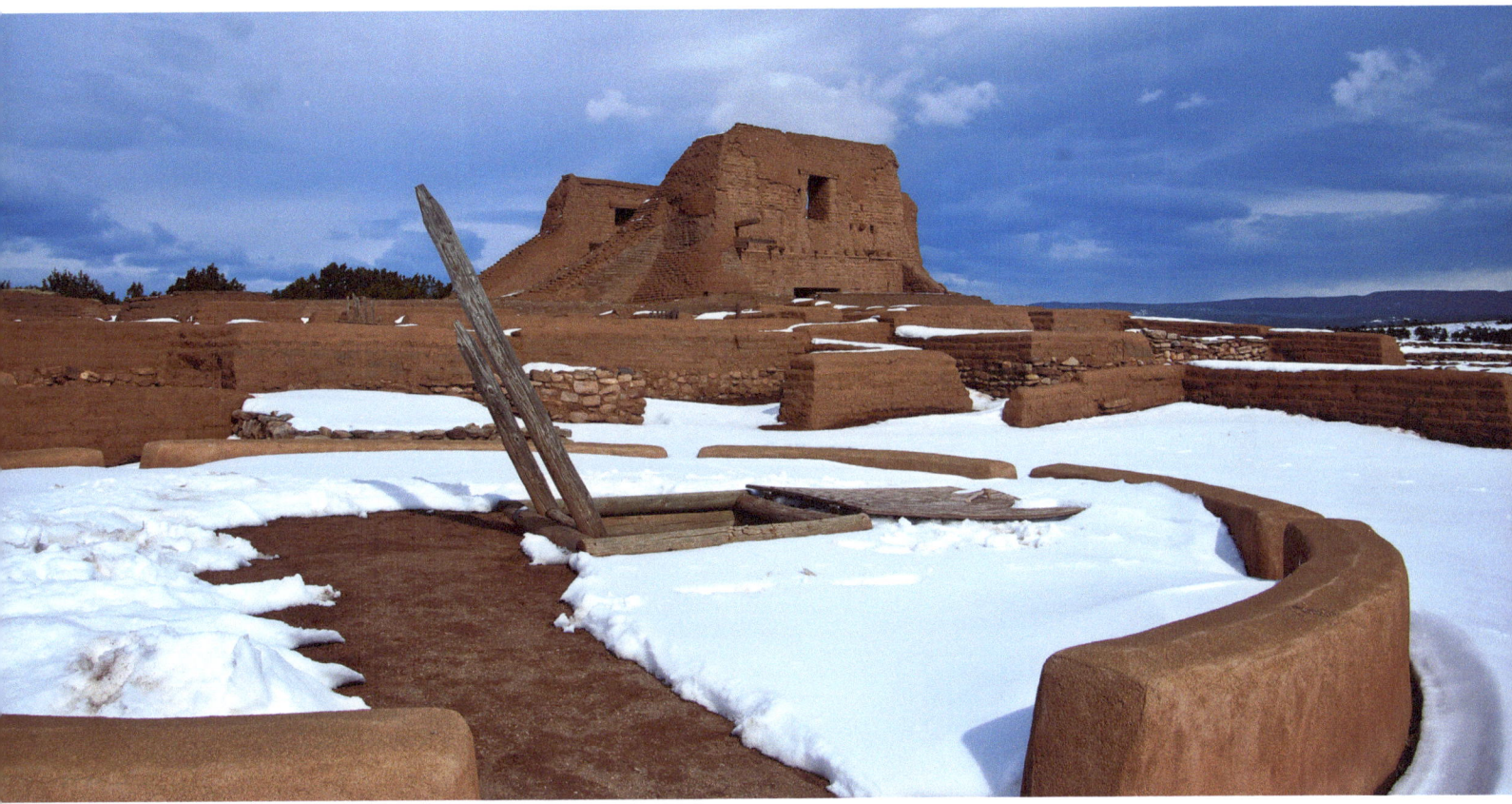

Pecos National Historic Park in New Mexico is a place where cultures collided and time tried to stand still. Neither of these efforts worked out well.

Pecos "began" somewhere around AD 800 when the first settlers in the Rio Grande Valley area moved into this almost perfect environment. By AD 1200 the first pueblo had been built, and by AD 1300 the area was in full swing. It featured a fairly significant multi level pueblo, with upwards of 700 rooms, and the Tiwa Indians called it home. Situated in between the Rio Grande Valley and the plains, Pecos had an ideal location. Francisco Vasquez de Coronado, when he rolled through the area in the early 1500s, thought so too, although the Europeans stayed away until 1590. By 1618, a mission had been built at Pecos and the cultures meshed and collided over the years. Today the remains of a Great Kiva and the mission stand side by side. The stormy skies remind us that the past here was not always tranquil, yet Pecos endures, despite the storms, just as it always has. May we always remember, respect, and celebrate our past.

Supersterious Reverence

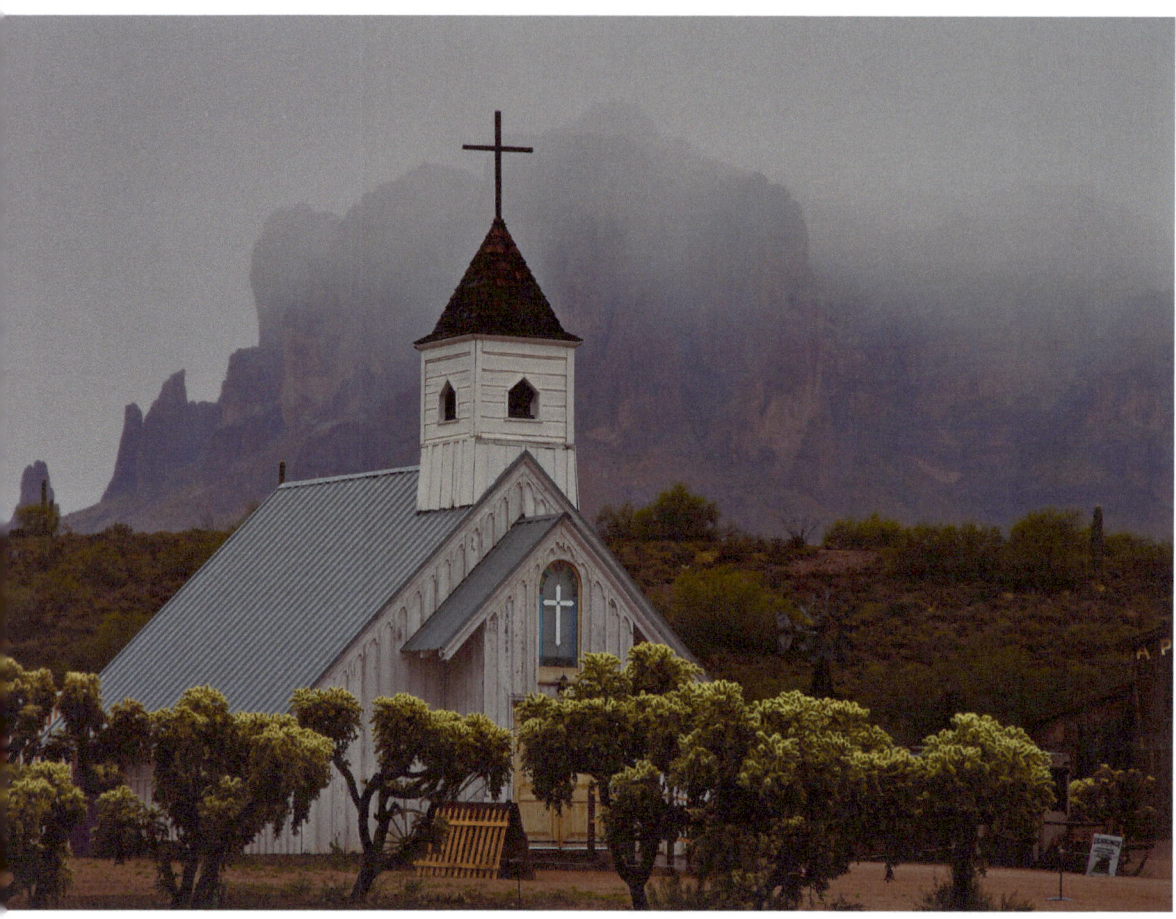

The mountain stood a vigilant watch, day in and day out. A presence and sentinel behind the church, the guardian provided a comforting constant. The days came and went, but the church and mountain were always there—always. Each tended to its own flock; the church, its congregation, which found comfort within its walls, and the mountain its church, which found comfort beneath its mass.

This day was different than most. Although spring had come, so had winter. This year winter had grown jealous of spring and decided to supplant it, once and for all. Suddenly, winter swept back in with a vengeance, bringing cold and snow with it. The mountain, however, would have no part of this shift and certainly would not let its friend feel the effects, for the church was at winter's mercy. Summoning all the effort within it, the mountain drew winter unto itself, and a battle ensued. The resulting fog and mist enveloped the mountain, almost obscuring it, making it almost menacing, but the church knew better. It knew that it was safe and that the grasp of winter would not be felt this day around its steeple. Eventually, winter retreated until the right and proper time, and church and mountain went back to sunny days, each holding in its heart the most precious gift of all: hope.

Welcoming Santuario

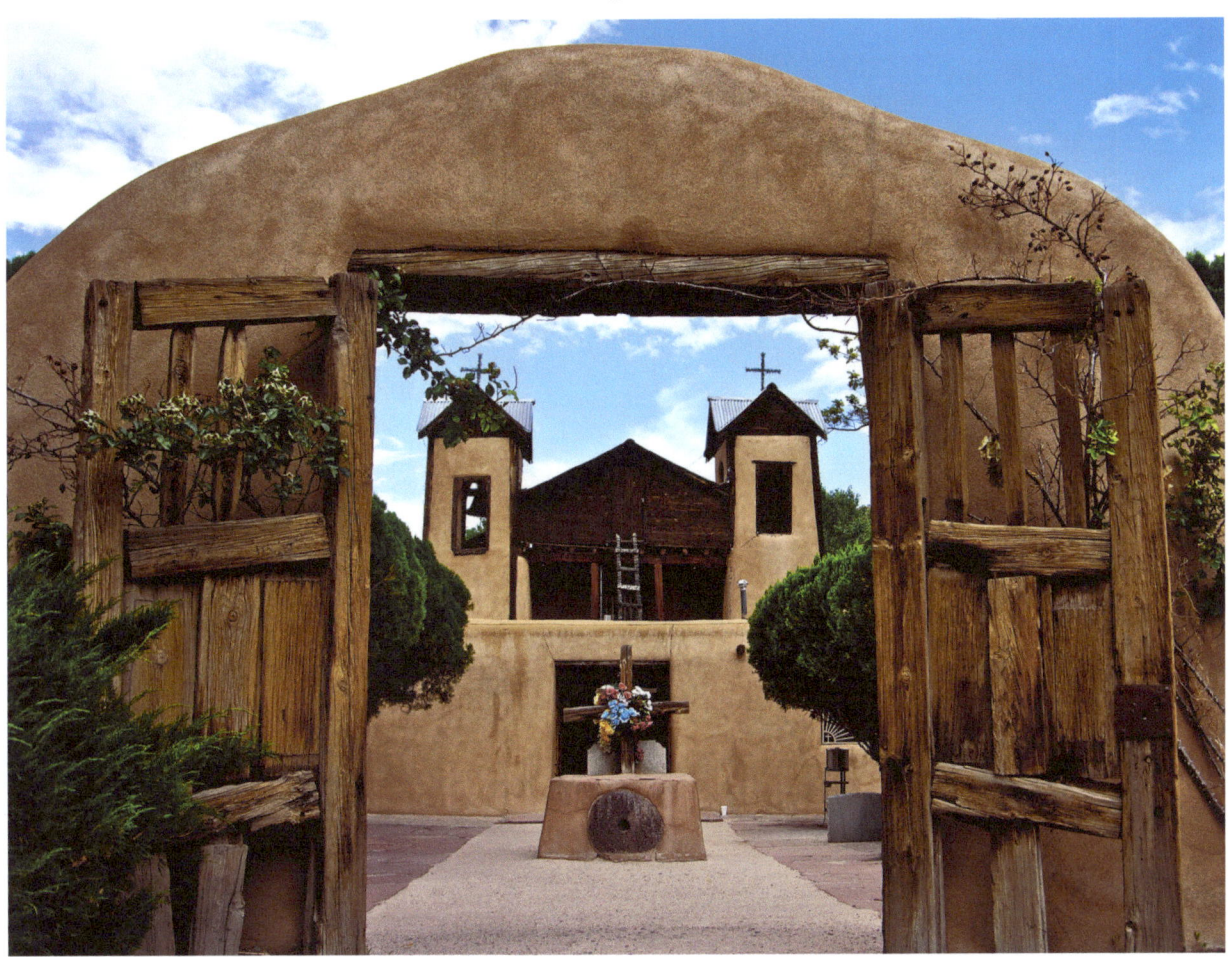

The legends hold he was healed by faith alone, through the vehicle of the sacred dirt. Free from sickness, free from disease, free from the ailments that held him back, he stood straight and walked tall as only the righteous walk. At El Santuario de Chimayo, nestled in the Sangre de Cristo Mountains of New Mexico, the legends may not be legends at all, and instead may well be fact and miracle.

Sometime around 1814 or so Fernando Abeyta built a small chapel, and no sooner had it been built than testimonies of cures began pouring in. To this day, visitors to the chapel are free to take a small amount of holy dirt to effect their own cures. As to the veracity of the miracles, the Church is silent on the subject, taking no position. In any event, this serene sanctuary stands today as a testament to those who believe; past, present, and future.

Tyuonyi Pueblo

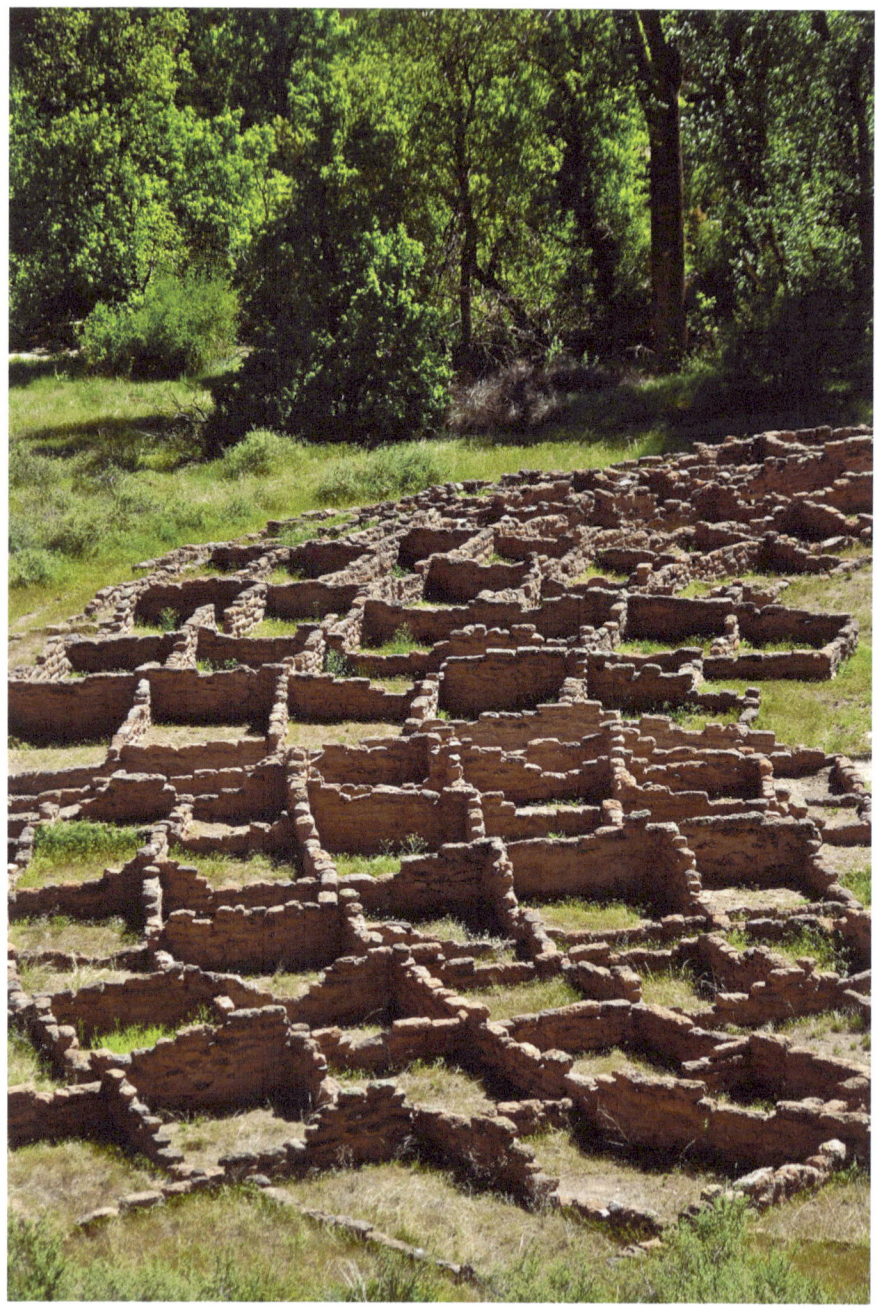

Life for those who came before us was not easy. Hardships abounded, and it didn't take much to tip the balance from survival to the alternative. One misstep, one illness, even one poor hunting season, could invoke disaster, yet mankind survived and thrived, and in the process, did what we do so well: build.

These ruins of Tyuonyi Pueblo lie in Frijoles Canyon, in the heart of Bandelier National Monument in New Mexico. The ancestral Pueblo people who built Tyuonyi knew how to build for the ages, and more than 500 years after it was abandoned, the remaining walls still stand proud. At its height, Tyuonyi stood at least two stories tall, possibly three, and had somewhere around 400 rooms. More than one hundred people, possibly many more, called it home, for in the family and community we find safety and succor, just as it has always been and as it always will be.

Walls may eventually crumble back into the earth, but the foundations remain, a standing testament to the resilience of man.

Kiva Memories

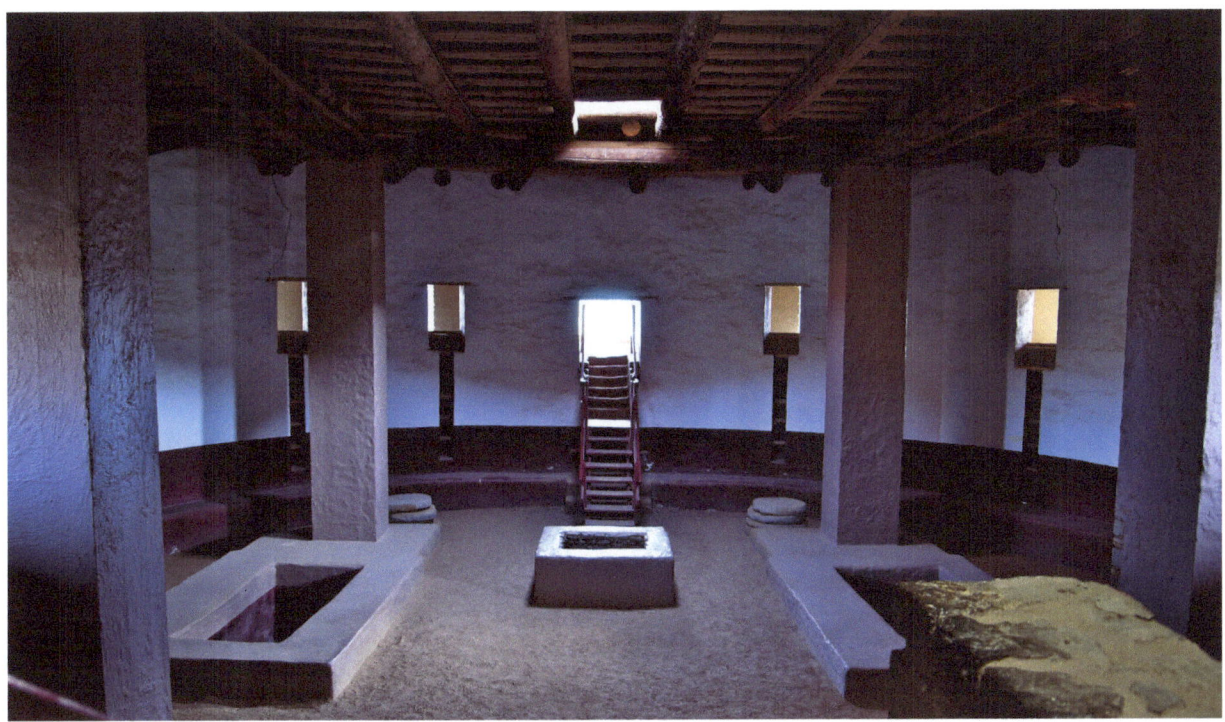

We celebrate those who have come before us in many ways. We honor them by taking some of their lexicon unto ourselves. We incorporate their knowledge and their wisdom into our own. We perform some of the same rituals and ceremonies, some unchanged throughout the years, we venerate their ancient homes, visiting with respect and awe. We pay homage there, and remember them well.

Crumbling walls serve as stark reminders of the footsteps echoing in the past. Nevertheless, sometimes it is instructive to see and experience ancient places as they once truly were.

This is a restored great kiva in the Aztec Ruins National Monument in northern New Mexico. Although we cannot say for certainty that it is exactly what the kiva looked like, we have restored this one as faithfully as we can, based on the historical records, archeology, and clues that have been unearthed.

Walking into the great kiva, you can connect, deep in your soul, with those who originally built it. You can, if you listen carefully, hear their whispers through time. It is one of a handful of restored great kivas, yet these powerful icons still speak as powerfully as they always have. The memories live on.

Winged Rock

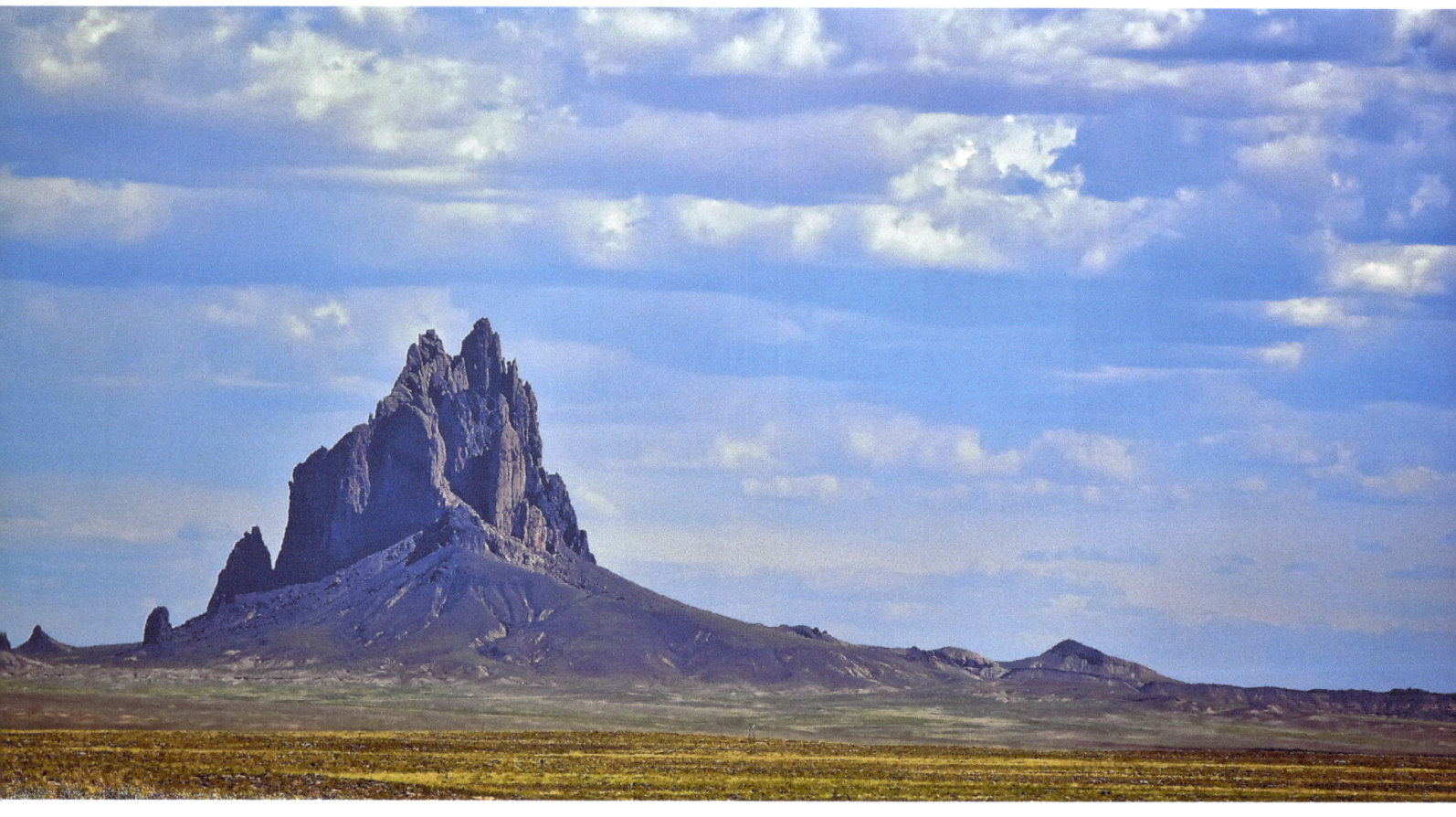

Near the center of the Ancient Pueblo People's civilization stands tall the monolith of Winged Rock. The Navajo have known and celebrated Shiprock for as long as they can remember, which is a very long time. Standing alone in the northwest corner of New Mexico, the winged rock is a place of mystery, legend, and culture.

The Navajo have many legends about the rock, and many revolve around the rock's role in bringing the Navajo to the Southwest in the first place. Initially, the Navajo lived on top of it, coming down only to tend to their fields. Alas, one day lightning struck, stranding the women and children on top and the men below forever. An old, senseless tale? To some, perhaps, but to stand at the base of this towering feature is to feel the spirits of the past around you. There is a powerful presence here, of this there is no doubt. No one is allowed up on the peak, to avoid the real risk of stirring up the ghosts of those who remain. Really, there is no need, either, for some spirits are best admired from afar.

Bonito Doorways

Near the center of Chaco Canyon, in Chaco Culture National Historic Park in New Mexico, lies Pueblo Bonito. Long since abandoned, it still plays an important role in Native American history, culture, and tradition.

Although no one is sure what purpose, exactly, Pueblo Bonito served, most agree that it was a gathering place for important events and occasions. Native Americans from throughout the Southwest gathered at Chaco, and it was the center of their Southwest.

A series of doorways from room to room in Pueblo Bonito lead the length of a long wall. To what purpose these rooms served, who can know? Although large sections of the pueblo have collapsed, these doorways, standing since AD 828, still withstand the test of time.

It was with reverence, then, that the Bonito Doorways photograph was made, and processed in traditional black and white to preserve the feel and antiquity of the pueblo. May your own doorways withstand the passage of time, remaining ever open.

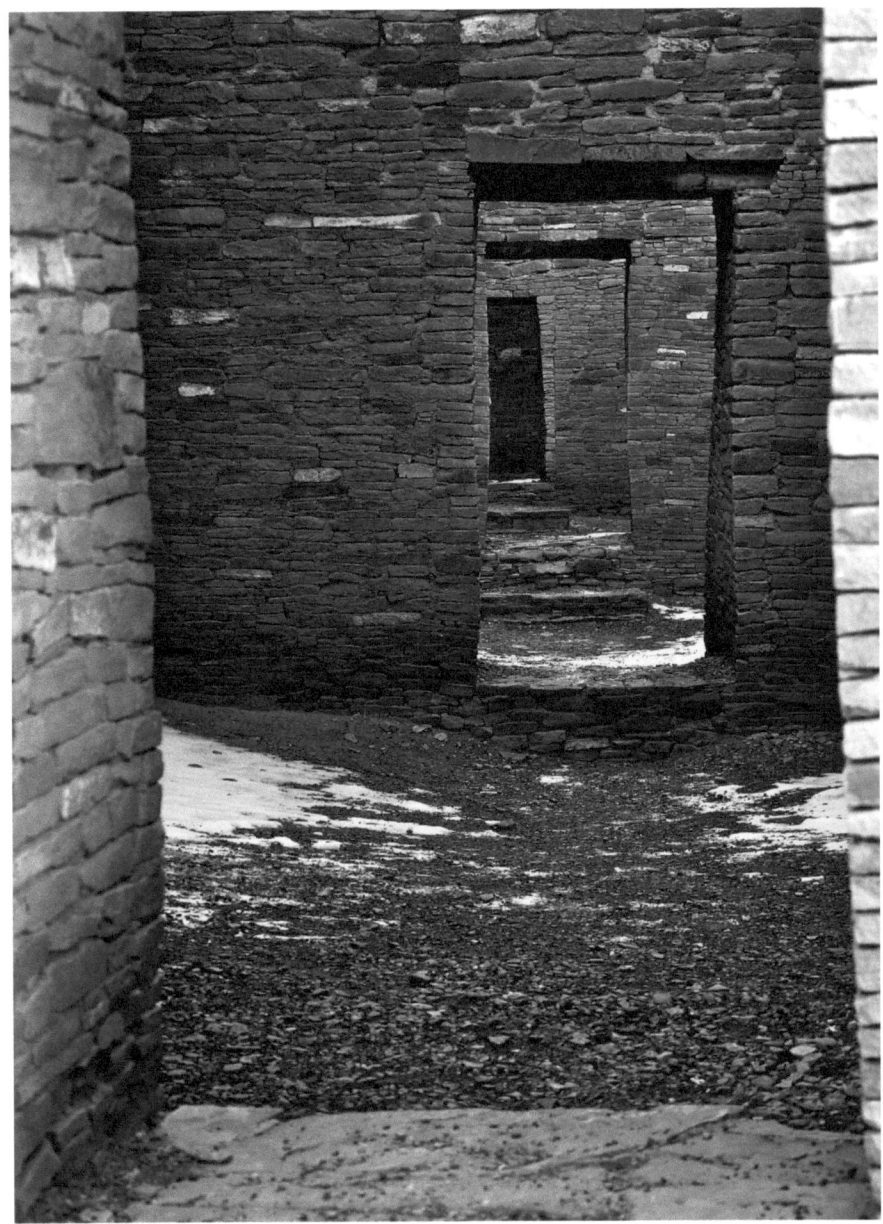

Kiva's Ghost

Kivas were present in almost every pueblo and central to many aspects of life. Kivas came in all sizes, but they all shared some basic features; they had reasonably tall walls, they were often built into the ground, and, most importantly, they were covered. They typically had access ladders into them.

Imagine, then, the anticipation that one must have felt waiting for an elder to come down the ladder. The ladder would stand empty, patiently waiting. At first, the slightest tremble might be seen, and then a foot, and then two, and then the elder himself.

Sometimes, in just the right lighting and circumstances, you might feel, even today, the presence of the elder upon the ladder. Echoing throughout time, the rituals and ceremonies continue. In this instance, the kiva gave me a gift, a true gift, across space and time. It is a powerful and poignant reminder that even today—especially today—kivas are far from empty.

Backstory

Kiva's Ghost is absolutely, exactly, 100% straight from camera. The ghost is as real as a man can possibly be and is not superimposed, Photoshopped, or otherwise altered. This is, indeed, the gift that the kiva gave me. Here's how:

I had decided that a photo of a ladder going into a kiva would be a good subject for me and set out to make one. In New Mexico, there are only a handful of rebuilt or restored kivas, so it wasn't hard to decide on which one: Pecos National Historic Park. I bundled up my gear and off I went. Inside the kiva it was dark, very dark, as expected. This kiva is cov-

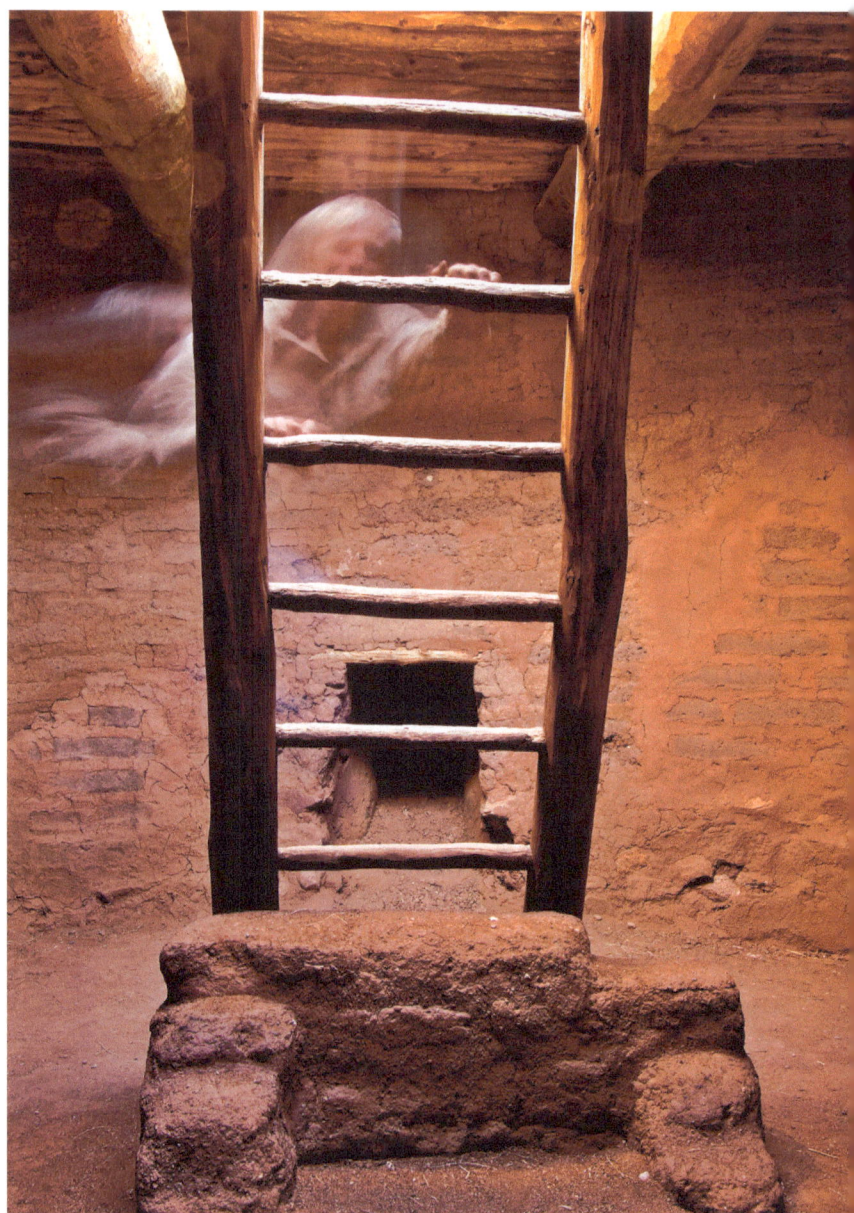

ered in the style of the ancient ones, and it has a ladder, but importantly for me, the rest has not been restored. I took my camera gear down into the kiva, set up my tripod for a very long exposure, and set to work preparing the photograph. The process was not quick; it took time to expose each photo, about thirty to forty seconds, time to review it, time to make adjustments, and so on. Besides, being in a hurry isn't a good thing. I was mostly alone there, which suited me fine, but now and then someone else joined me.

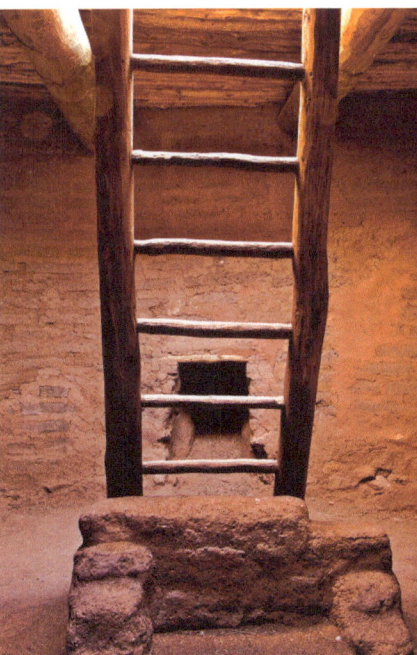

One such gentleman was as much intrigued by what I was doing as he was intrigued by the kiva itself. He watched me as I worked and we chatted a bit and generally enjoyed each other's company. He was respectful of what I was doing, too, for which I am grateful, and stayed out of the way of the photograph. Eventually, I had it all dialed in and it was perfect. I pressed the shutter release, stood back, and folded my arms in satisfaction.

At this point the gentlemen decided to leave. Uh-oh! He went up the ladder quickly, but when he reached the top, he must have seen my expression. "Are you taking a picture?" he asked with genuine concern.

"Yup," I responded.

"Am I in the picture?" he asked, his voice hesitant.

"Yup," I responded.

"Did I ruin your picture?" His voice registered alarm.

"Nope!" came back my cheerful response. "I'll just make it again in a moment."

He nodded and was up and out of the kiva.

That's when the kiva gave me the gift. During the long exposure, we had our conversation above, and when the photo was done, Kiva's Ghost was the result. I stared at it for the longest time, not knowing what to think, but there was but one answer.

The gentleman had white hair; he wore a white shirt and blue jeans. If you look carefully at the top of the third rung down, you can just make out his leg—blue doesn't show up well in a long exposure in a kiva, for whatever reason. A very keen eye can discern his other leg at the top of the fourth rung down. The ethereal flowing was merely his slight movement.

I've thought long and hard about this photo and what happened that day. There is, of course, the technical explanation. There is also the realization that the echoes of our past still swirl around us, if only we open our minds, our hearts, and our spirit.

Motioning Stillness

Sometimes one is completely in the moment, blending every element of the day together, creating a scene of such utter serenity and tranquility that it almost overwhelming. In contrast, sometimes the raw power of motion is also extraordinary. Our avian friends often exemplify that power. These are a few of their stories.

Cloudy Crane

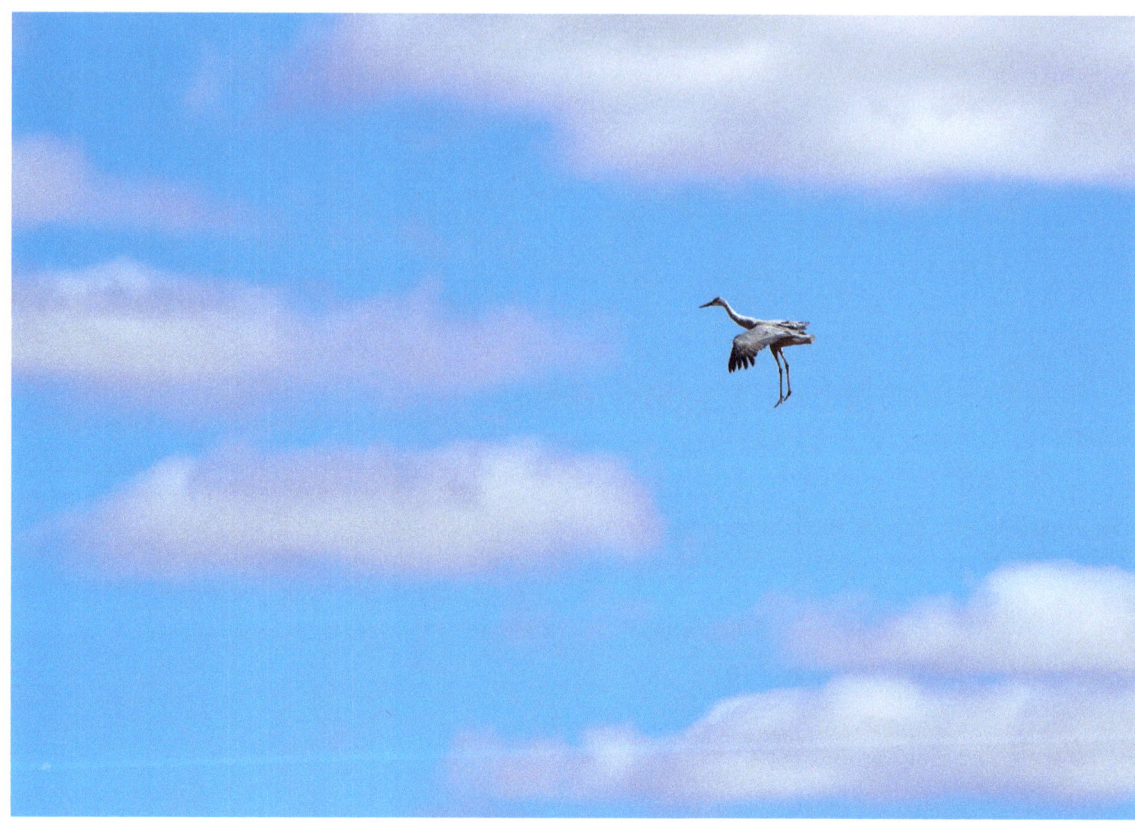

Sometimes a picture, or so they say, is worth a thousand words. You see it and you instantly know the entire backstory, the story at hand, and have a reasonable chance of predicting the future. Sometimes a picture gives you reason to think and ponder deep thoughts. Sometimes a picture simply makes you feel.

And then we have Cloudy Crane. This whimsical picture caught a sandhill crane preparing to land at the Ladd S. Gordon Waterfowl Complex near Socorro, New Mexico. Captured against the blue sky and cloud combination that looks more like it belongs in an animated show instead of a photograph, the crane was spreading its wings wide, lowering its flaps, er, feet, and gliding into a perfect landing.

Your own imagination can easily finish the story here, providing whatever ending is fitting. You can even fill in the backstory of the crane, if you wish. Where was it? What was it doing this fine day? Why was it coming back in the middle of the day, instead of the end?

In any event, or in any story, the cloudy crane provides the perfect character.

Soaring Eagle

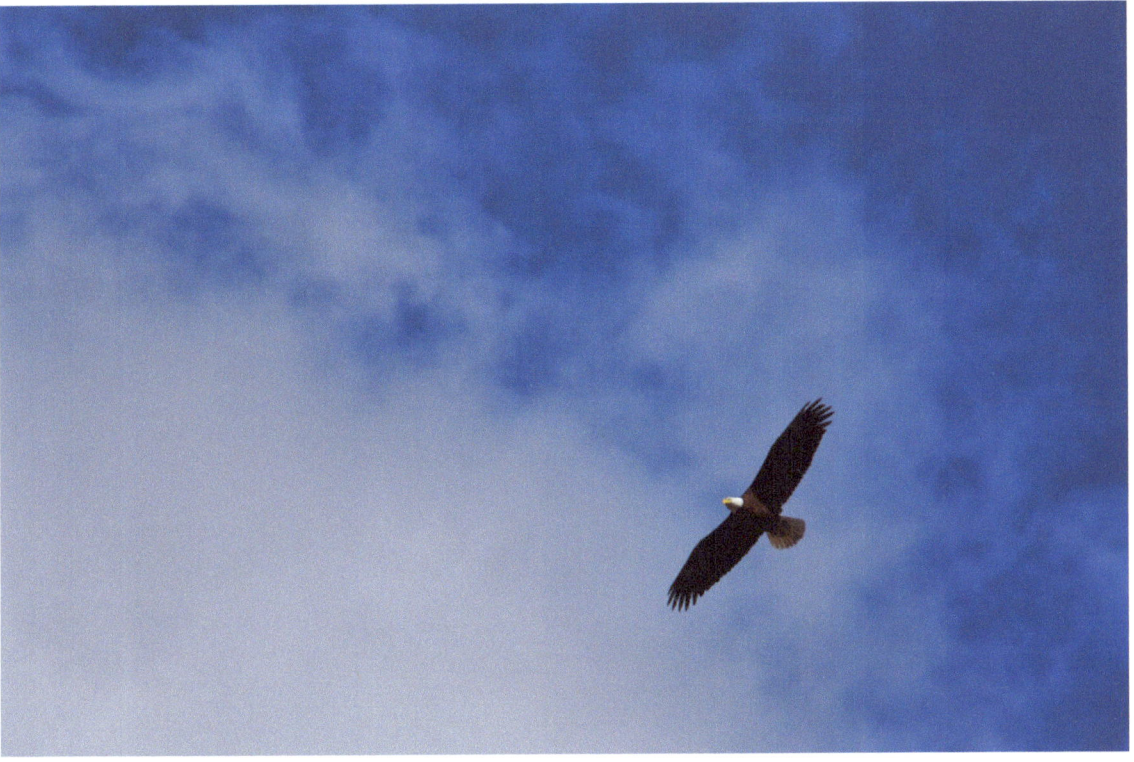

Nothing, perhaps, is more incredible than a bird, wings outspread, soaring high above. Oh, to be free from the constraints of the ground! To be able to spread your wings wide, catch the faintest of breezes, and survey your kingdom from high above! No pity is given to those stuck on the ground.

Nothing, perhaps, is more awe inspiring than a bird of prey, a raptor, with wings outspread, soaring high above. With its wings spread wide, eyes intent upon the ground for prey, the hunt happens silently from high up above. For those on the ground, safety is not assured.

Nothing is more majestic than a bald eagle, with wings outspread, soaring high above. The sight of one on the hunt takes one's breath away; the eagle itself takes no notice and remains focused on the task at hand. Back and forth, it swoops up and dives down, all the while its eyes directed intently on the ground.

At long last, the eagle returns to its catch, resting briefly. In a moment, its wings unfurl and catch the breeze, and the eagle soars again.

Crane Gathering

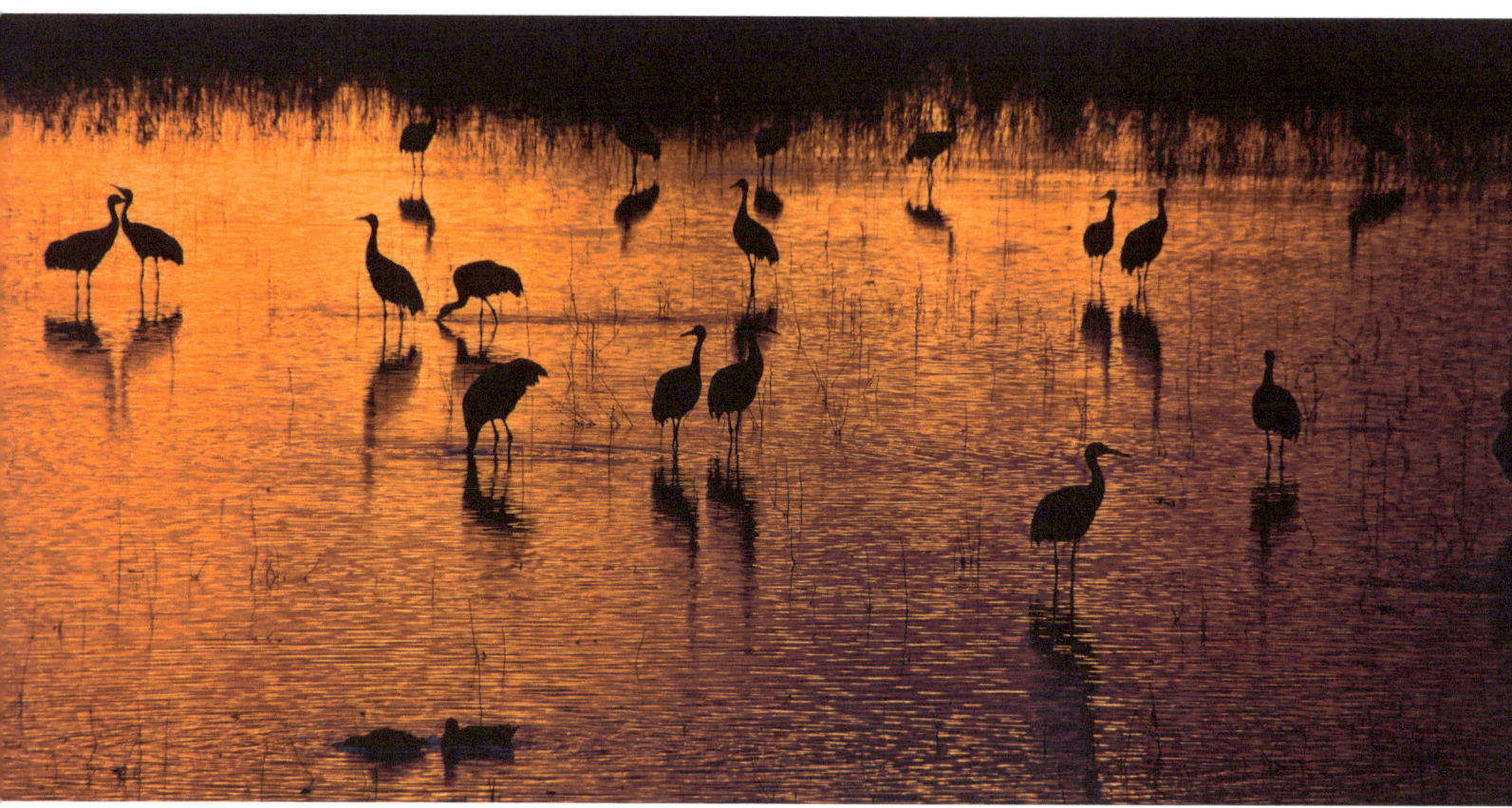

The Bosque del Apache National Wildlife Refuge is replete with birds of all sizes and types. Tens of thousands, if not more, birds descend upon the refuge to spend the winter months. Everything a bird could want is provided: fields planted specifically for feeding in the day, called refuge fields, and plenty of ponds for the evenings. The ponds are vastly important, for the birds spend the night there. Birds are easy prey at night, so they need some sort of defensive mechanism, which the water provides. Predators dislike going into the water for their meal.

Near the end of each day, near sunset, the "fly-in" happens, when the birds return from the fields where they have been feeding to the ponds. The birds settle into the pond for the evening, but just like humans, they take a little time to settle in. They move about, feed a little, and generally, or so it appears, relax. As the sun was slipping below the horizon, the daily crane gathering took place. Peace and serenity remained throughout the early evening, broken only by the occasional crane calling to its mate. Eventually, even those sounds faded away into the gentle evening.

Indigo Afternoon

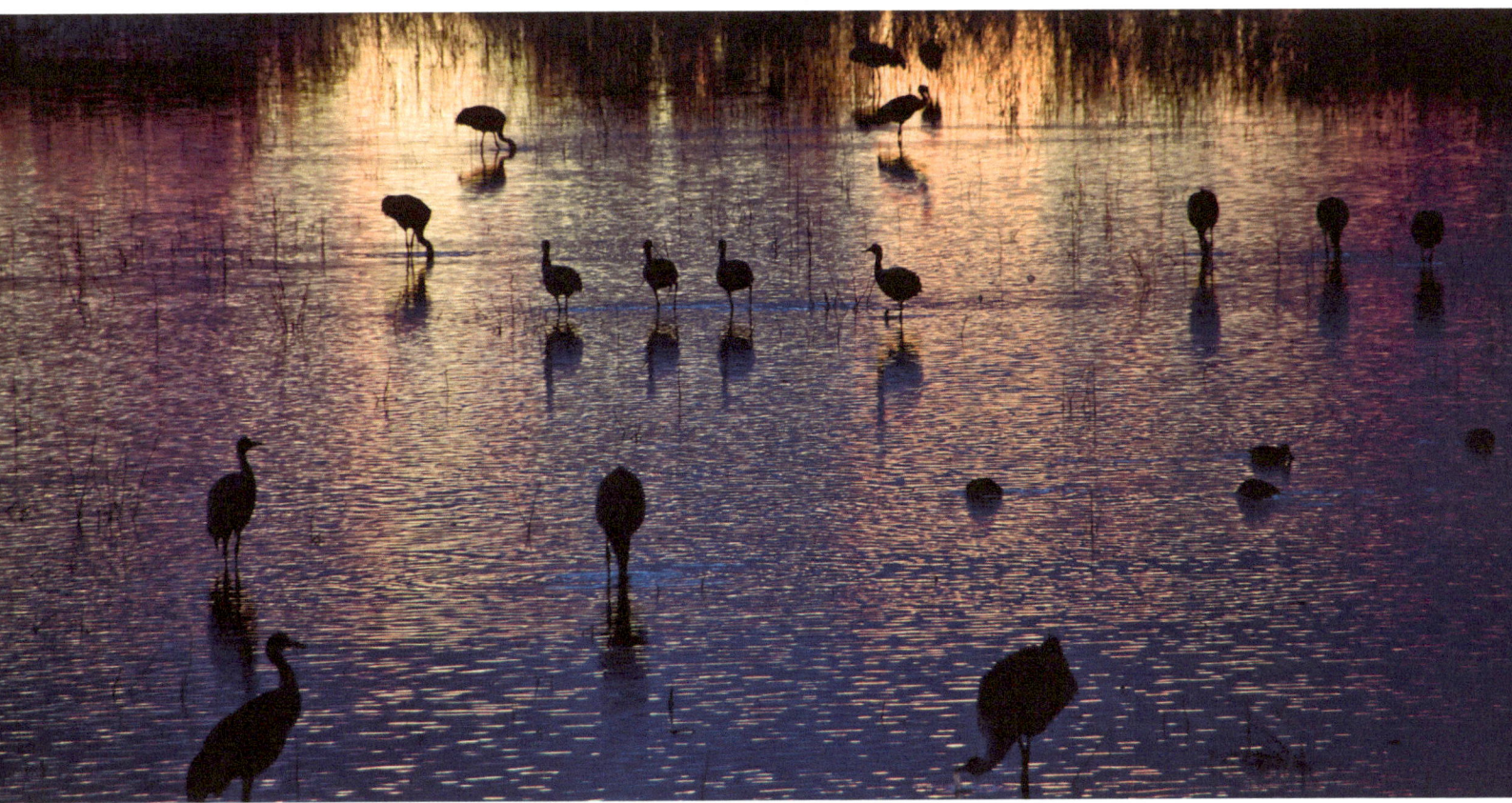

As birds of all sorts begin to return from the refuge fields where they have been feeding, the once-tranquil ponds around the Bosque del Apache spring to life. Ducks, snow geese, sandhill cranes, and even the occasional blue heron all take their place in their pond of choice and begin to settle down for the evening.

New Mexico is known for its colorful sunsets, as well, and every now and then a sunset of over-the-top color happens along. When an such a sunset meets the fly-in, magic happens.

The day had been cloudy on and off; there was plenty of moisture and clouds still in the air, setting the stage for a colorful sunset. The sun began to dip below the horizon, giving off its deepest hues. For just a moment—the briefest of all brief moments, the mere wink of an eye—the colors dipped into the indigo range. That brief moment became Indigo Afternoon.

Dawn Flight

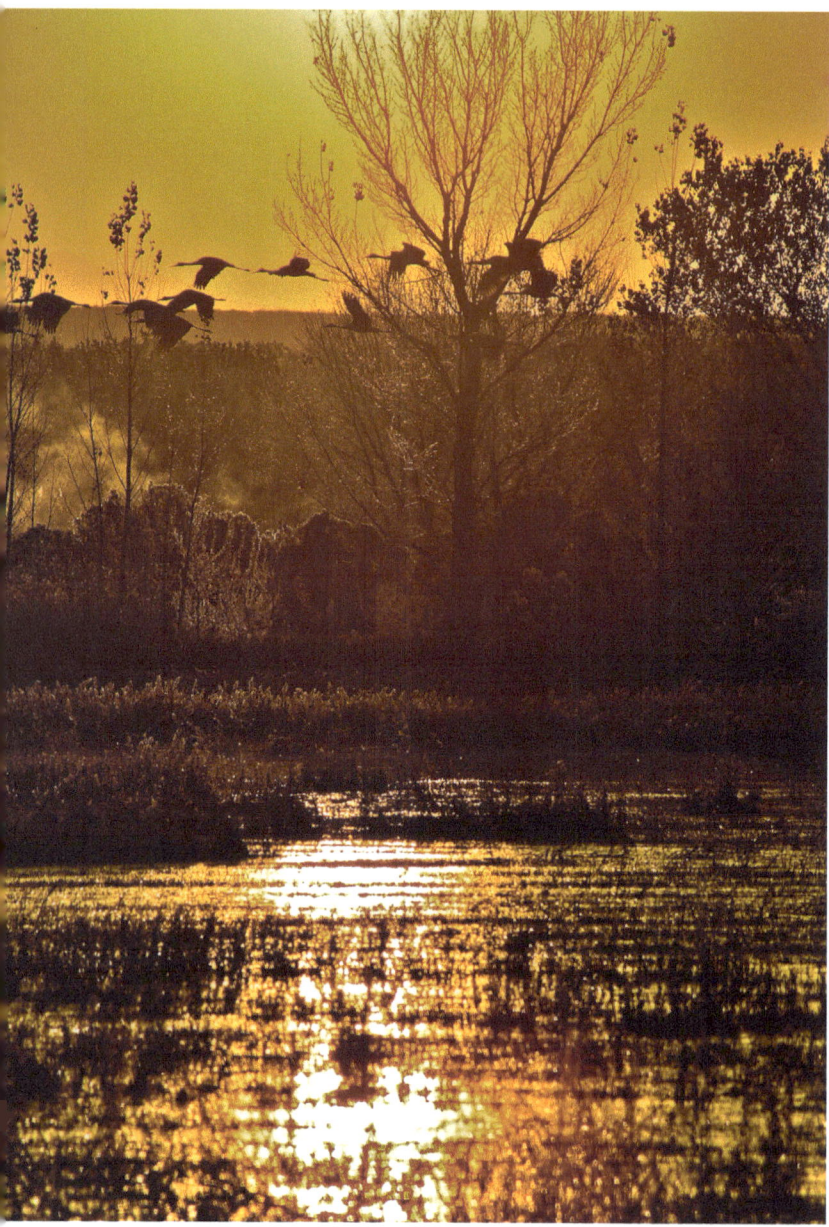

Dawn.

The general problem with dawn activities is that they generally happen at, around, and sometimes even before, sunrise, and the problem with sunrise is that it happens first thing in the morning, and we all know the problems with mornings. If you happen to combine a dawn activity with a winter month, you can see the dilemma. Before making this photograph, I thought I knew what was cold was. I was wrong.

The location in question is the Bosque del Apache, and time is a bitter cold November morning. It is an awe-inspiring experience to watch more ducks, geese, cranes and other winged critters than you can count suddenly take to the sky. The sound is akin to thunder and transforms a peaceful, serene pond into a storm of activity that lasts mere moments before all is tranquil again.

To see this event, you need to stand around for a couple of hours in the pre-dawn darkness, waiting. It feels almost one thousand degrees colder, too, when you are just standing and waiting for the sun to begin to rise and the birds to take flight. You wait for your toes to give up and leave you in search of someplace warm. You wait for things to happen. You shiver, trying to stay warm, and wonder why you are there watching birds sleep, but mostly you wait for an extraordinary spectacle to unfold. Once it does, you realize that all that discomfort was nothing compared to what you just witnessed. When you do, it is just indescribable.

Golden Takeoff

Evening.

The afternoon, and warmth, eventually find their way to the Bosque del Apache. Warmth might not seem like it will make it, when you are enduring the morning, yet patience is rewarded. Everyone, sooner or later, thaws out. Usually.

As the sun begins its journey into the western sky and daylight fades, photographers pop out from everywhere for the magic of Golden Hour, that time of day when the sun provides deep, rich, colors. No matter how hard you look, you'll not see photographers during the day, but at one minute into Golden Hour, there they are, looking as if they had been there forever. Once the time has past, so go the photo folks, and they fade once again into the landscape as if they were never there.

How do I know this? Because I am one of them. Oh yes, I'll probably be drummed out of the corps for admitting it, but I am one of the Golden Hour seekers.

Why not? Plentiful opportunities abound during this time. Let's take a perfectly random example to illustrate my point. Take, oh, a pond, and the sunset throwing long copper and golden rays. Interest. We need something of interest for the pond. Oh! I know! Let's use, hmmm, a crane. Yes! A sandhill crane! As long as we're at it, we might as well have the crane taking off, too. If we let our imagination run with this pond, sunset, and crane, it might look something a little like this photograph.

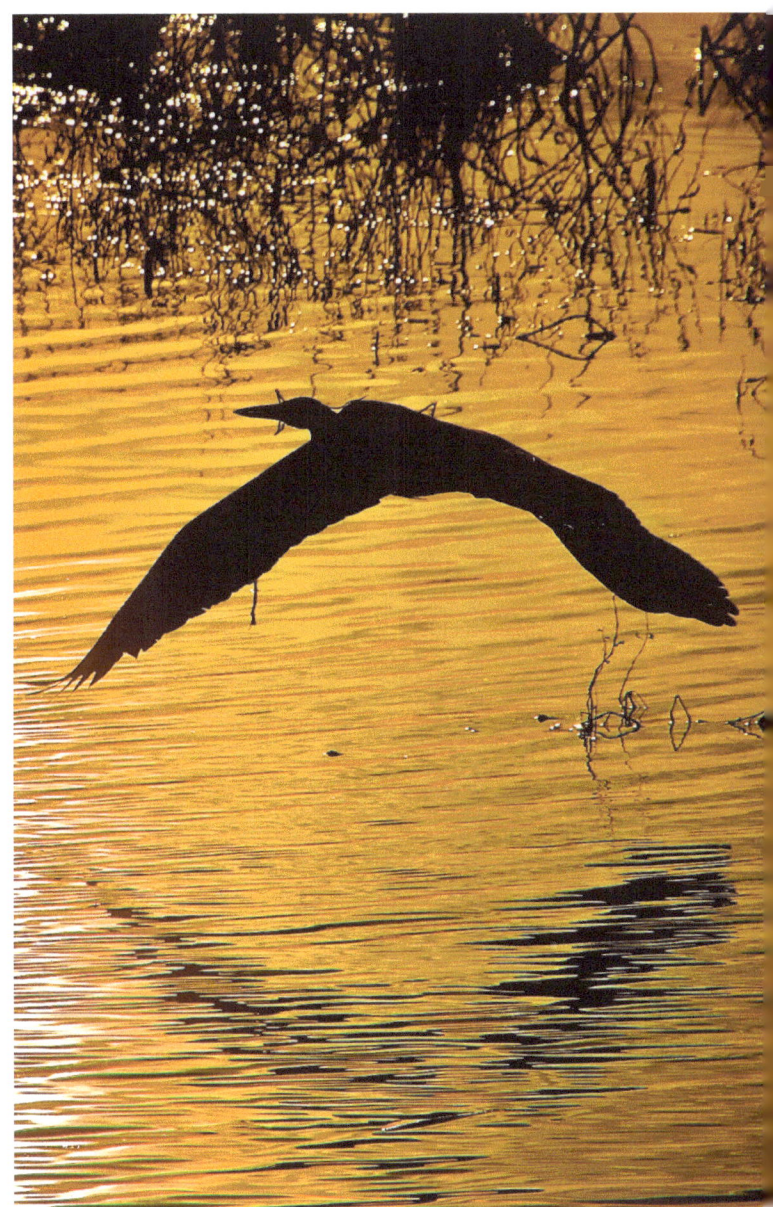

Hummingbird Flight

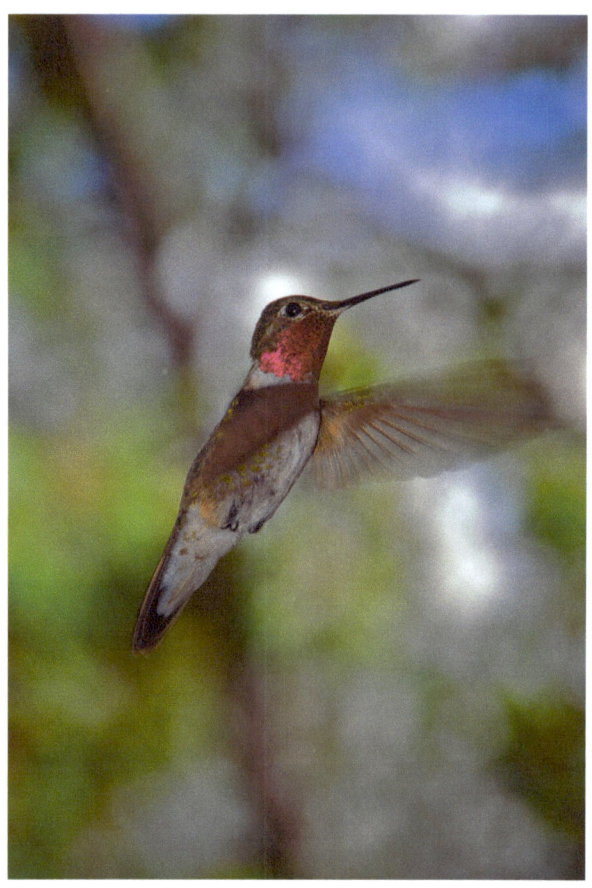 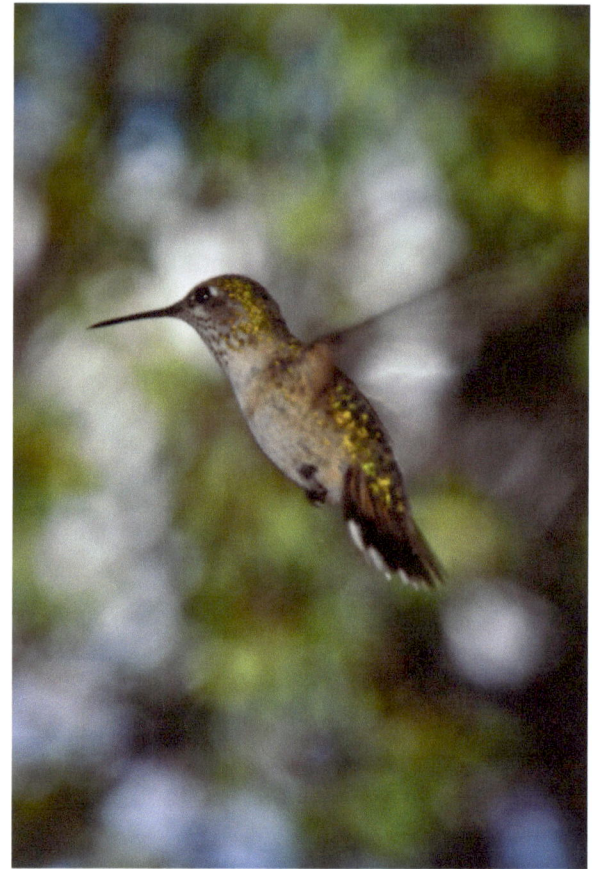

Hummingbirds are not the easiest bird in the world to photograph. They tend to be exceptionally fast, as you can imagine, and don't stay in one place for long. Catching one in flight, then, is even harder. Oh, it might seem simple at first. Walk outside with camera in hand, set up, wait a moment for the perfect bird to come right to you, take the picture, and head inside for a good glass of refreshing lemonade. It didn't work out exactly as planned.

In real life I ended up being exceptionally patient, sitting as still as could be, thinking thoughts like "I am a hummingbird. I am a hummingbird. I am crazy. No, er, a hummingbird." Eventually the hummingbirds that wandered by started to accept that I was in fact, crazy, no, er, a hummingbird and largely ignored me.

At long last, a gorgeous male (left) and female (right) Anna's hummingbird were in the right place, and at long last I could make the photographs. The lemonade never tasted so good.

Taking Flight

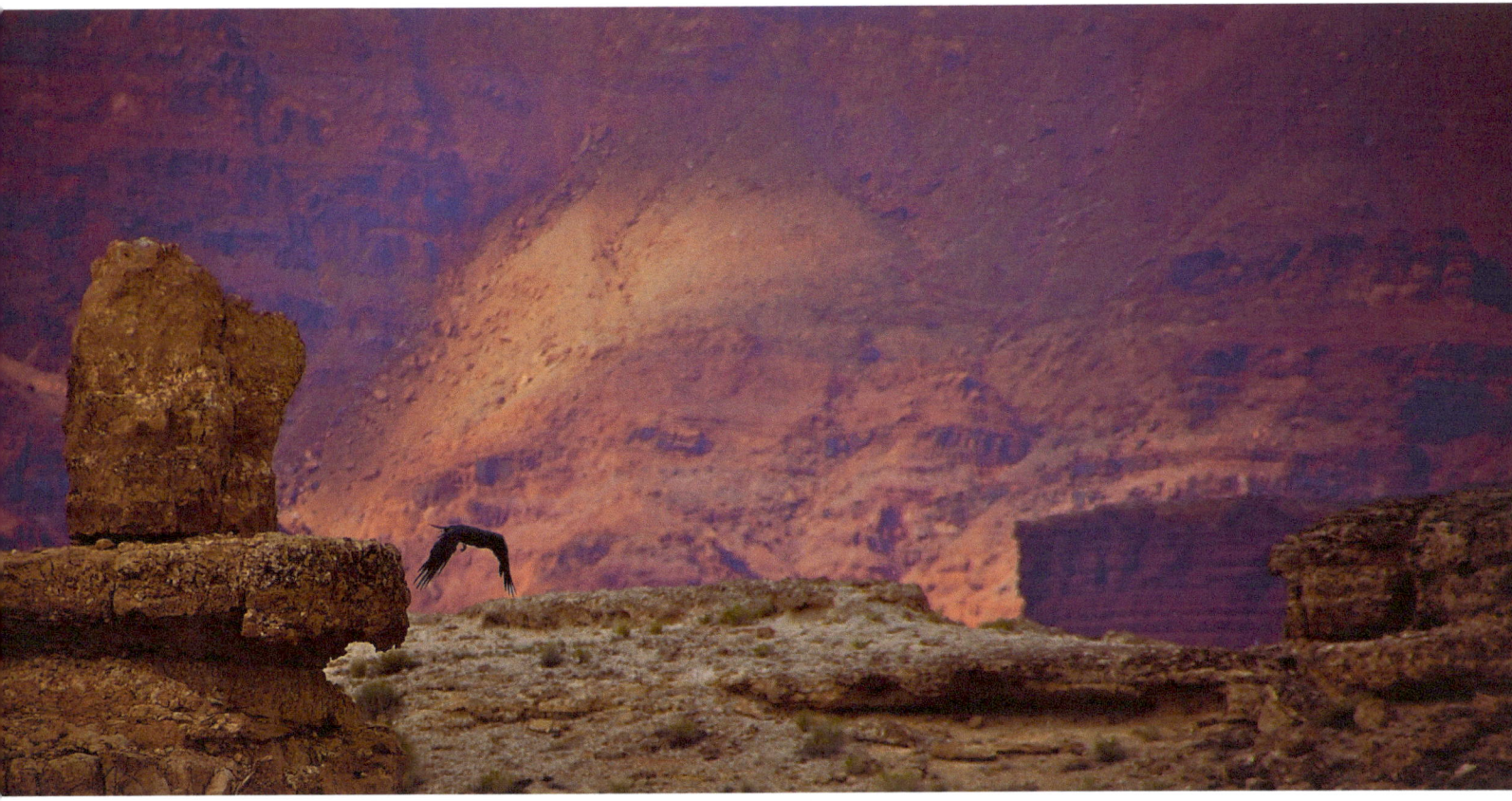

The afternoon was silent—nothing except the whisper of the wind disturbed the canyon's peace. If you used your imagination, you might hear the gentle roar of water from the Colorado River, or perhaps it was just wind again. The heat was oppressive, it being summer, and not many creatures had the desire to stir.

The afternoon was getting a little long in the tooth. Although it was not quite time to go to bed, the sun was hot and tired and decided to call it an early day, which worked out well, because the canyon walls, with unusual mauve shades to begin with, came alive in an effort to get in all the day's color at once.

One bird decided to move from here to there. The "whoosh" of its wings broke the silence, and the afternoon's quiet was no more. The bird took off from a large rock outcrop and headed off in search of prey, or maybe just a change of view. After a moment, the sound faded into the distance, and silence descended once again.

Snow Jay

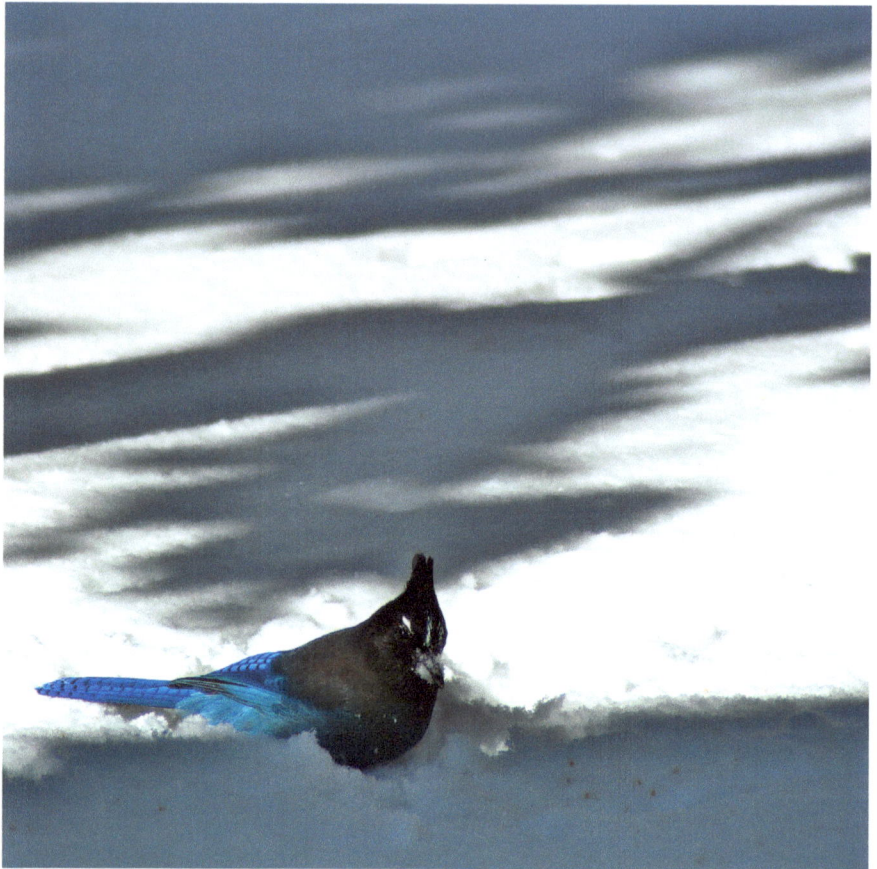

Who doesn't love a good snowfall? Don't answer that if you are the one tasked with the snow shovel.

The world is fresh and white and new right after a good snow; the ground sparkles, glistens, and gleams, unbroken whiteness wherever you look. The trackless world transforms into a landscape full of magic and discovery.

All of these things are great if you are a human. Perhaps not so much, though, if you are a bird, for the birds have to scrounge to get the day's meal. I encountered this Stellar's Jay as he was digging around; the flurry of his bobbing in and out of the snow caught my eye, and the camera lens caught him shortly after that. He looked up and here we are.

Snow, clean and fresh and white. And full of stellar's jays, too.

Beep! Beep!

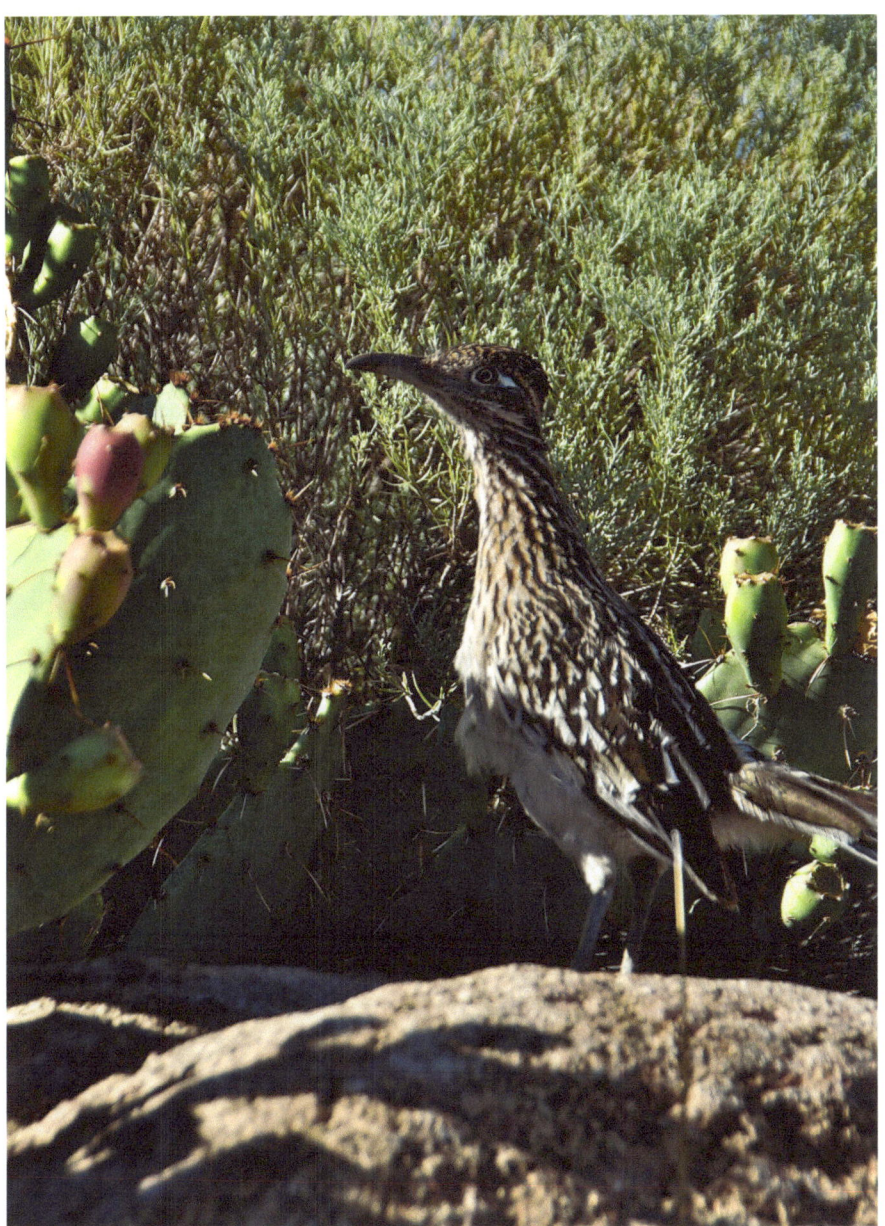

"Beep! Beep!" That's all I heard as I was ducking for cover.

One moment I was enjoying a beautiful afternoon. The next moment, something was moving toward me at about a billion million zillion miles an hour, and I was diving for cover. I dove behind the nearest boulder, as anyone would in my position, and then quietly peeked out. There, on the next boulder over was, of all things, a roadrunner!

How lucky I was! First, and foremost, because I was not run over, always a good thing. Second was the fact that seeing a roadrunner is a lucky portent. The Hopi deeply understand the roadrunner wards off evil spirits, and rightly so, for what evil spirit could hope to keep up with a roadrunner? In any case, this one chose to pose for me, although, when pressed, I might concede it was simply enjoying the afternoon sun. We both were, come to think of it.

A proud bird, fast as all get out, lucky, and it didn't run me over. All in all, it was a superb day. With a faint "Beep! Beep!," it was off again, like the wind.

Living Life

From the smallest lizard to the larger mammals, everyone has a story. It may be a story of tenderness or playfulness, and sometimes it is a story of courage and hope. To those who stop and listen to each, life is revealed, story by story.

Petrified Lizard

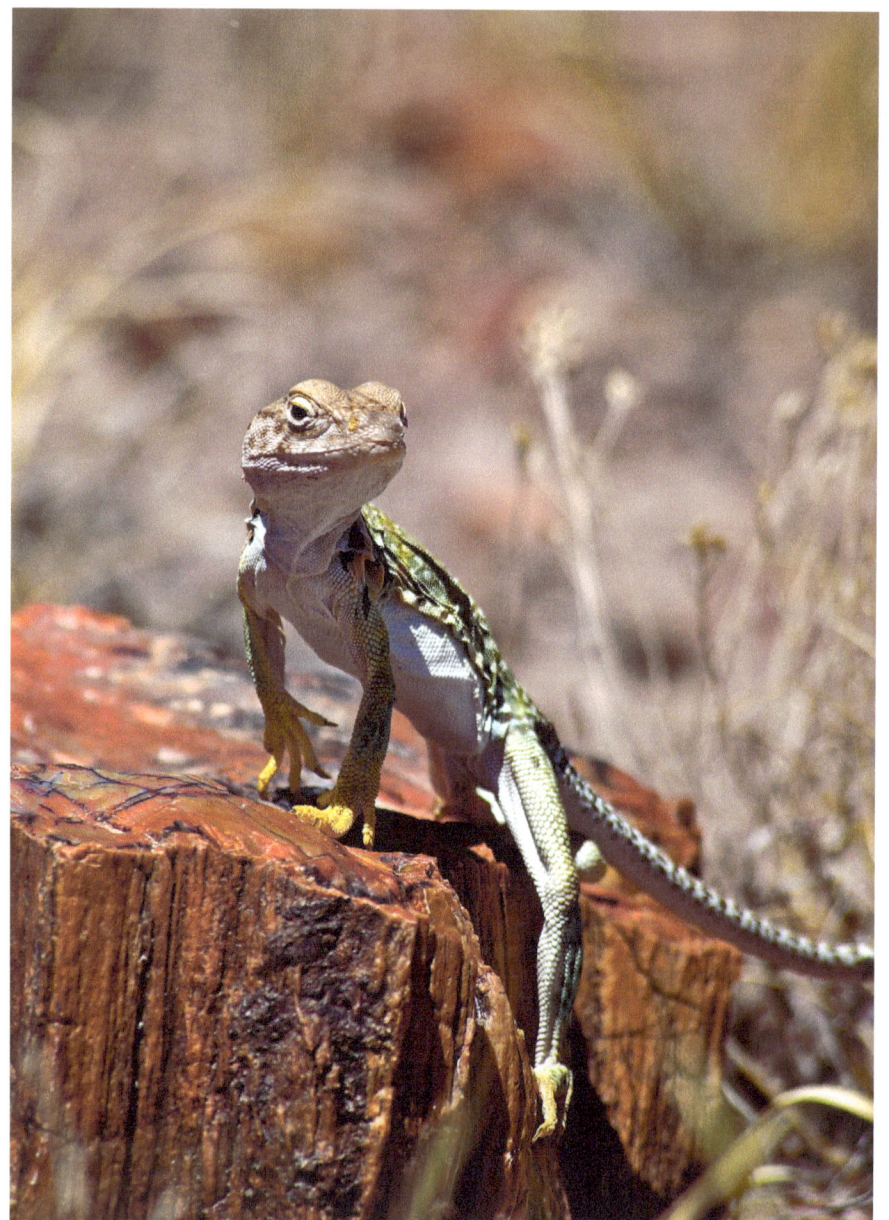

In the desert, patience and the ability to be motionless pays off. This collared lizard, in the Petrified Forest National Forest in Arizona, has learned that lesson well. Perching motionless on a piece of petrified wood, he waits. And waits. And waits. And waits.

He is so still that he blends into the background, and even when looking right at him, he fades away from sight. His bright yellow feet do not give him away, for they meld perfectly with the petrified wood he stands upon. And he continues to wait.

His stillness was good for me, for it gave me a perfect opportunity to get close enough for this photograph. I liked the way he was perched, with his head cocked just so. He was looking at me, but not at me, and although he knew I was there, I, apparently, posed no threat at all to him. The sun continued to beat down on us both, but he didn't flinch.

After a time, he must have decided that a different piece of petrified wood would provide a better vantage point, and without a sound or whisper, he was gone. The photograph of him remains, petrified in time.

Duckness Monster

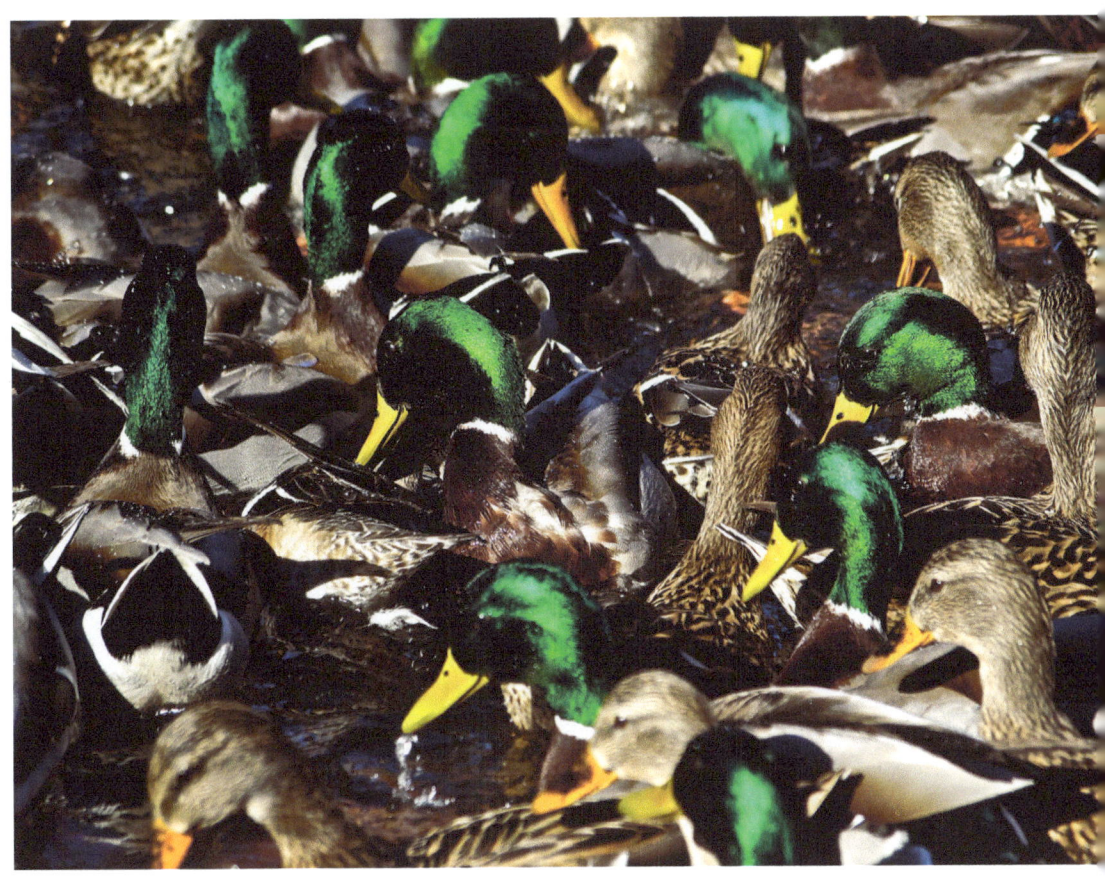

They seem gentle, don't they? Gliding along serenely and silently in the water, the humble duck is known by all, loved by all, and watched by all. Who doesn't turn his head to watch a duck glide by?

I had always thought of ducks as gentle creatures. They move from one side of a pond to the other so effortlessly that it is beyond reason they would be anything other than dignified. I have heard tales of the mysterious monster that ducks can become, but I dismissed it as an old duck's tale. Duckness Monster? Hah! Ducks? Monsters? Are you trying to tell me a funny story, and not a scary story? Perhaps you picked up the wrong fairytale book. Ducks are gentle and peaceful animals, don't you know? Now if you will excuse me, please, several ducks are on that pond and they demand my attention.

How wrong I was! My illusions were completely and forever shattered, when I witnessed what happens to ducks at feeding time. Gone are the gentle ducks of a moment earlier. In their place, right before my eyes, was the dreaded Duckness Monster. Run!

Peek-A-Boo Deer

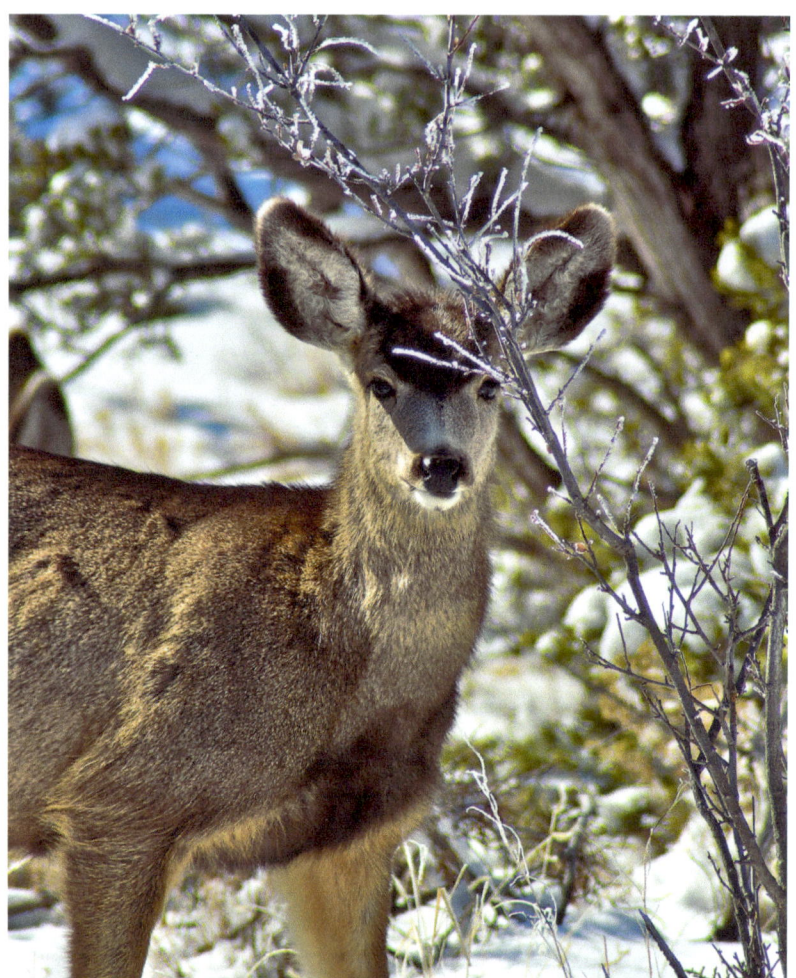

When we are small children, there are many games we love to play. Perhaps, though, one of the more popular ones is the venerable game of Peek-a-Boo. You know, the one where you hide your face in your hands and then reveal your face yelling, Peek-a-boo in a loud voice, scaring the child in question, drawing puzzling looks from everyone around you, and summoning help, all in one fell swoop?

The point is that you hide behind something that certainly doesn't hide you, on the assumption that the child won't figure it out.

As best as I can figure, this deer knows Peek-a-Boo, too, because clearly, hiding behind that small branch in Bandelier National Park in New Mexico didn't work out well for the deer. On the other hand, it worked out really well for me.

Peek-a-Boo! (But I said it in a really quiet voice.)

Peek-A-Boo Elk

"Whatcha doin?"

I about jumped out of my skin, for I wasn't expecting to be spoken to just then. All my attention had been focused on the sunset in front of me, and most of the time elk don't talk much. Turning to the young fellow, though, I explained that I was trying to make a photograph of an amazing sunset here at the Grand Canyon.

"Oh," was all he said in response, and he continued to peek over the top of the other elk, who was enjoying the sunset and paying me no nevermind. The sun continued to creep lower, and in a moment it would be perfect, but as I was finally ready to create the photograph, a loud, and startling "Now!" broke the spell. I jumped about a mile, straight up. The camera went flying, but I caught it, and I was left breathless. I glanced at him with a questioning look. He said, gently, this time, "Now it is perfect." Indeed it was, so the moment was recorded, the camera put away, and equipment quickly stowed.

Afterward, in companionable silence, we all watched the sun slip below the horizon.

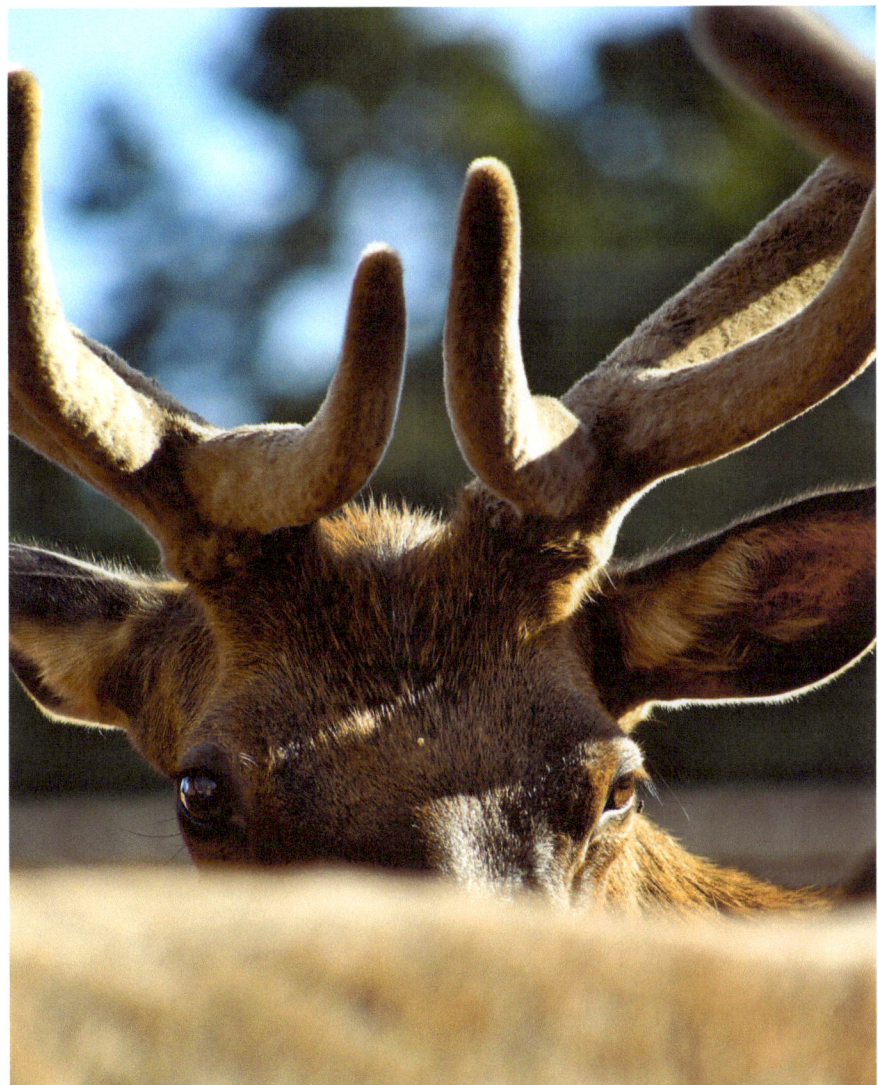

Peek-A-Boo Mustang

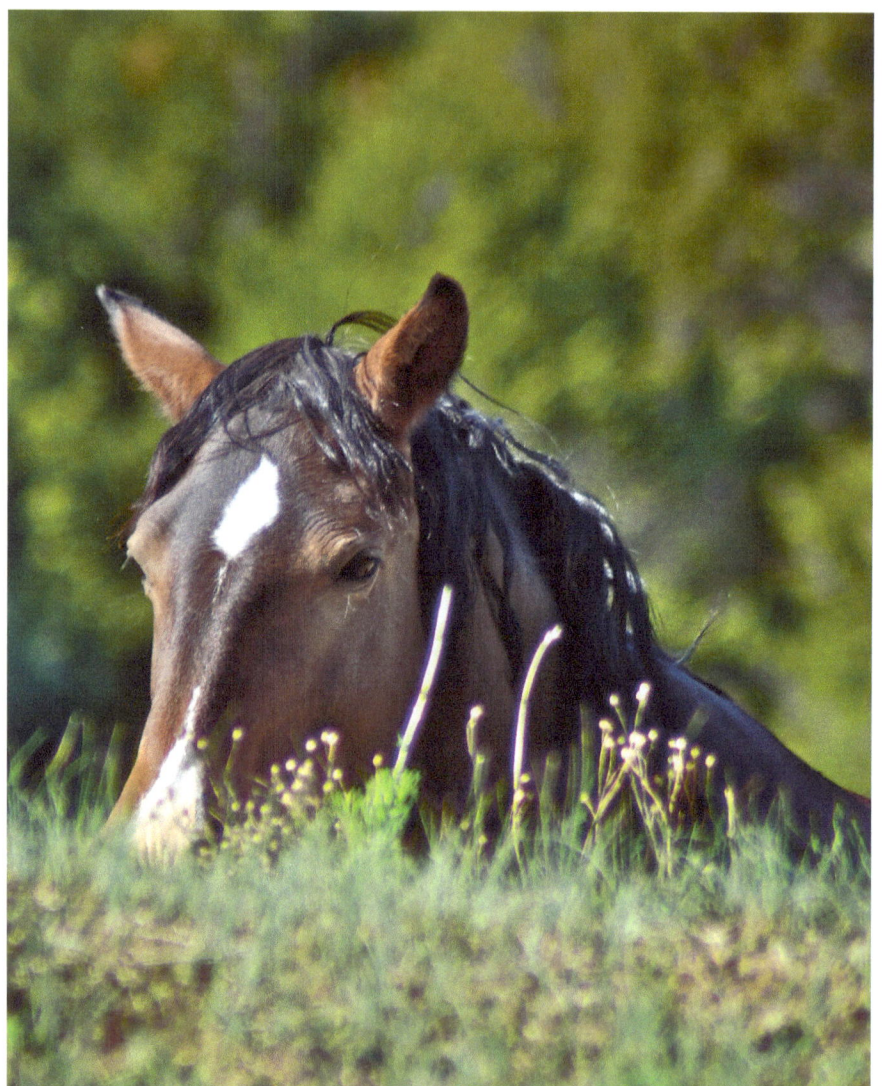

Within the Monero Mustangs Sanctuary in northern New Mexico lies a small watering hole. It isn't a big watering hole, but it does include the most important bit: water. It also includes another important bit: a berm that partly shields the water hole from the surroundings. Where there is water, wild mustangs will come, but these are wild mustangs living within the sanctuary. Although familiar with humans, they are not accustomed to the human hand and certainly not in the mood to be domesticated. They maintain a good deal of caution around us, and rightly so, since many of the mustangs have been rescued from human abuse.

This is La Vieja, a mare caught peeking over the berm next to the water hole, just to see what, or who, was out there. The "who" was me, camera in hand, capturing the moment. We looked at each other for a brief moment, acknowledging each other, and then La Vieja turned away from the berm for her much-needed and ever-so-pleasant drink.

Postscript: A couple of days after this photograph was made, La Vieja became a mother to a filly. You can bet that both of them are now at the water hole, playing peek-a-boo.

Dos Amigas

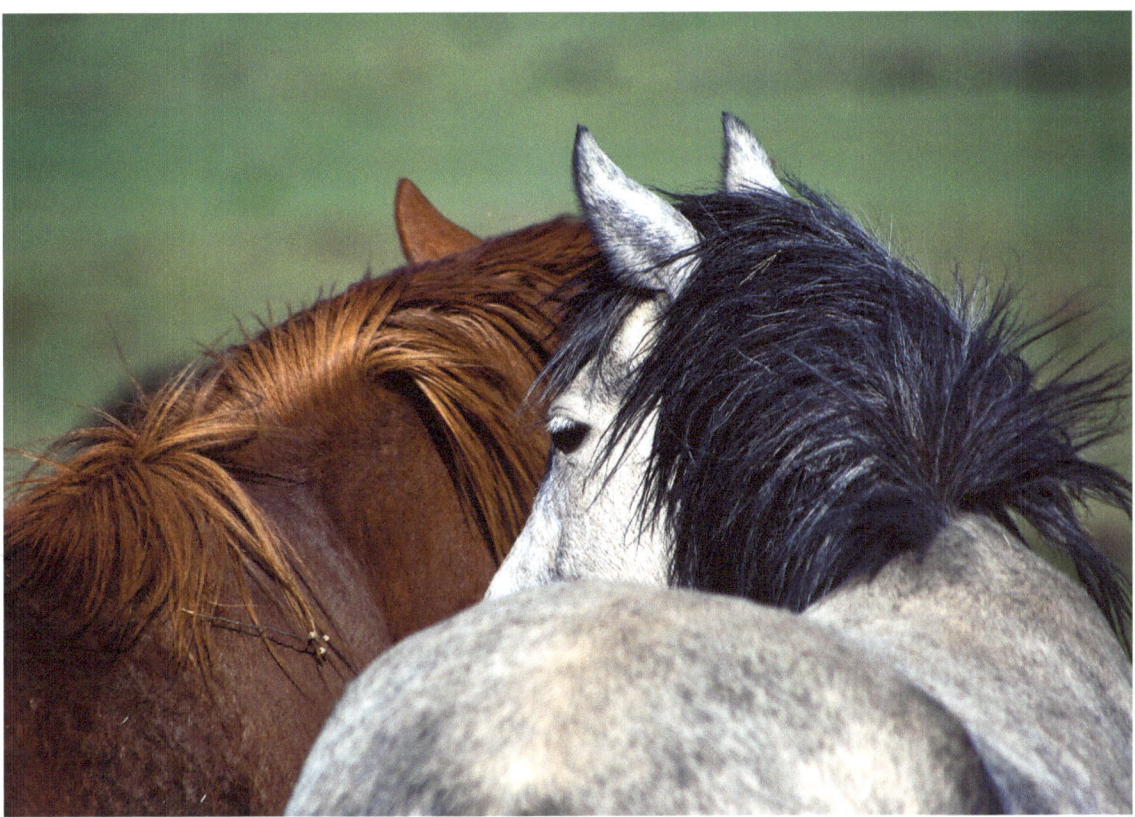

There are moments in life that are tender and touching. They are fleeting, gone before you know it, yet these moments define us. Unsurprisingly, these moments are not exclusive to humans.

Take the case in point with Clarisse, the red on the left, and Tizne, the blue-gray on the right. Part of Milagro's band at the Monero Mustangs Sanctuary, these two mares are enjoying a tender moment out in the open fields of the sanctuary. To be sure, the rest of the band is close by—very close by, especially Milagro himself, who would not let these two out of his sight. Nevertheless, Clarisse and Tizne, slightly apart, share a special bond of togetherness and companionship.

The Monero Mustangs Sanctuary in New Mexico rescues mustangs from terrible fates and restores to them a large measure of freedom. Safe from the predations of humans, they are able to again form bands as they are meant to do and freely roam about the sanctuary. Thanks to the loving and care from the folks who run the sanctuary, their worries are few, leaving these two friends free to enjoy the afternoon sun and tender moments.

Explora Gosling

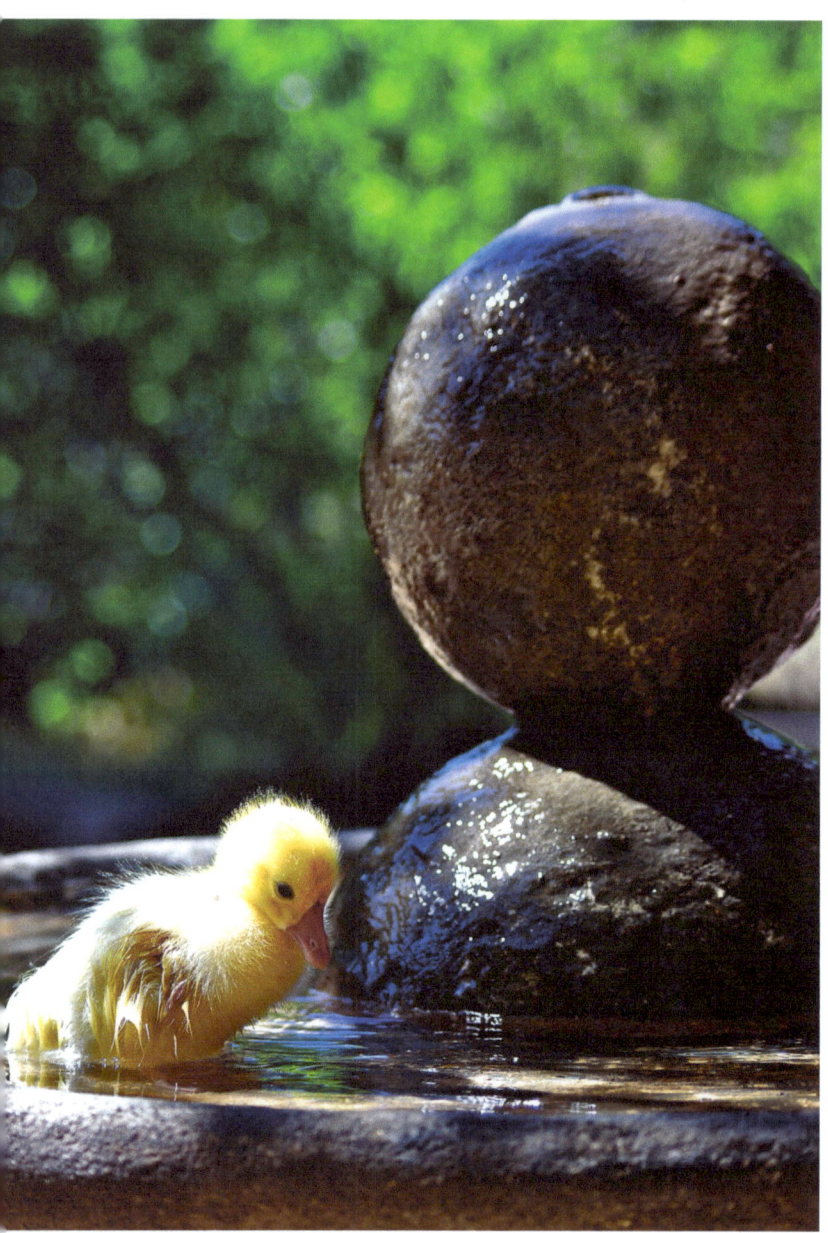

The explorer crept through the dense jungle, pressing onward. Somewhere, somewhere up ahead, lay her ultimate goal: the fountain of youth. Many tales were told of the fountain. Many had heard of this fabled fountain. Many had mounted an expedition to the fountain, yet none had found it, or if they did, none came back to tell of it. This old and experienced explorer goose knew she would prevail, though.

The explorer continued onward, despite her weary bones. She had been on far too many expeditions, been in far too many dangerous situations, and had enough close calls to last a lifetime or two, but this expedition was special.

It was near; she could sense it. In all her years of life, she had never undertaken such a trek, but then again, for all her life she had trained for it. She was as prepared as she ever would be.

At first she heard the faint trickle of water. Her hopes soared. She pressed onward through the dense vegetation, the sounds of water splashing and running growing louder and louder. There! Through a break in the forest, she saw it. She had found the Fountain of Youth and her name would live on forever. Rushing forward, she dove headlong into the pool without a second thought.

As she splashed in the fountain, laughing and happy, she could not remember feeling so refreshed. She felt young and vibrant and the energy of youth flowed through her. She felt as if she were just a five-day-old gosling, splashing about for the very first time. Explora Gosling found her youth.

Sunny Chipmunk

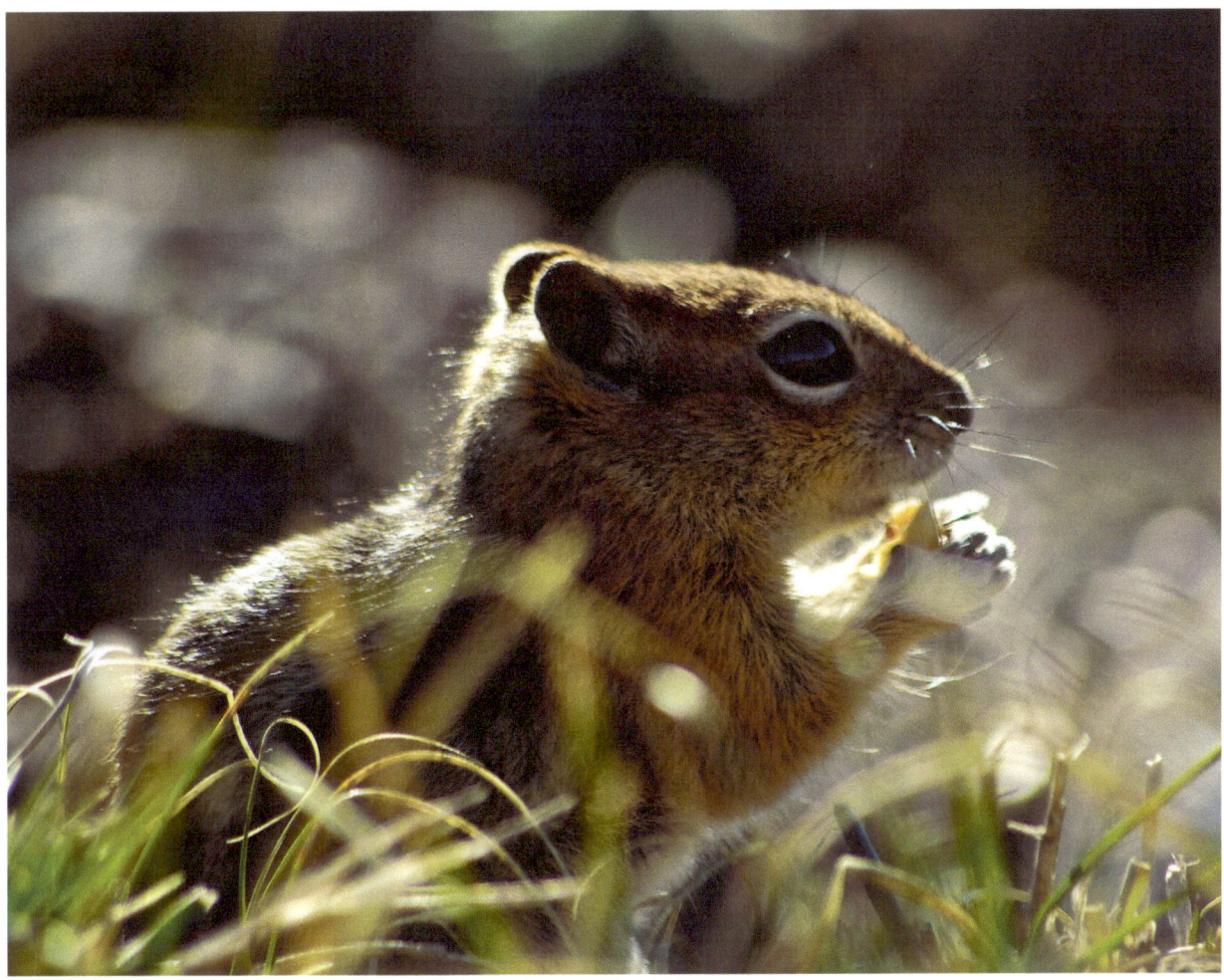

What a delight the afternoon sun is. Its warmth provides cheer, no matter what else the day may have brought. Its rays soak into your fur and on through to your skin, giving you a sense of comfort. You could, after all, sit and soak it up all day, especially after a long, cold winter. Ah, there is nothing better.

Well, wait! Come to think of it, there is something better than the afternoon sun, and that would be having a snack, a tasty snack, while sitting in the sun. Two delicious things, combined! As all chipmunks know, this combination cannot be beat.

A spring day, a snack, the sun; who could ask for anything more?

Proud Raven

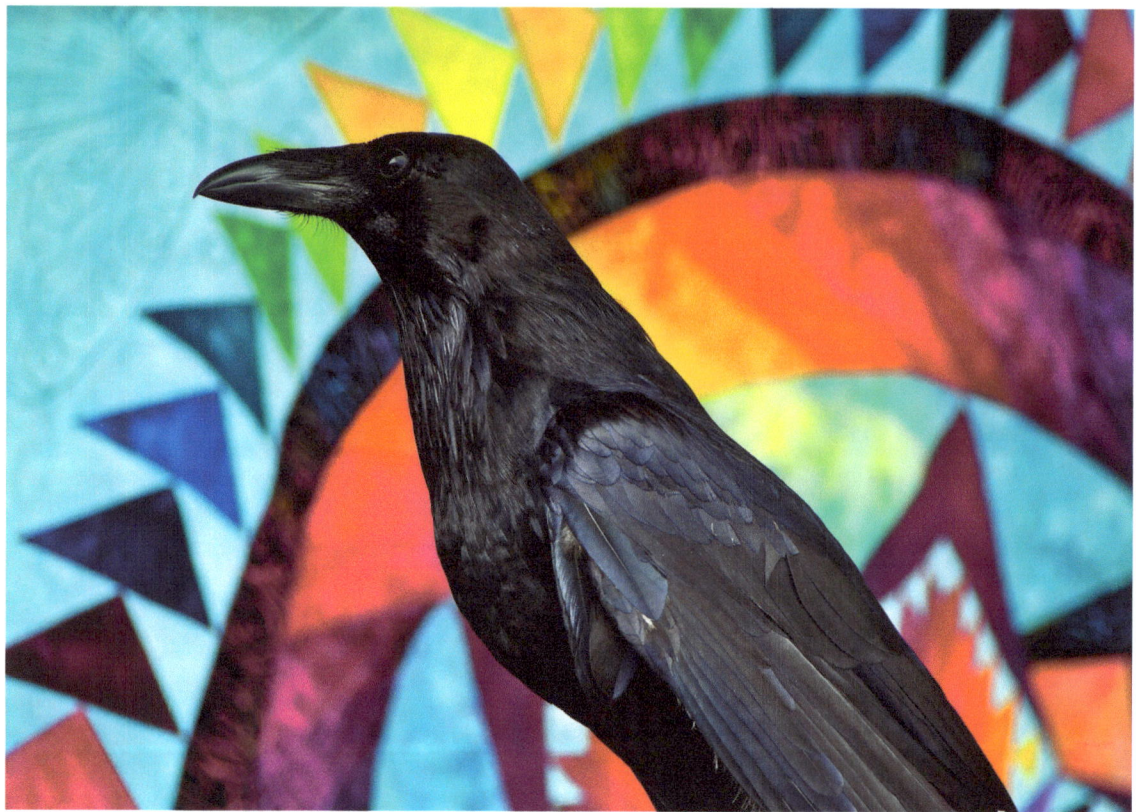

"Once upon a daytime bright, while I pondered strength and joy…" That opening was the original version, but it was a little too upbeat. Looking for darker inspiration, Edgar happened upon a raven, and the rest has been immortalized.

Ravens are bright. They are clever, and they are intelligent. They can solve problems, and they have such a look that you just know they are thinking deep thoughts. They don't have the bright colors that other birds sport, but that doesn't mean they aren't dignified, as this particular raven can attest. Against a bright blanket, with a design that compliments the raven perfectly, the raven looks proud and regal.

Quoth the Raven: "Once more."

Three Honketeers

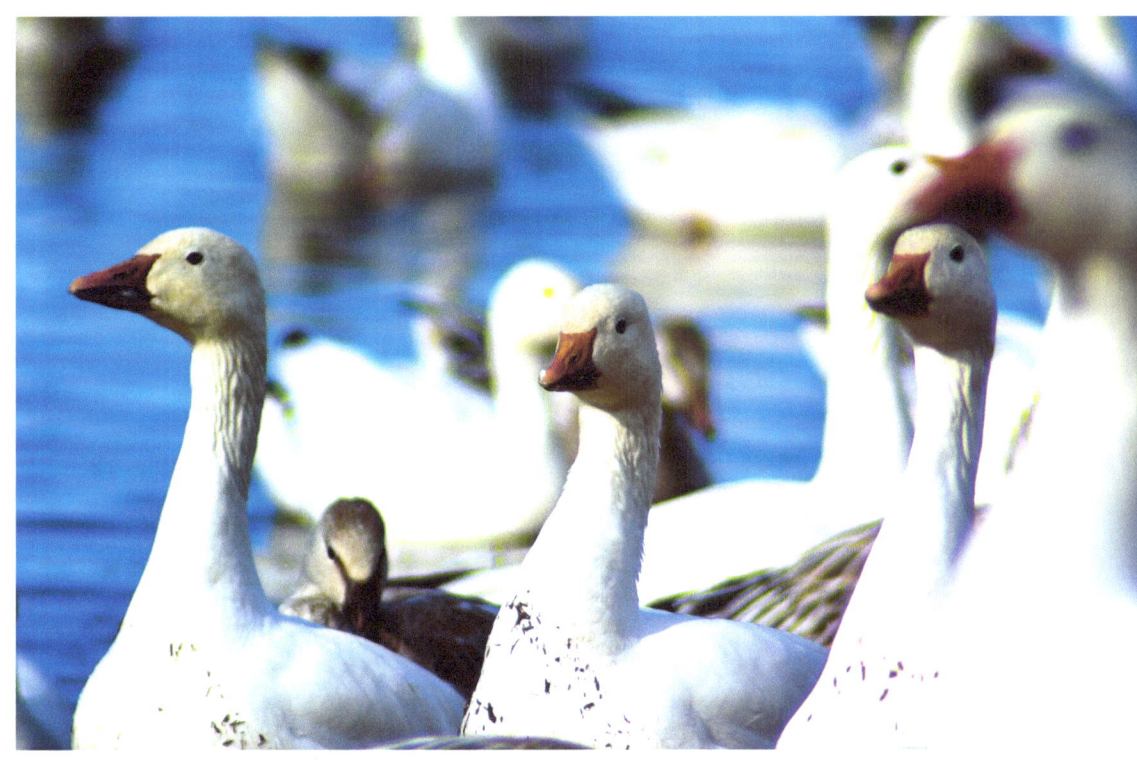

I've been known to live on the edge of focus, and more often than I would care for, I fall off that edge. In this case, however, I achieved what I set out to, getting those three geese in the middle spot-on, while leaving the rest tantalizingly out of focus.

How did I get this photograph? By going completely against my nature, which is to say, by having patience. Just outside of the Bosque del Apache National Wildlife Refuge, there is wonderful pond. It's not a big pond, but neither is it small, and it was like a siren call to me once I saw the snow geese clustered on the far side. I promptly headed to the shoreline and plopped myself down to wait to see what developed.

For no explicable reason, the snow geese started swimming my way from across the pond. "Wonderful," I thought as I continued to sit there. Then, to my utter astonishment, they started getting out of the pond close to me. There was no moving, no getting up, and no way to think about any other piece of equipment except the nice telephoto lens I happened to already have, which made sense at the time, since they were originally far away. One makes do with what one has, and thus was born my idea of very selective focus.

Time passed, and eventually, the snow geese did, too. But between the time they landed to my right, then passed me on land to my left, this particular photograph presented itself. The Three Honketeers led the way from there to here. What an incredible experience to be part of! The memory of being in the middle of a gaggle of snow geese will be with me for a long time to come.

Young Bull

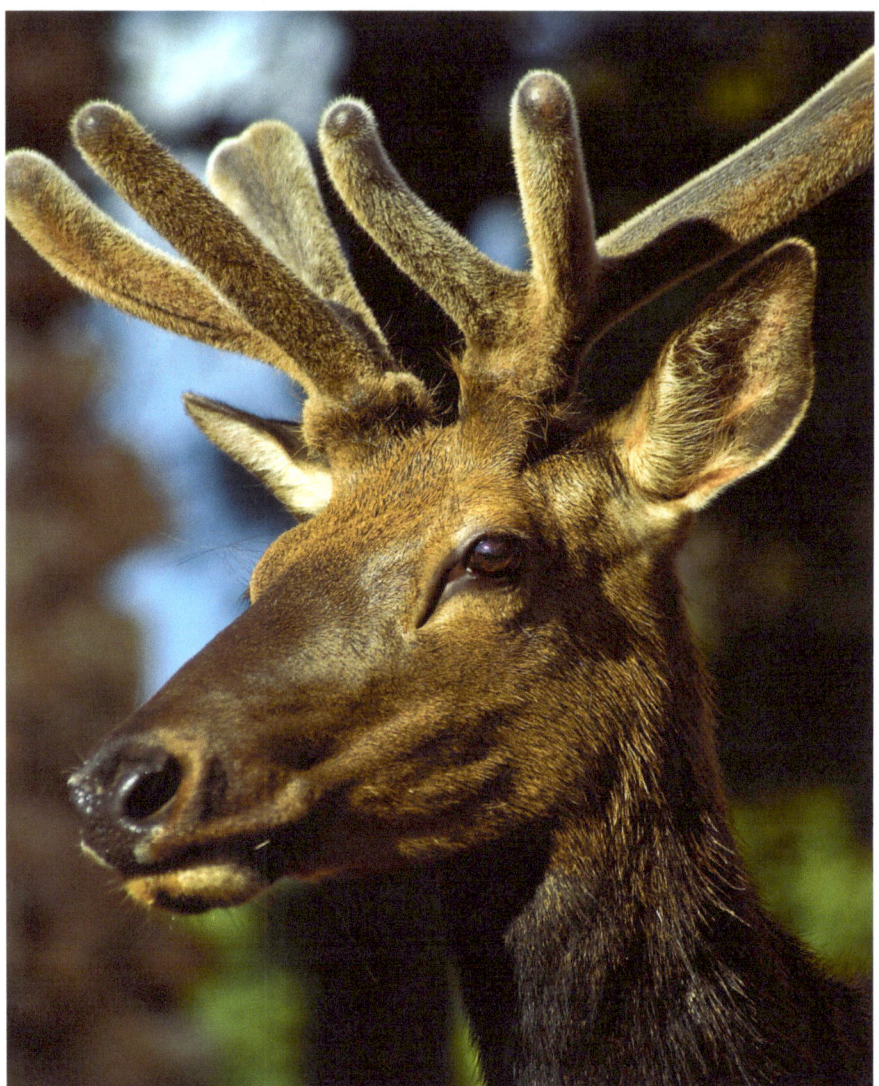

Ah, to be a young elk. Could there be anything better?

The world is fresh and new, full of wonder and surprise, and new adventures await around each and every corner. It is a time for learning how to be a young bull elk and how to wield those antlers, which are coming along nicely, getting bigger every day. It is a time for life. It is the time of the elk.

This fine young fellow was photographed at the South Rim of the Grand Canyon National Park, a fine place for seeing elk. It was early in the spring, and the winter snows had faded from memory. There was plenty to forage, and the world around him was as green as can be. The rains had just come in, and water was not a concern. The end of a spring day, in the late afternoon sun, is a grand time to pose for your photo.

Man and elk had an enjoyable encounter that day. Both were calm and enjoying the day. Each was curious about the other, and both thought: "Ah, to be a young elk. Could there be anything better?"

Wounded Antelope

I had the pleasure of looking through my library to select some of my favorite images for this volume. I have focused on the beauty and majesty of the Southwest, and I wanted to represent the creatures at their best, yet this haunting image, seemingly out of place, remains one of my favorites. It is one of hope and perseverance, thus it belongs here, at the end of this chapter, to remind me what it is important.

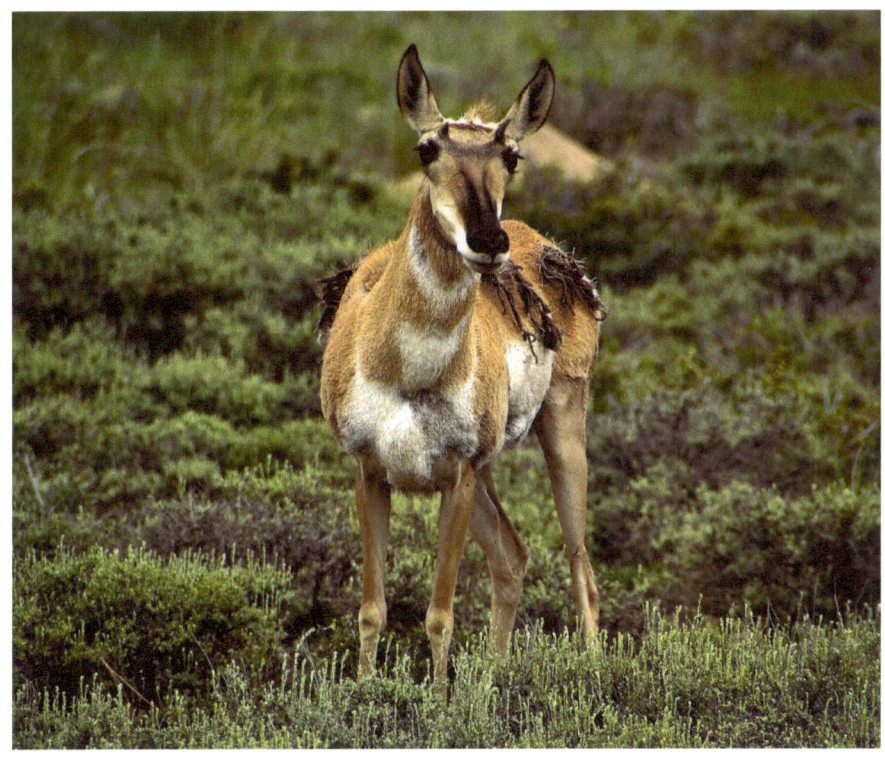

This deeply wounded, yet recovering pronghorn antelope at Fairyland Point in Bryce Canyon National Park, bears witness to what is possible. On its back you'll note what looks like some growths. They aren't growths, they are what is left of this antelope's hide after it survived a near-fatal attack, possibly by a mountain lion. The wounded, torn flesh is a result of the attacker's claws sinking into the antelope's back as it attempted to pull it down. Somehow or other, this antelope broke free of that attack, managed to escape, and managed to live, against long odds.

The animal was wary as I approached, always keeping a safe distance. It took me for what seemed like forever, but I managed to make this photograph without spooking it. I departed as carefully as I came, and left with the deepest respect for the antelope.

An antelope doesn't have a good chance once its attacker has it in its grasp. I cannot begin to imagine the sheer and unrelenting terror it felt as it was chased, then caught, then the claws sunk in and raked across its back. Once the attack came, the outcome was preordained, and the circle of life would continue, yet the antelope never gave up. It had a very different outcome in mind and continued to fight with all its might, even as the end was coming.

The end didn't come. The antelope may not look the best right this moment, but it will heal in time. I included this photo of this brave creature to remind myself, never to, no matter what may be happening, give up.

Flora's Allure

The flora around us sometimes are unnoticed, yet, they provide backdrop of beauty as far as the eye can see, and well beyond. For beauty and magnificence are all around us, to those that stop and see and listen.

Sky Reach

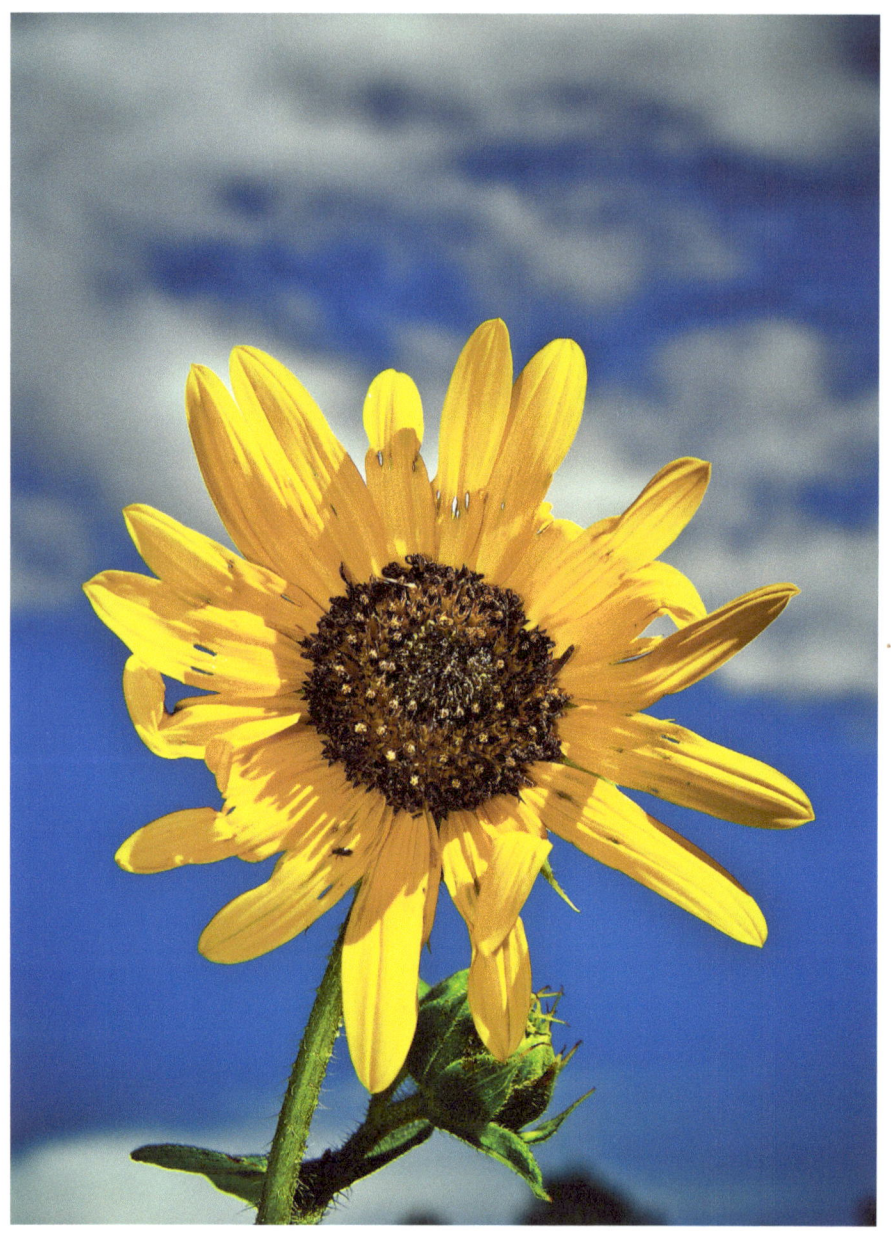

What better way to start Flora's Allure than with a sunflower?

The Southwest in general, and New Mexico in particular, has a plethora of sunflowers. In some areas, they are everywhere, absolutely everywhere, and you can turn in any direction and see them. The vast fields of sunflowers swaying gently in the breeze are an overwhelming sight.

It is hard to describe the feeling you get when you see the endless sunflowers reaching for the endless sky. Everywhere you look, from right in front of you to the edge of everywhere, the sunflowers look toward the sun, greeting it en masse, making for an awe-inspiring and breathtaking sight. Surely, then, the massive invasion makes the perfect photograph, and the more sunflowers that fit into the photograph the better, right?

Despite the myriad of flowers, one in particular caught my eye. There was something poignant about this specific one as it reached for the sky by itself. Alone among many, it stood just a little bit taller than its brethren, and was able to get a little bit more light. It caught my attention, and I made this photograph. An equal trade, I think.

Glorious Columbine

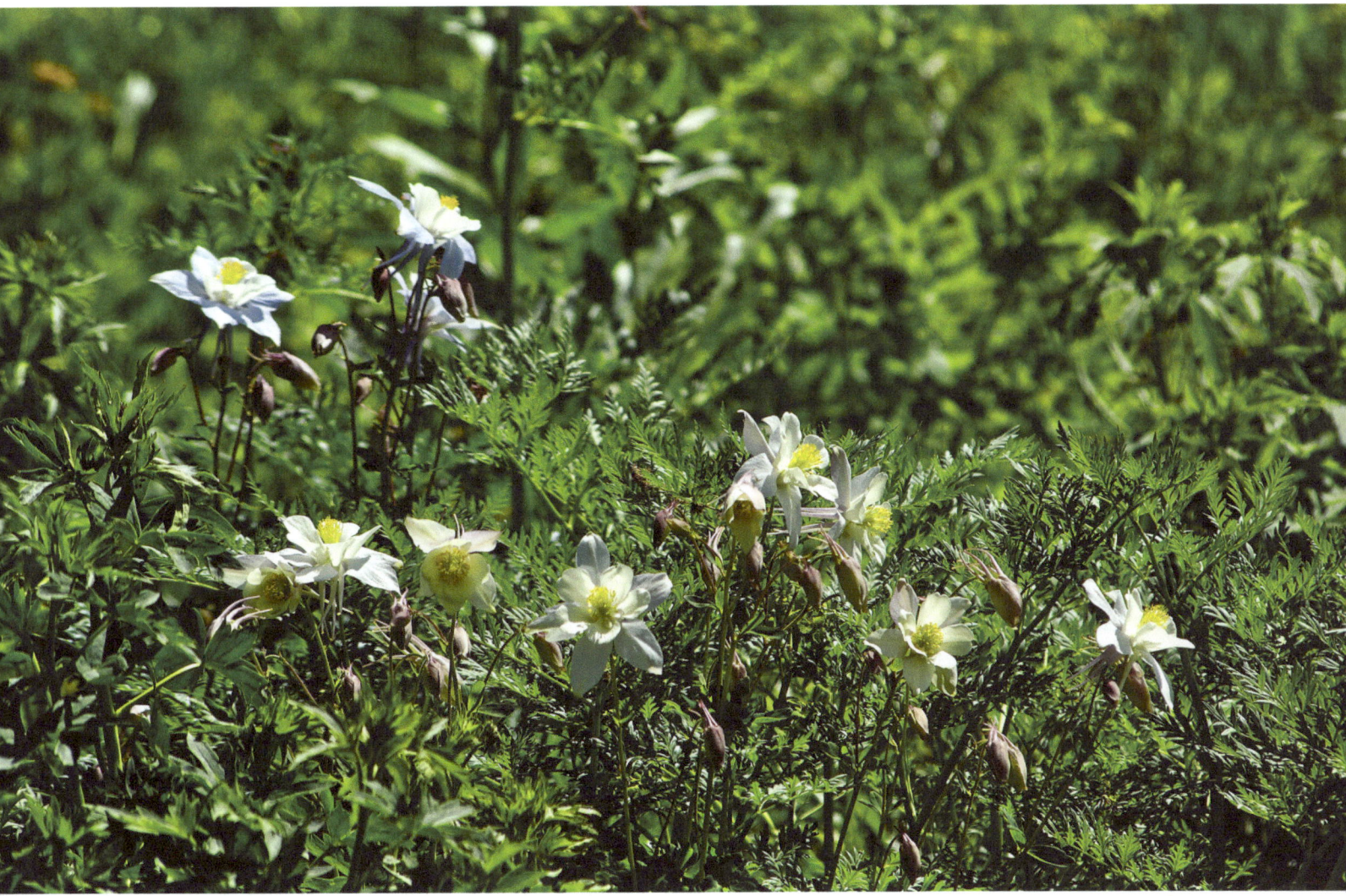

Sometimes, beauty is found in groups. Take, for example, this simple, yet exquisite grouping of columbine in the northern Colorado mountains. Basking in all their glory in the day's bounty of sunlight, they have not a care in the world and give off untold glory. It is hard to describe the feeling you get when you see endless columbine reaching for the endless sky, everywhere you look, all around you, offering a breathtaking sight.

Flowering Cane

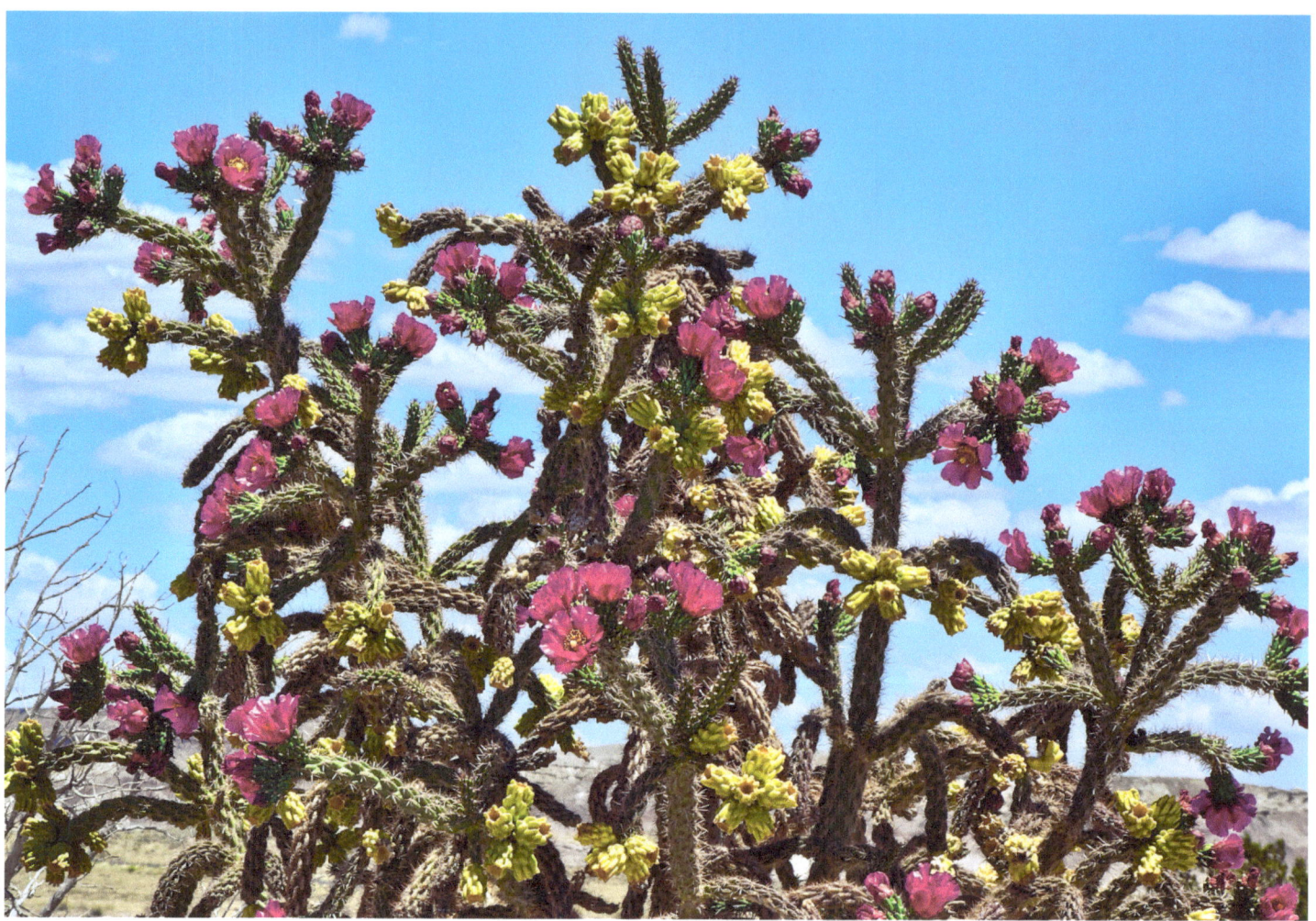

Near the edge of the Painted Desert in Arizona, there sits a cane cholla. Small and quietly unassuming, it is usually overshadowed by the multitude of colors in the Painted Desert. Most of the year, it grows without complaint, without calling attention to itself, in a lovely, if subdued, shade of green, the same shade of green seen all across the desert.

Spring, though, creates a completely different story, for the unnoticed cholla transforms into vibrant yellows and shades of magenta. It flowers, and it flowers a lot, bringing forth a burst of colors that don't normally exist in the Painted Desert's palette. For a short while, the flowering cane owns the color crown.

Coniferific Tenacity

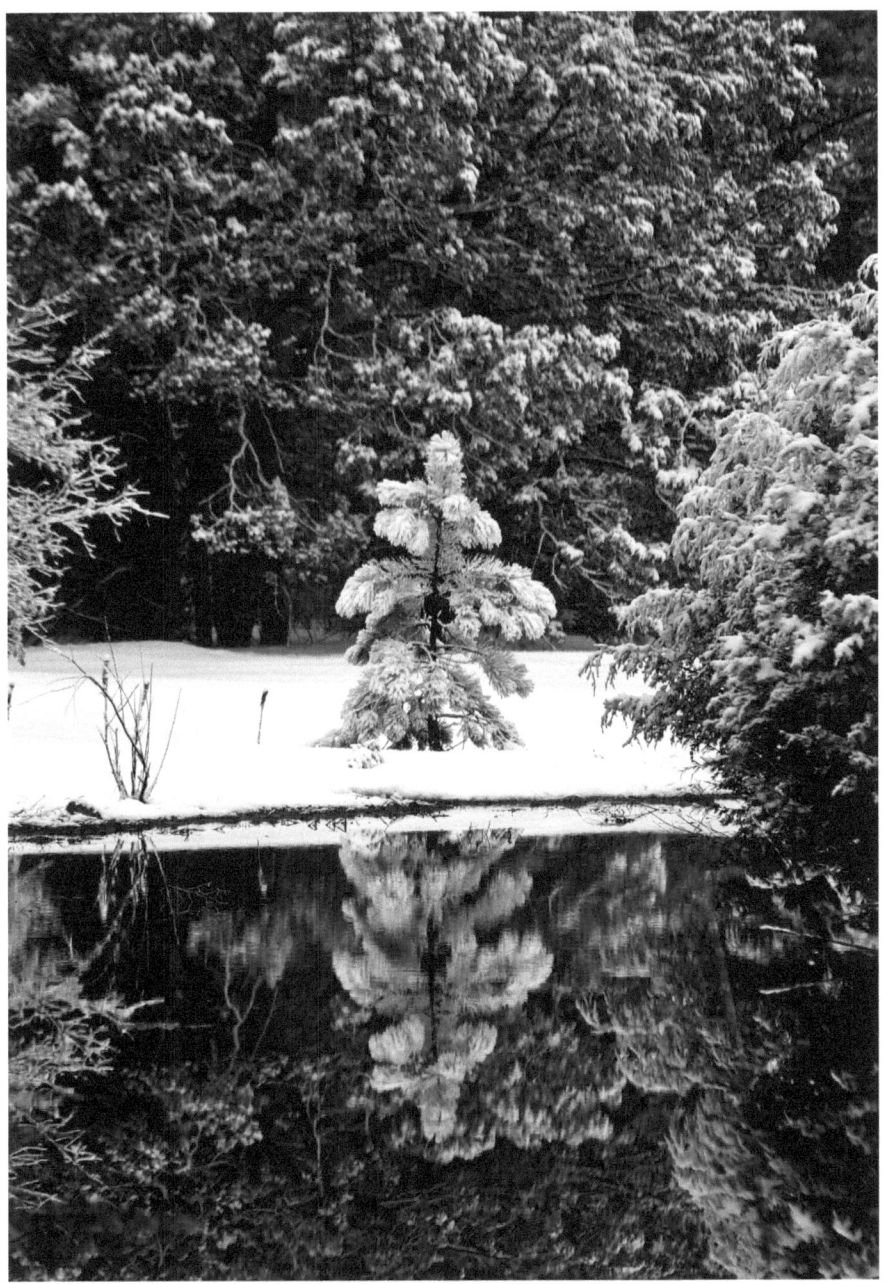

It was, to put it mildly, bitterly cold. The winds came from everywhere, blowing colder air in on top of already frigid air. The sun decided enough was enough and abandoned the day, and all unlucky enough to be in it to their individual fates—which, as it happened, turned out to be a heavy snowstorm. It was one miserable winter day.

The next day, the sun made a brief appearance and managed to warm everyone up, almost. Finding the effort too much, all it ended up doing was melting some snow into a few desultory puddles. The world was flat and gray and lifeless, for even the wind wanted a day off.

This small conifer persevered and endured. It had within it the strength of a one-hundred-foot tree, and moreover, it knew it. Deep inside, it knew it was big and strong, and this bit of weather bothered it not. It rode through the cold and into the spring, where once again it began to reach for its true destiny.

Author's note: I was struck by this small scene when I came across it, and the story seemed fitting. This is actually a color photograph; the day was indeed lifeless, and there was no sun, no color, no shadows—nothing except a dreary gray. Still, this tree seemed anything but gray, and it has the barest hint of green to it. A simple photograph, yes, but one that speaks of persevering.

Sandy Yucca

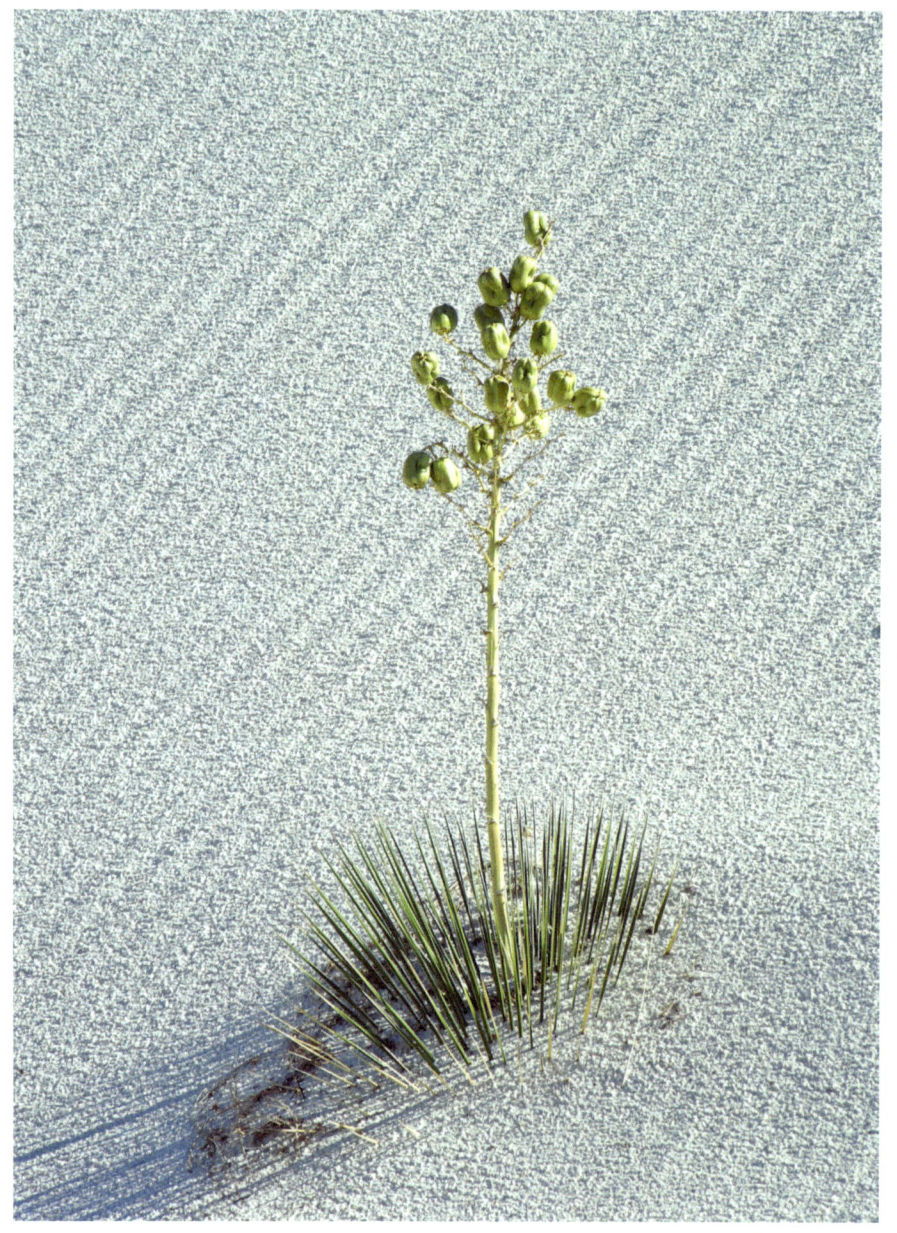

We live our lives. Each of us leaves our mark on this world, each in our own way. Time passes for us, sometimes quickly, and sometimes not so quick. We continue in our lives, always moving forward.

It is not this way for everyone, however, and it is certainly not this way for the yuccas that attempt to survive in the White Sands National Monument in New Mexico. Theirs is a constant race against the sand and a constant race to survive. As the winds shift and move the dunes—and oh, yes, the dunes move, and sometimes quite a lot—the yuccas must always reach light; failure to do so means the yucca will not survive. The yuccas are not so much concerned with leaving their mark on this world as they are merely staying in it.

Sometimes, though, the winds do not bury the yuccas and instead leave gentle ridges across the dunes. The lines are as precise as any gardener would make and have a style beyond compare, with an elegant symmetry. The ridges in the sand, along with the almost blooming yucca itself, reminds us that beauty is always all around us, and always leaves its mark.

Yucca Dune

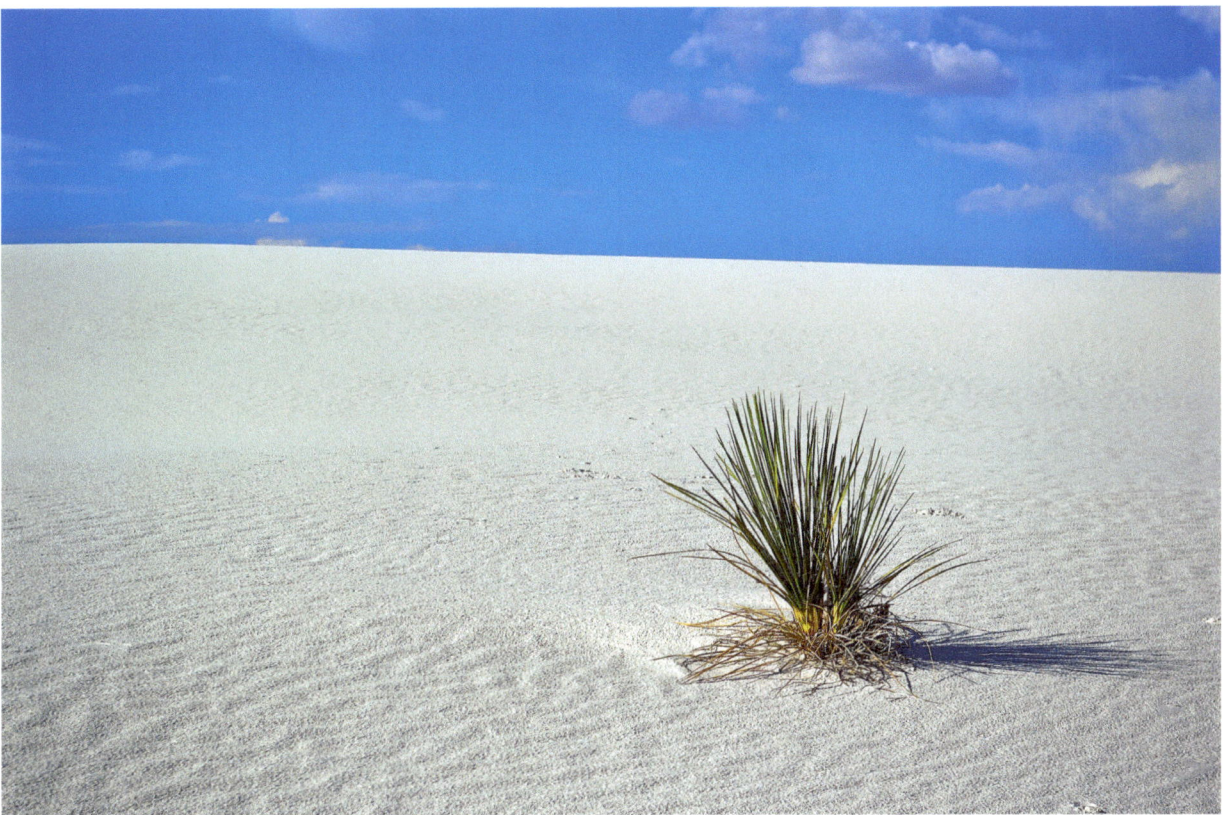

The emptiness, when seen from just the right angle, is absolute and complete. The white gypsum sands stretch for infinity, never beginning, never ending, always continuing, always stretching, endless emptiness.

In the middle of this emptiness, life finds a way. Growing in the middle of nowhere and everywhere, the yucca, alone on its dune, perseveres. It is undaunted by the endless emptiness and continues its race against the sands. Make no mistake about it, either, for it is a race against life. If this soapstone yucca cannot grow quickly enough or tall enough, the shifting sands of the dune will cover it, overwhelming and consuming it.

In the White Sands National Monument, this race happens throughout the dune field, with many victors and many losers. Some dunes have many participants on them; others, like this dune, sport one isolated yucca, which leads the way for others yet to follow. For now, though, the race for survival continues on Yucca Dune; the sands continue to stretch to infinity, and the outcome far from certain.

Saguaro Amigos

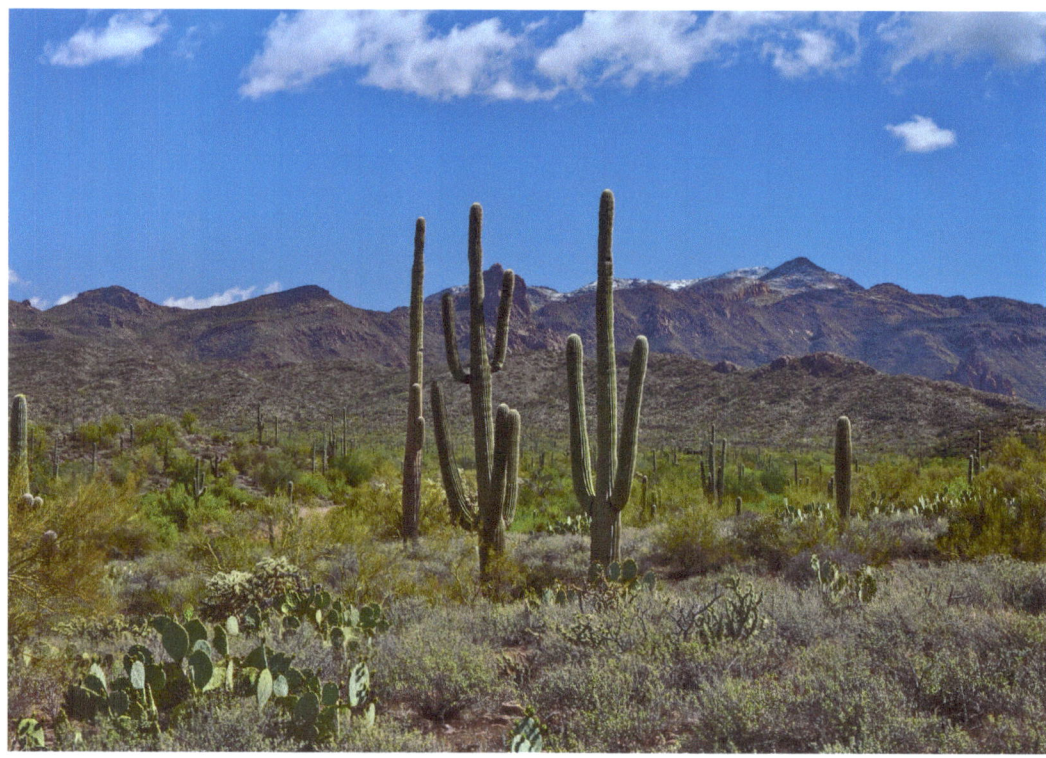

They stood there, stalwart against time. Year after year, year in and year out, they stood on their desert—their desert, mind you—standing tall. Every year, year in and year out, year after year, they grew ever so slowly. The saguaros were in no hurry at all, and a century or two was not that big a deal in the grand scheme of things. Saguaros tend to think very long-term thoughts.

At first, it was a lone Native American creeping by, now and then, stealthily and quickly, slipping past without a whisper in the night. Later it was more Native Americans, on horses, this time, and they cared not who saw them transverse the desert. As the years rolled by, it was a Spaniard who took note of them, but seeing as they had no gold, he kept going. Later still, an entire expedition of Spaniards came through, but again, no attention was paid to the friends in their desert. Prospectors, intent for the gold in the Superstition Mountains, walked by without noting the amigos. Later, the distant whistle of a train echoed through the hills, only to be supplanted by the sounds of automobile engines, but only if a plane wasn't overhead.

The saguaro amigos stand together, stalwart against time, year over year.

Snowy Aspens

The woods went on forever.

Standing in the nearly un-broken snow, aspens stretch toward infinity, and possibly, quite possibly, beyond. The late afternoon shadows played across the trees and the snow, creating sharp lines that stood in contrast to the trees. And the trees! Those in front of me leaned at an angle, just so, inviting me to lean with them, or at least, drew my eye that way.

That's when I saw it! A path! A single trail blazed through the snow to my left. It went past me, further into the woods, following the aspens to the edges of the world. What brave explorers had gone before me? What was their fate? The path went in a single direction in the woods—deep. It went deep.

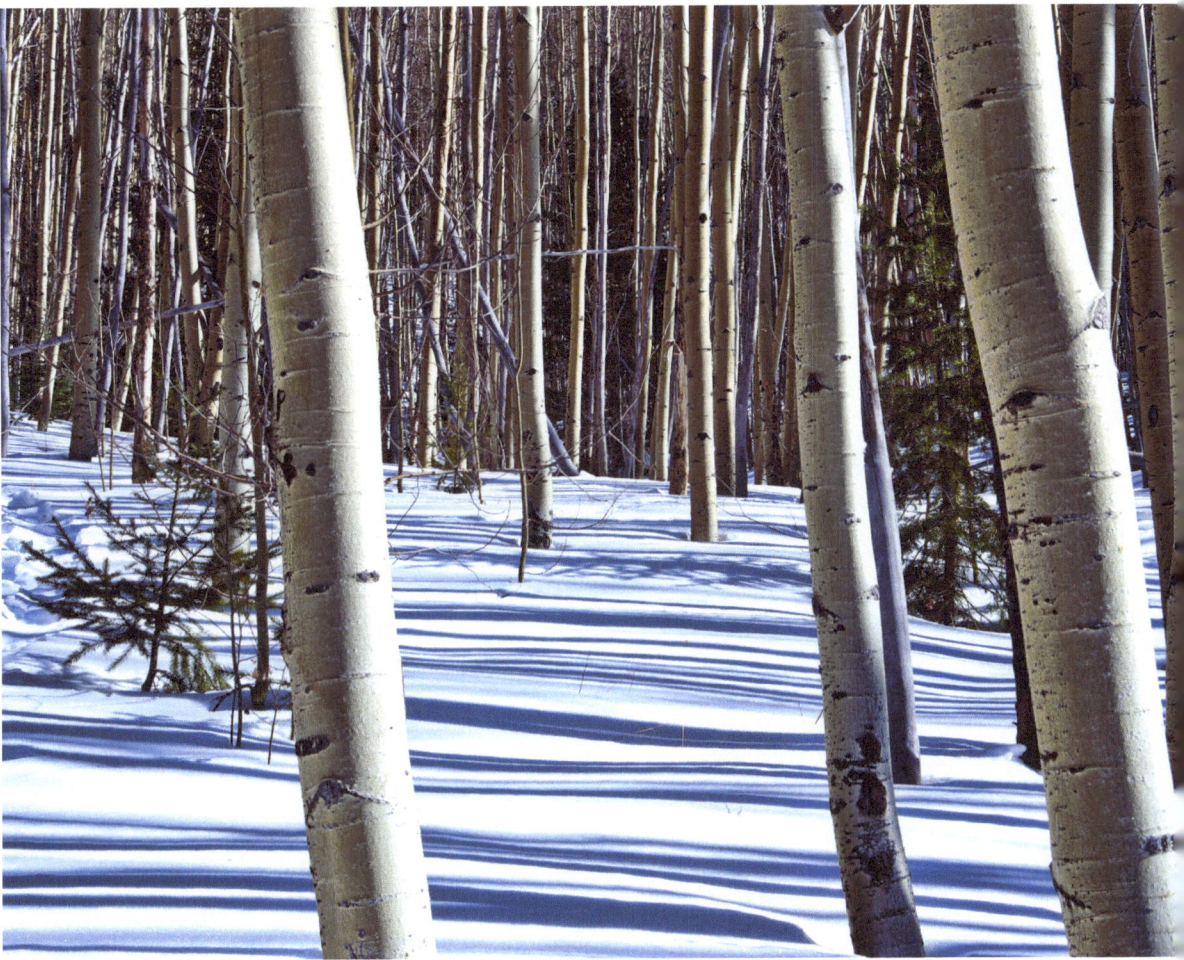

The sun continued to shine brightly as it moved, and the shadows moved with the sun. No one came back from the woods. No explorer returned with tales of what lay beyond.

The woods simply went on forever. Eventually I turned away into the evening.

Aspen Wood

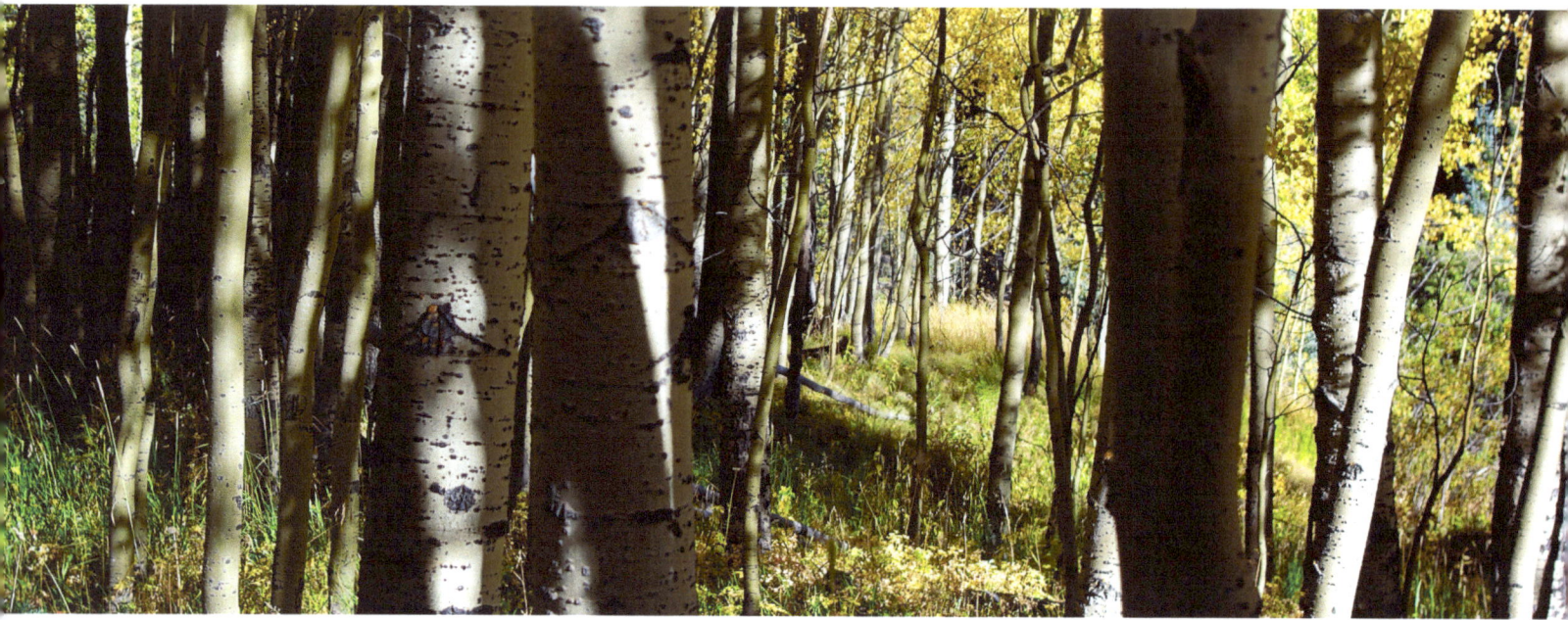

Aspens in fall, what an incredible sight!

Aspens in the fall in Colorado are an even more spectacular sight. Everywhere one looks, the leaf colors are bright and vivid, and in every hue of vibrant yellow and orange. As far as the eye can see, the scene is intense.

This photograph is one of my favorites. Taken in September along the Million Dollar Highway, the aspens caught me off guard. I was, frankly, looking up at the sky and pondering interesting clouds, when I looked off to my left, and then I was taken by the way the strong sunlight filtered down below into the woods. I loved the shadows that played along the aspen trunks. I adored the fall colors in the background, yet also the greens of summer still hanging on in the foreground.

As I look back, the memories of that perfect fall day come flooding back to me from where I stood, lost in the Aspen Wood.

Aspen Wall

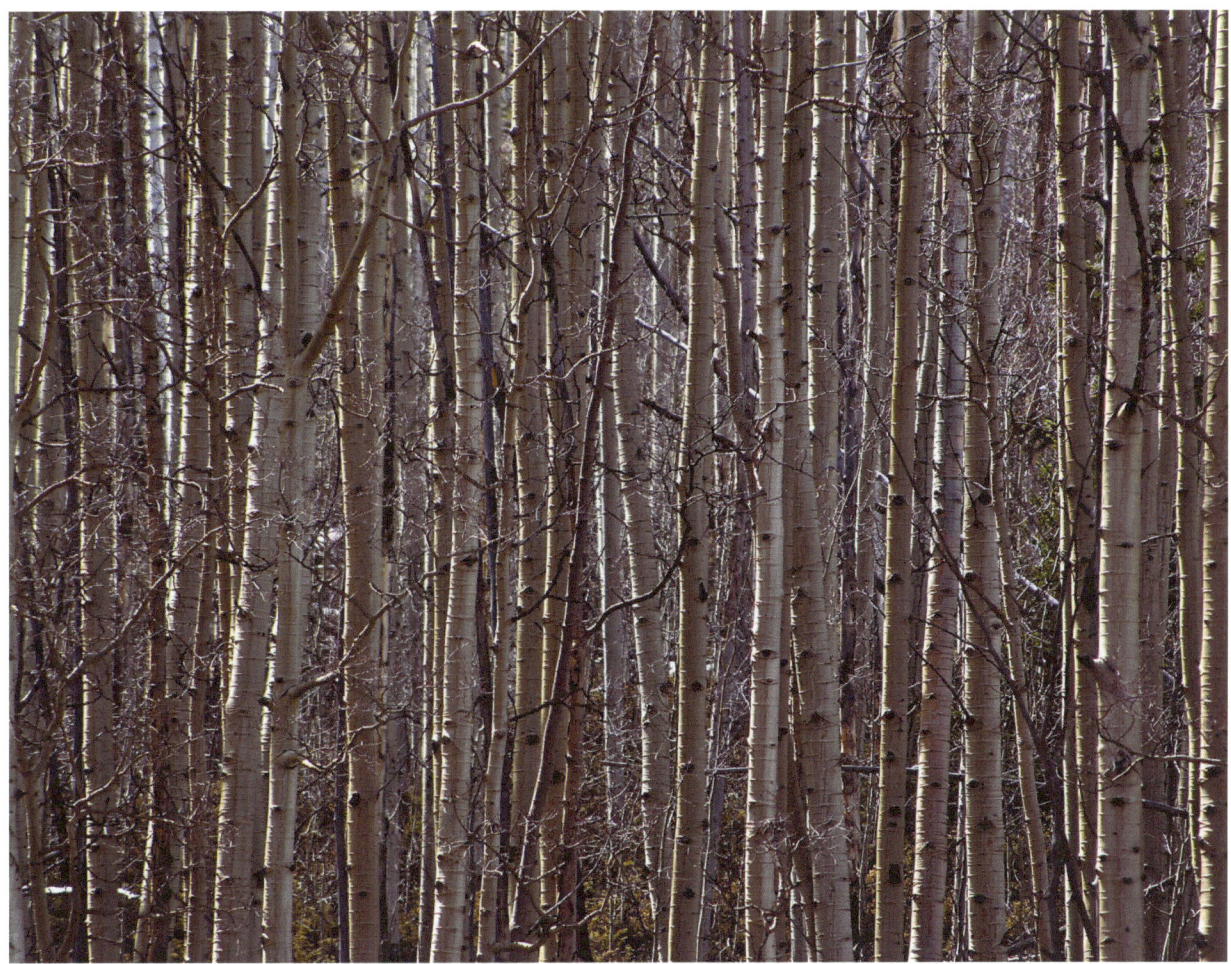

You've heard the expression, maybe, "You can't see the forest through the trees." The expression is based on an ancient Chinese proverb that says "Sometimes you lose a forest through the trees." Either way, the quote works well here.

I had been looking for a solid, perfect, wall of aspens for a good long time, because I thought it would look exceptionally interesting, but then I realized that perfection is highly overrated, and I took the saying to heart. I modified my search from the "perfect aspen wall" to "an aspen wall with a whole lot of great character," and the result is this photograph. Sometimes it is good to remind ourselves, too, that we lose sight of the obvious things because they are obvious. Sometimes it is good to take a step back, breathe, and keep the important things in mind.

Day's End

The passing of each day is a regular occurrence. Still, the day does not have to go quietly, peacefully, or without a struggle. Night overthrowing daylight is a time of mystery and magic. And a time of great opportunity. Here are a few of those stories.

Leaving Afternoon

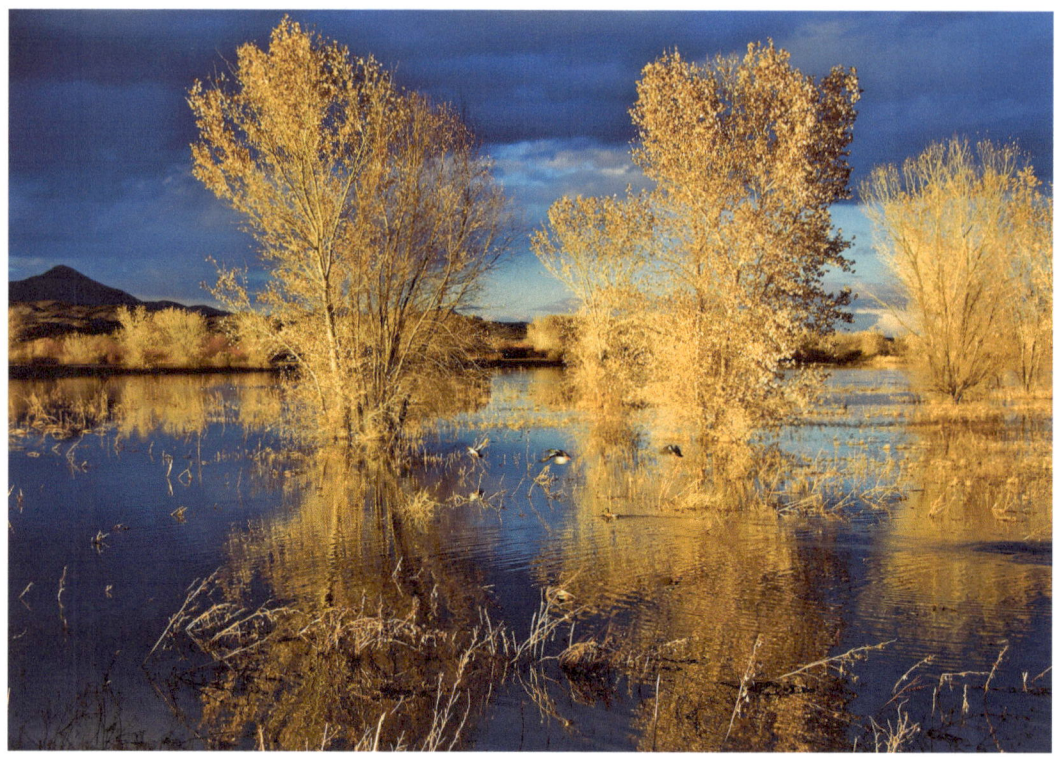

The end of the day is always an enchanting time, and especially so in the Bosque del Apache National Wildlife Refuge in New Mexico.

The Bosque del Apache is dedicated to providing a safe winter home for migratory waterfowl, such as sandhill cranes, snow geese, and a variety of ducks, among other birds. Actively managed, it provides a safe winter habitat as well as plenty of refuge fields, making it the perfect destination for its winter inhabitants. Perhaps they know this, too, for a feeling of peace and serenity reigns there, a place of safety and refuge, a place where time seems to stand still.

Time does go by, though, and eventually each day must end. This particular day's end, as the afternoon was leaving and evening entering, was full of rich golden colors and tones. The trees reflecting on the pool also reflected the rich light, and in turn everything reflected the end of an absolutely stunning day.

If you look closely, you'll see a few ducks in the middle also leaving the afternoon. Moments after this scene, darkness stole the day away.

Branching Sunset

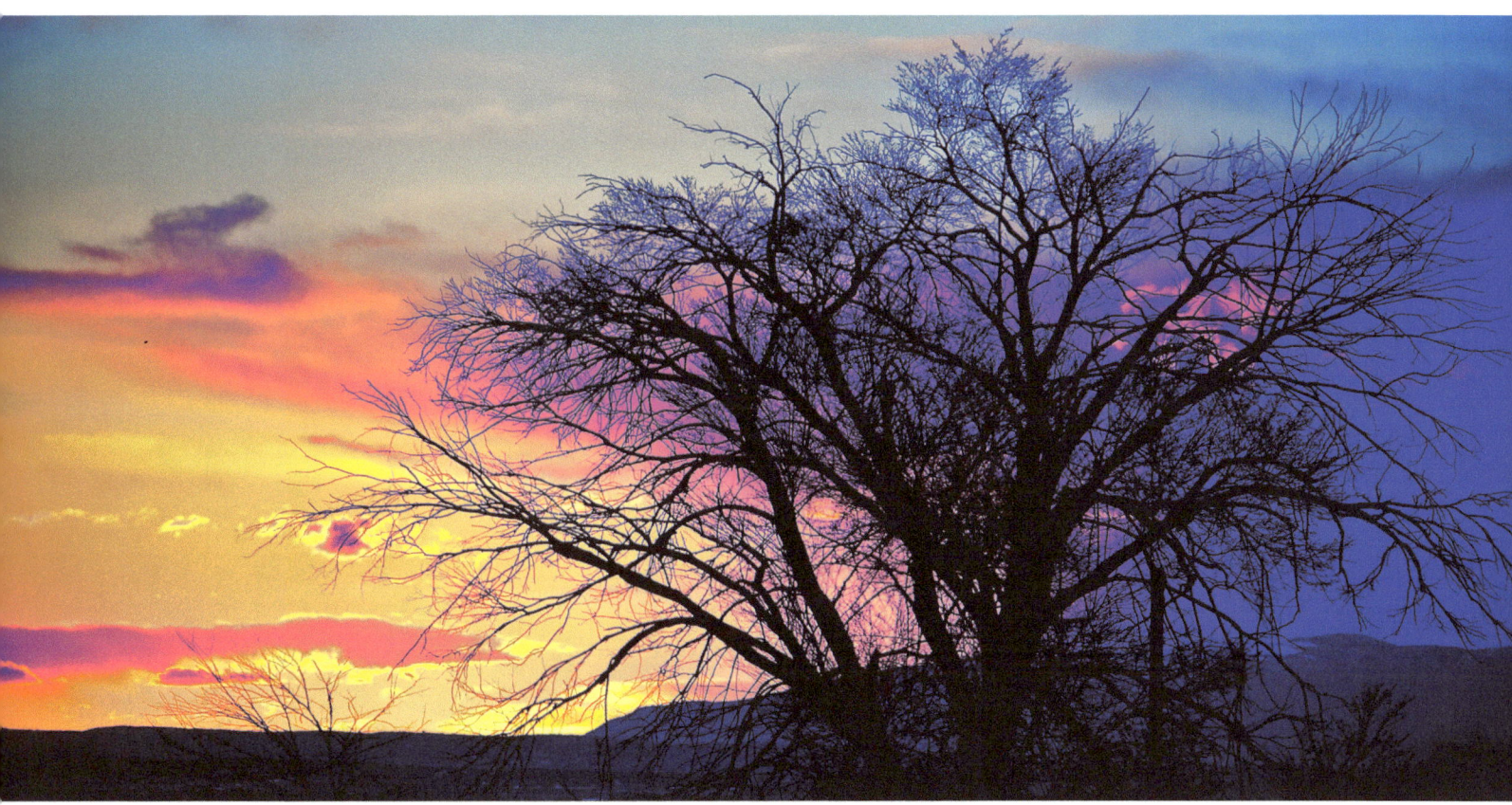

The sun made a last gasp and dove behind the distant mountain. The world wasn't quite ready to see it go, but the weary sun was through for this day. The clouds, sure that there was more time left to them, were caught unprepared, and their myriad colors bore stark witness to their outrage at being left alone so quickly. After all, the sun was not supposed to go suddenly, and certainly not without fair warning. The clouds glowered and vowed to stay lit all night long, if need be, until the sun came back and apologized.

The tree, however, stood fast, for it suspected that the sun was up to something sneaky; it gave up its own color quickly, welcoming the night with an inky blackness all its own. It stood, patiently waiting the outcome of the battle between the sun and the sky and decided in the end that the victor mattered not. Trees, being wise, were long accustomed to these conflicts, and having seen too many of them, remained fast in their dark neutrality. Before anyone could do much of anything about it, darkness claimed all.

Rainbow Point

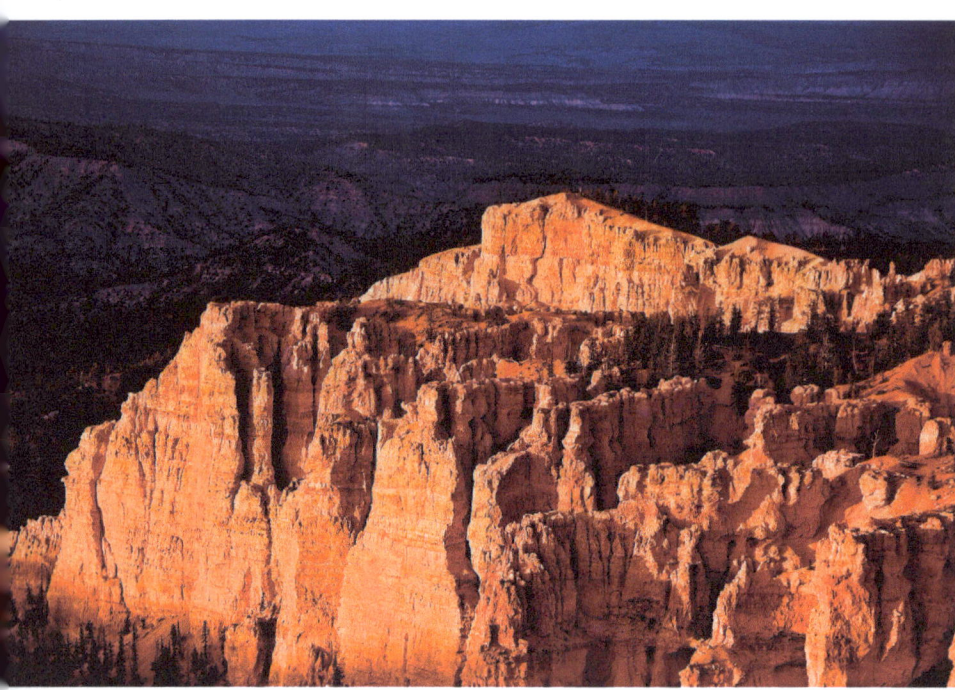

Rainbow Point, far within Bryce Canyon, is a spectacular overlook. Caught here in the very last rays of the day, the sun snagged the tips of the hoodoos and lit them up, bringing the canyon alive, and for a moment, highlighting the inherent orange coloration of the hoodoos.

Bryce Canyon is a phenomenal place, and it is hard to be anywhere in the park and keep your breath. Located in Utah, a place known for its awe-inspiring rocks and formations, Bryce Canyon has a charm uniquely its own. As you drive through it, rising higher and higher, the views become more and more bedazzling, and each time you round a corner you are presented with a sight that is more breath-taking than the last. The last turn on this road, and, in fact, the end of the road itself, is Rainbow Point. It is the grandest of them all.

The moment lasted all too briefly however. The sun slipped below the horizon, and the canyon slipped into the dark of the night.

Sunset Walker

White Sands National Monument in New Mexico is a vast, empty, tract of white gypsum sand dunes. Stretching forever, the pure white dunes are unbroken, except by the occasional brave yucca, toward the edges of the dune field.

As the sun drops from the sky, these few yucca are even more pronounced, silhouetted against the evening sky, standing tall against the encroaching night. To a photographer, they make an ideal subject, and this photographer had the same thought when he began his trek toward a small clump in the distance.

What a beautiful scene it all made: the golden and orange tones in the sky with some high clouds for contrast, the silhouetted yucca, and the silhouetted walker over the gently rounded dunes.

The walker reached his goal with just enough time to spare; he photographed his image as he saw it, his small journey apparently a success. The sun was also successful, completing its daily transit of the sky, and darkness fell over the dunes.

All was calm and peaceful, and the day ended flawlessly.

Taos Violicious

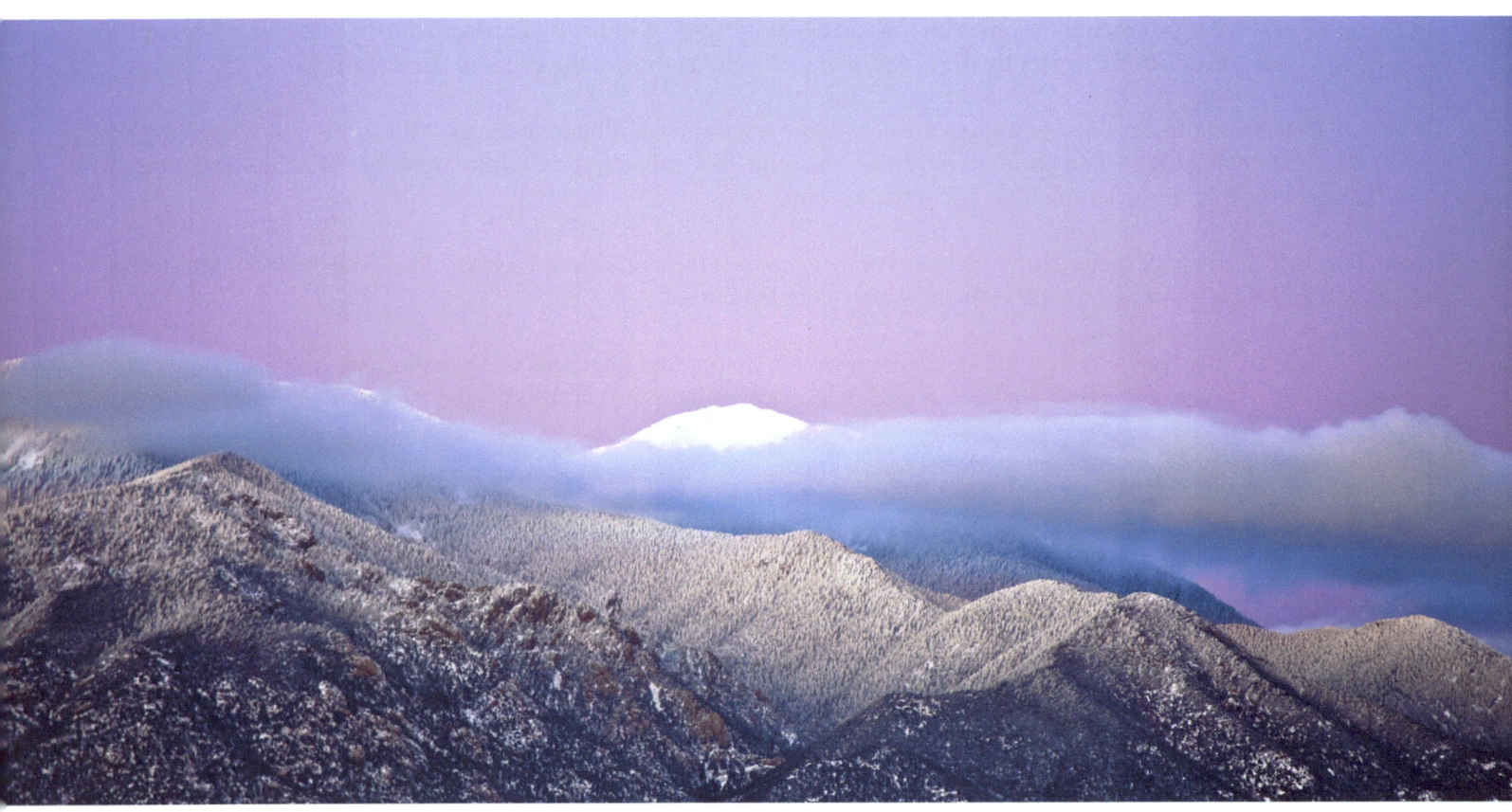

New Mexico sunsets provide some of the richest colors imaginable, ranging from deep indigos to pinks to reds to every color you can name, and some you can't. The recipe for the ideal New Mexican sunset couldn't be easier:

Start with a distant mountain near Taos, New Mexico. With plenty to choose from, just reach in the Carson National Forest, select the preferred mountaintop, and top it with snow, sprinkling a little extra around the base as well. You might also want to add in a low cloud for that decorative flair. Simply drape the cloud over the mountain (be sure to leave the mountaintop exposed, of course), layering it just so. Wait as the sunset develops, check the scene often, and keep a careful eye. If everything comes together, you will be treated to a violicious sunset, replete with hues of violet.

Alas, the color doesn't last long, and it is fleeting at best. The color flairs for a brief moment, but in that moment, the perfect sunset happens.

Angelic Sunset

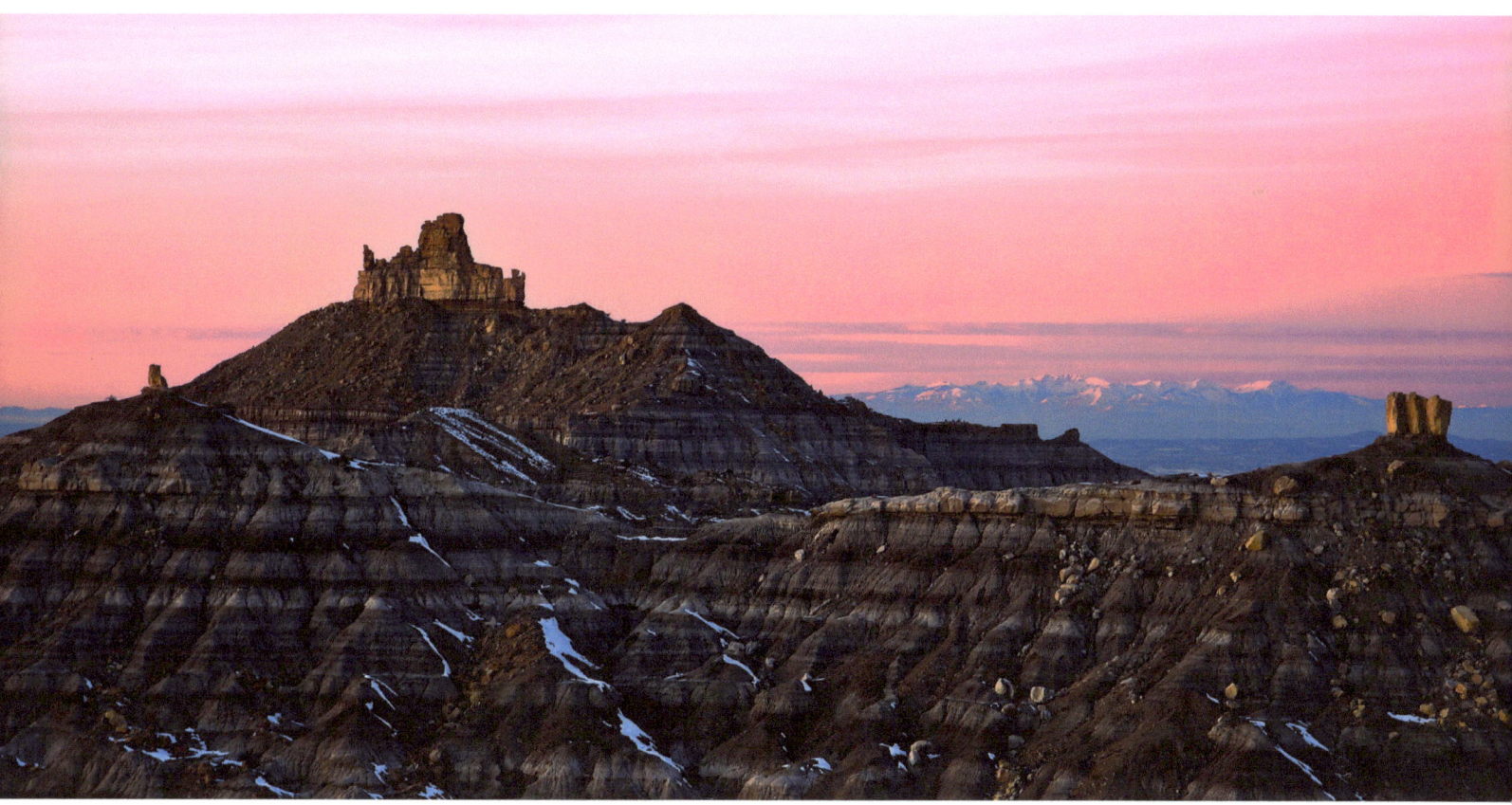

When most people think of New Mexico, they probably think of the deserts, and with good reason. As any New Mexican can tell you, deserts are common. Many people realize that New Mexico has mountains, too, and some of them are good sized. Mountains and desert: to many, these words describe the entirety of New Mexico.

New Mexico has magnificent hidden treasures, too. Eons ago, it was close to the equator and home to a vast tropical rainforest, and yes, the dinosaurs roamed here. With the shifting of tectonic plates, New Mexico drifted northward, away from the tropics, and time buried that part of her history. The treasure trove remains for those who know where to look. Within the state are several badlands, filled with hoodoos, rugged landscape, and twisted rock formations. True beauty is found everywhere; you just have to know where to look. Like Angel Peak, especially at sunset, and even more so when the sky flashes watermelon for a moment, as happens from time to time. Add in the snow-capped Ute Mountains in the background, and you have an Angelic Sunset.

Fiery Bisti

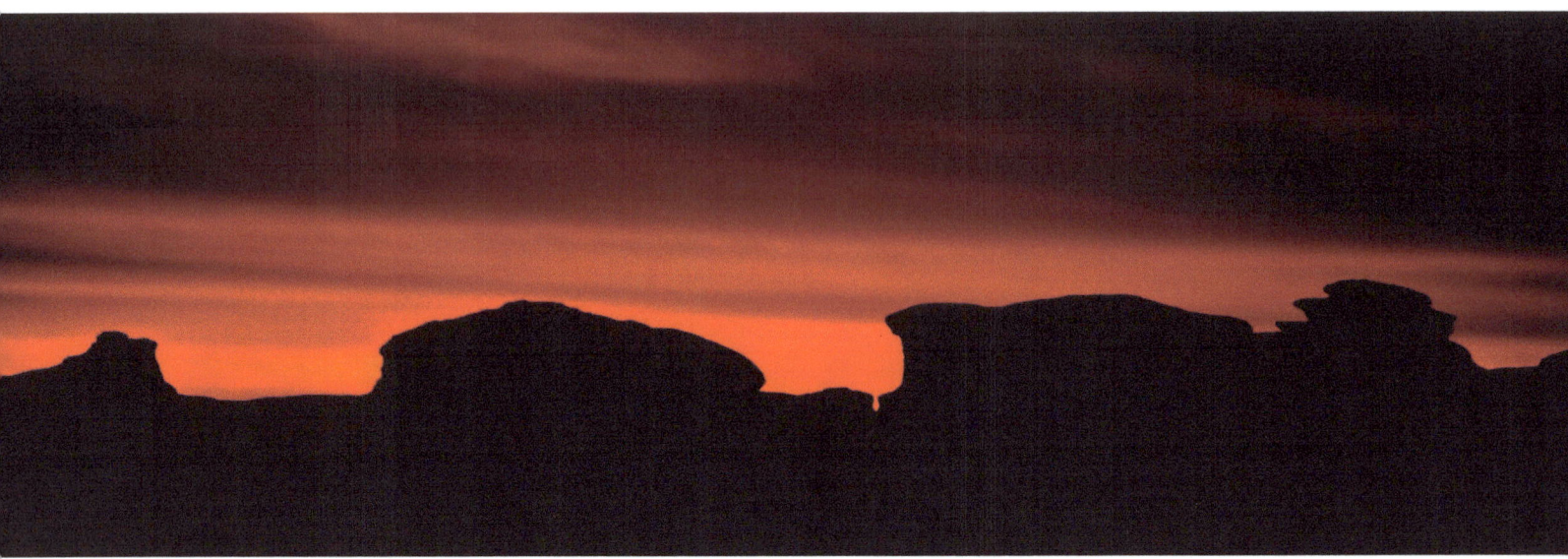

Scattered throughout the Bisti Wilderness in the New Mexico exist the strangest and most tortured of shapes. Everywhere you look, another bizarre and weird rock formation waits for you; everywhere you glance, you see another impossible shape. The Bisti is well known for its extraordinary, stark, beauty.

For all of that, though, the true real beauty happens as the sun begins to set and gives up its turn in the sky. Each sunset is different; unique and unpredictable. It might be routine (whatever a beautiful "routine" sunset is), or it might be the most amazing sight imaginable.

The magic in this particular sunset happened well after the sun left the sky, leaving in its wake a distant fire. The shapes of the Bisti silhouetted against that inferno provide a striking counterpoint, bringing to life the fiery Bisti.

Monumental Goodnight

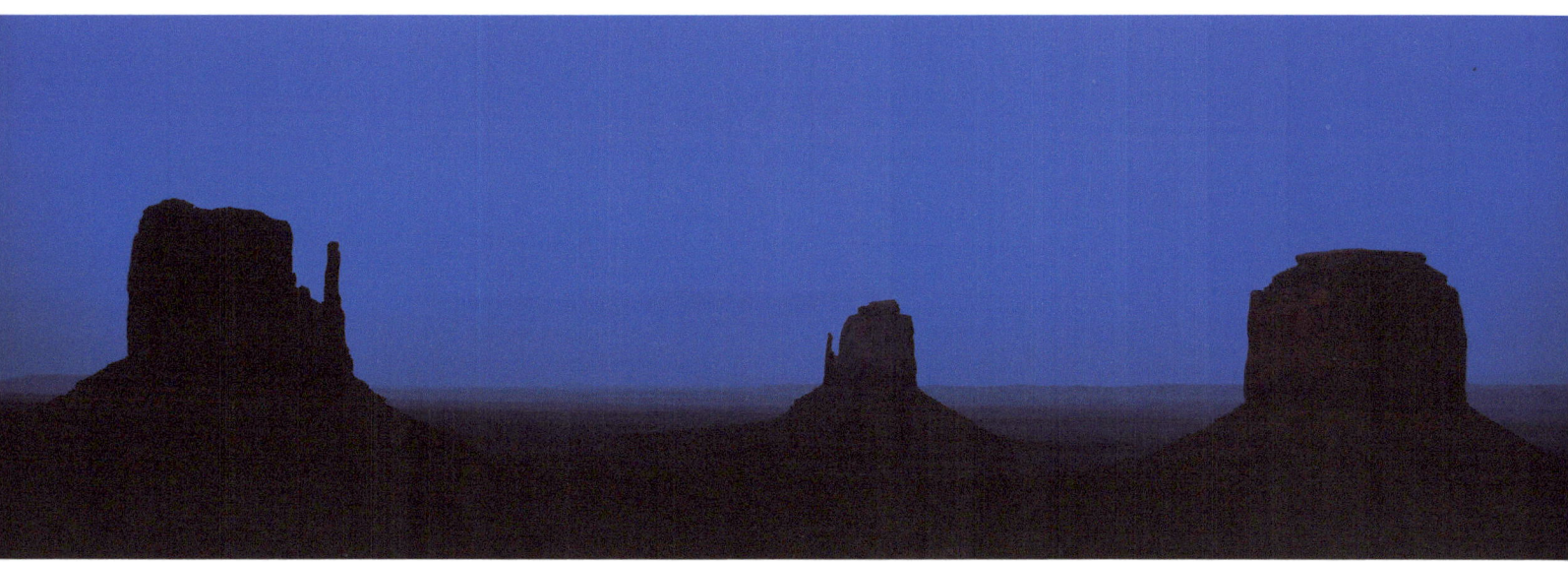

The world, just after the sun sets, changes completely. Creatures and denizens of the daylight hours give way to the mysteries and mayhem of the night. Who knows what lurks in the darkness?

The time of transition is also a time of fascination in the land. The colors ebb and flow quickly, transforming, sometimes, from the golden yellows to the purples to the reds and beyond. Once the sun sets, the nighttime blues and deeper tones come alive—briefly, ever briefly—as darkness claims and rules the land.

This is Monument Valley after the sun has begun to set. Little color is left in this particular tableau, except the very one I wanted the most, blue.

This photograph is a personal piece for me. It represents the last gasp of the day. Long after most people have stopped looking, that's when the best photographs are made. The peace, the serenity, the feeling of the evening all come alive. Rather than photograph this scene while there was more light, this is far more representative of what it looks like the moment before darkness reigns supreme. It is a time of reflection, of contemplation, of silence.

May you have a Monumental Goodnight.

Hello, Moon

"Hello, Moon," said the tree. "It's been a while since you've been around."

"Hello, Tree," said the moon. "I've been a little bit busy around the other side. I hurried back as soon as I could, and here I am."

Tree understood, for this cycle had been happening for as long as it could remember, and quite probably longer than that. Still, Tree missed Moon when it was away, and the nights were a little bit colder and much more lonelier. The sky was just so much more alive when Moon was there.

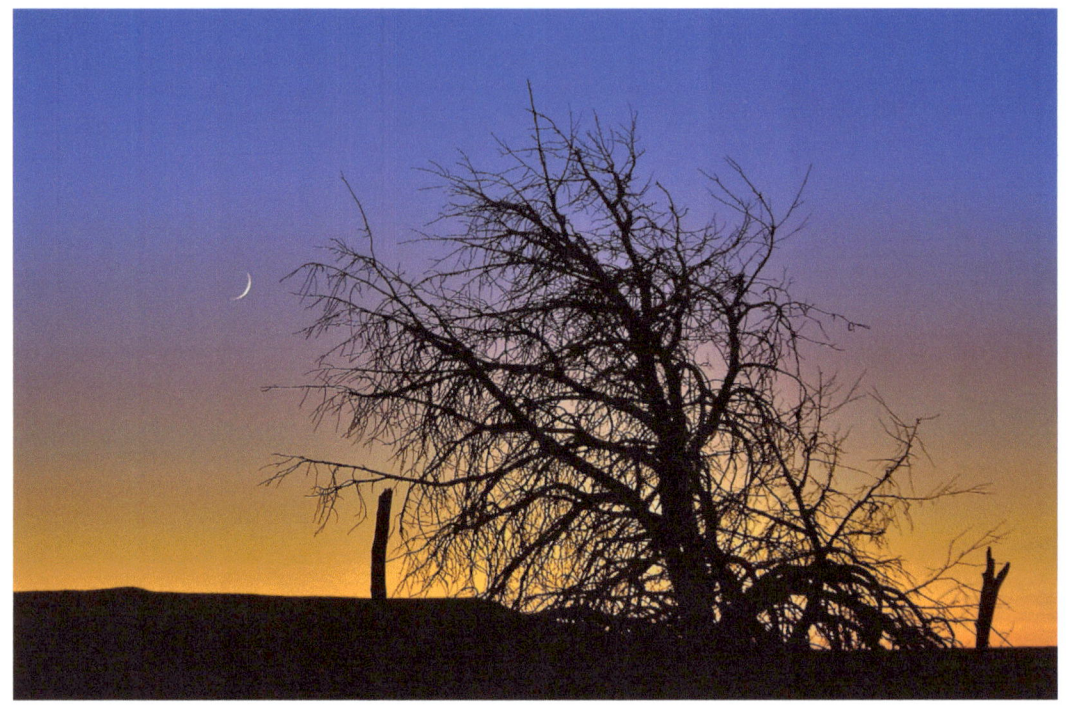

The two enjoyed the companionable silence for a little while. Good friends that they were, words were not always needed. Moon continued the ascent into the sky. Tree leaned a little closer, so as not to miss a word, should a word be said. It wasn't. Neither seemed to mind. Tree continued a slight lean; not so much that a passerby would remark, but enough that one, if so inclined, would notice.

The evening began to pass, all too quickly. "See you again tomorrow, Moon?" Tree whispered into the night.

"Of course," came the gossamer response on the breeze.

Floating back came, "Goodnight, Moon."

Wolf Moon

'Twas a Wolf Moon out there, a time of mystery, a time of danger, a time when sensible folks stay inside, lock the doors, bar the windows, and hide under the bed, because the wolves be a'calling out there. Wolf Moons are nothing to fool around with, that's for sure, for many an odd thing happens during them.

Nah. It was merely the first full moon of the year, the Wolf Moon, and I was, where else, camera in hand when the clouds parted for a moment, allowing this shot as the moon was rising just to the left of the Sandia Mountains in New Mexico. Left, in this case, is defined as my being in the west looking east, with the mountains to my right, which makes this moon to my left, and my head hurt trying to describe it all. It was in wonderful color for this moonrise.

Wolf Moon, what a moon! Now, if you'll excuse me, it is off to hide under my bed.

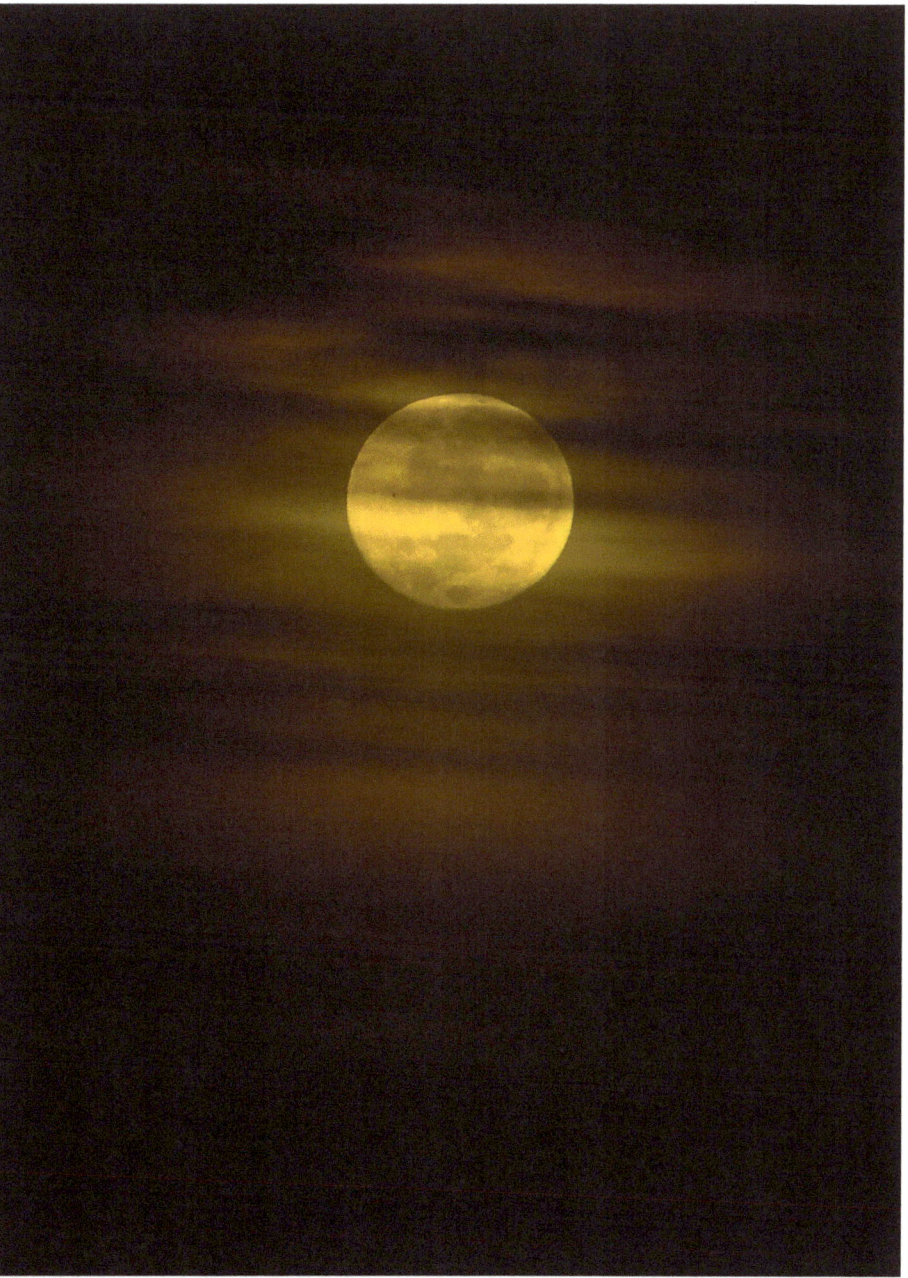

Photograph Locations

Cover
> *Infernally Yours* Sandia Peak, New Mexico

Introduction
> *Dawnting Shadows* Tijeras, New Mexico
> *Ready, Waiting* Grand Canyon National Park, Arizona
> *Sand Tracks* Great Sand Dunes National Park, Colorado
> *Bisti Silhouette* Bisti Wilderness, New Mexico

Southwest Wonders
> *Open Road* near Winston, New Mexico
> *Telluride Peak* near Telluride, Colorado
> *Snowy Vista* Sandia Peak, New Mexico
> *Snowhere Trail* Sandia Peak, New Mexico
> *Foggy Garden* Superstition Mountains, Arizona
> *Desert Snow* Superstition Mountains, Arizona
> *Snowbound Ranch* Valles Caldera National Preserve, New Mexico
> *Dune's Edge* Great Sand Dunes National Park, Colorado
> *Hanging Lake* Hanging Lake National Landmark, Colorado
> *Ancient Forest* Petrified Forest National Park, Arizona
> *Silverton Afternoon* Silverton, Colorado
> *Crystal's Summer* Crystal, Colorado
> *Capilla's Joy* Clines Corners, New Mexico

Red Rock
> *Classic Wave* Paria Wilderness, Arizona
> *Wave Way* Paria Wilderness, Arizona
> *Inspired Valley* Monument Valley, Navajo Nation
> *Canyonlands Overlook* Canyonlands National Park, Utah
> *Delicate Arch* Arches National Park, Utah
> *Grosvenor Arch* Grand Staircase-Escalante National Monument, Utah
> *Bryce Point* Bryce Canyon National Park, Utah
> *Evening Bluffs* El Malpais National Monument, New Mexico
> *Antelope's Light* Antelope Canyon, Navajo Nation
> *Sand Falls* Antelope Canyon, Navajo Nation
> *Monte Rojo* Ghost Ranch, Abiquiú, New Mexico

Visionary Eyes
> *Saw-Whet Pose* Bosque del Apache National Wildlife Refuge, New Mexico
> *Owl Eyes* Bosque del Apache National Wildlife Refuge, New Mexico

Blue Hoo Albuquerque, New Mexico

Intense Pygmy Corrales, New Mexico

Wolf Prowl Wild Spirit Wolf Sanctuary, Ramah, New Mexico

Wolf Eyes Wild Spirit Wolf Sanctuary, Ramah, New Mexico

Sunny Fox Wild Spirit Wolf Sanctuary, Ramah, New Mexico

Mischievous Fox Wild Spirit Wolf Sanctuary, Ramah, New Mexico

Hawk Eye Bosque del Apache National Wildlife Refuge, New Mexico

Hawk Standoff Bosque del Apache National Wildlife Refuge, New Mexico

Kestrel Takeoff Valles Caldera National Preserve, New Mexico

Kestrel Landing Albuquerque, New Mexico

Reverent Visions

Iglesia Solitaria near Espanola, New Mexico

Stormy Mission Pecos National Historic Park, New Mexico

Supersterious Reverence Apache Junction, Arizona

Welcoming Santuario Chimayo, New Mexico

Tyuonyi Pueblo, Bandelier National Monument, New Mexico

Kiva Memories Aztec Ruins National Monument, Aztec, New Mexico

Winged Rock near Shiprock, New Mexico

Bonito Doorways Chaco Culture National Historic Park, New Mexico

Kiva's Ghost Pecos National Historic Park, New Mexico

Kiva's Ladder Pecos National Historic Park, New Mexico

Motioning Stillness

Cloudy Crane Ladd S. Gordon Waterfowl Complex, New Mexico

Soaring Eagle near Payson, Arizona

Crane Gathering Bosque del Apache National Wildlife Refuge, New Mexico

Indigo Afternoon Bosque del Apache National Wildlife Refuge, New Mexico

Dawn Flight Bosque del Apache National Wildlife Refuge, New Mexico

Golden Takeoff Bosque del Apache National Wildlife Refuge, New Mexico

Hummingbird Flight Tijeras, New Mexico

Taking Flight Lee's Ferry, Arizona

Snow Jay Tijeras, New Mexico

Beep! Beep! Albuquerque, New Mexico

Living Life

Petrified Lizard Petrified Forest National Park, Arizona

Duckness Monster Albuquerque, New Mexico

Peek-A-Boo Deer Bandelier National Monument, New Mexico

Peek-A-Boo Elk Grand Canyon National Park, Arizona
Peek-A-Boo Mustang Monero Mustangs Sanctuary, Tierra Amarilla, New Mexico
Dos Amigas Monero Mustangs Sanctuary, Tierra Amarilla, New Mexico
Explora Gosling Tijeras, New Mexico
Sunny Chipmunk Clear Creek Falls, Colorado
Proud Raven Bosque del Apache National Wildlife Refuge, New Mexico
Three Honketeers near Bosque del Apache National Wildlife Refuge, New Mexico
Young Bull Grand Canyon National Park, Arizona
Wounded Antelope Bryce Canyon National Park, Utah

Flora's Allure

Sky Reach Tijeras, New Mexico
Glorious Columbine near Crystal, Colorado
Flowering Cane near the Painted Desert, Arizona
Coniferific Tenacity Cibola National Forest, New Mexico
Sandy Yucca White Sands National Monument, New Mexico
Yucca Dune White Sands National Monument, New Mexico
Saguaro Amigos Superstition Mountains, Arizona
Snowy Aspens Santa Fe National Forest, New Mexico
Aspen Wood near Telluride, Colorado
Aspen Wall on the Alpine Loop, Colorado

Day's End

Leaving Afternoon Bosque del Apache National Wildlife Refuge, New Mexico
Branching Sunset Stanley, New Mexico
Rainbow Point Bryce Canyon National Park, Utah
Sunset Walker White Sands National Monument, New Mexico
Taos Violicious near Taos, New Mexico
Angelic Sunset Angel Peak Recreation Area, New Mexico
Fiery Bisti Bisit Wilderness, New Mexico
Monumental Goodnight Monument Valley, Navajo Nation
Hello Moon North Acomita Village, New Mexico
Wolf Moon Placitas, New Mexico

Photograph Locations

Trail's End Bryce Canyon National Park, Utah

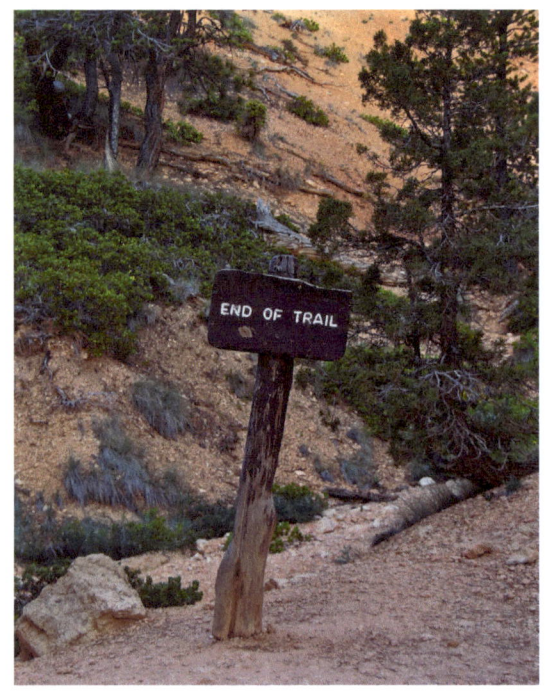

About the Author

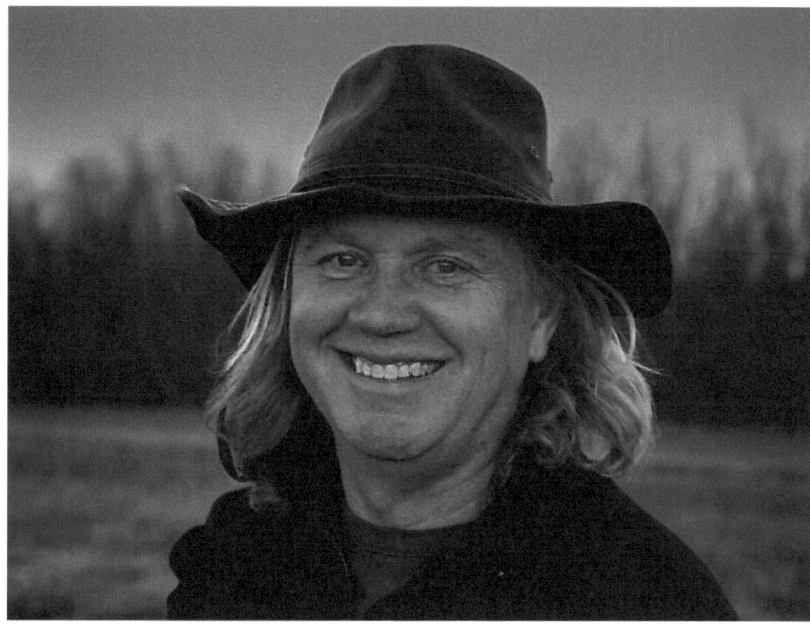

The sun sleeps on, not even thinking about rising yet. David, already standing out in a cold, wet field, waits for the sun and the wildlife to come alive. Seemingly the last place anyone else would want to be, this field springs to life with the dawn, and so does David's camera. Only the shot matters, in spite of toes threatening to move to the equator and fingers looking for a cup of coffee instead of wanting to hold the camera. He waits for exactly the right moment and then ... click. He has it.

David Schneider, a nature and wildlife photographer, focuses on bringing alive each scene and creature his camera sees. With a unique point of view and style, his prints capture the color, beauty and soul of his subjects. His affinity for nature extends into the scenic arena as well. His landscapes bring out the incredible emotion, beauty and grandeur of the Southwest and beyond; his photographs will take you from the tops of misty mountains to the shifting sands of the deep desert, letting you always be in the moment.

David lives in Tijeras, New Mexico, just outside of the Cibola National Forest. He prefers to be outside whenever possible, in his "studio"—the great outdoors. He believes in being one with nature, and not a day goes by that he doesn't find something new to be amazed and delighted by. With a lifelong interest in photography and nature, his passions combine, providing arresting photographs for everyone.

Photo by M.B. McClean

www.ingramcontent.com/pod-product-compliance
Lightning Source LLC
Chambersburg PA
CBHW042024200526
45159CB00036B/1125